Public Journalism 2.0

Where does journalism fit in the media landscape of blogs, tweets, Facebook postings, YouTube videos and literally billions of Web pages? *Public Journalism 2.0* examines the ways that civic journalism is evolving, especially as audience-created content—sometimes referred to as citizen journalism or participatory journalism—becomes increasingly prominent in contemporary media. As the contributors to this edited volume demonstrate, the mere use of digital technologies is not the fundamental challenge of a new citizen-engaged journalism; rather, a deeper understanding of how civic/public journalism can inform new citizen-propelled initiatives is required. Through a mix of original research, essays and case studies, this collection establishes how public journalism principles and practices offers journalists, scholars and citizens insights into how digital technology and other contemporary practices can increase civic engagement and improve public life. Each chapter concludes with pedagogical features including:

- **Theoretical Implications** highlighting the main theoretical lessons from the chapter,
- **Practical Implications** applying the chapter's theoretical findings to the practice of citizen-engaged journalism,
- **Reflection Questions** prompting the reader to consider how to further extend the theory and application of the chapter.

Contributors: Aaron Barlow, James K. Batten, Serena Carpenter, Cathy DeShano, Lewis A. Friedland, Tanni Haas, Kirsten A. Johnson, Nakho Kim, Suzanne McBride, Donica Mensing, Davis "Buzz" Merritt, Joyce Y.M. Nip, Sue Robinson, Jack Rosenberry, David M. Ryfe, Jan Schaffer, Burton St. John III.

Jack Rosenberry is Associate Professor and Chair of Communication and Journalism at St. John Fisher College. He is co-author of *Applied Mass Communication Theory: A Guide for Media Practitioners*.

Burton St. John III is Assistant Professor of Communication at Old Dominion University.

Public Journalism 2.0

The Promise and Reality of a
Citizen-Engaged Press

Edited by
Jack Rosenberry and
Burton St. John III

Routledge
Taylor & Francis Group

NEW YORK AND LONDON

First published 2010
by Routledge

Simultaneously published in the UK
by Routledge
2 Park Square, Milton Park, Abingdon, Oxon OX14 4RN

Routledge is an imprint of the Taylor & Francis Group, an informa business

© 2010 Taylor & Francis

Typeset in Perpetua by Wearset Ltd, Boldon, Tyne and Wear

Library of Congress Cataloging-in-Publication Data
Public journalism 2.0 : the promise and reality of a citizen-
engaged press / Jack Rosenberry and Burton St. John III, editors.
p. cm.
Includes bibliographical references and index.
1. Citizen journalism. 2. Online journalism. I. Rosenberry, Jack.
II. St. John, Burton, 1957-
PN4784.C615P83 2010
070.4'3—dc22   2009027647

ISBN10: 0-415-80182-6 (hbk)
ISBN10: 0-415-80183-4 (pbk)
ISBN10: 0-203-87677-6 (ebk)

ISBN13: 978-0-415-80182-9 (hbk)
ISBN13: 978-0-415-80183-6 (pbk)
ISBN13: 978-0-203-87677-0 (ebk)

Burton St. John dedicates this book to his mother, Joyce St. John, who often relayed Winston Churchill's motto: "Never give in, never give in, never, never, never." Although she always made sure to credit the source, she made sure I never forgot the message.

Jack Rosenberry dedicates this book to his favorite citizen journalist/blogger: his wife, Missy (http://blogs.democratandchronicle.com/webster), whose unfailing support makes all of his work possible.

Contents

Contemporary Civic and Citizen Journalism   67

6 News Quality Differences in Online Newspaper and
   Citizen Journalism Sites   69
   SERENA CARPENTER

7 The *Virginian-Pilot*'s Co-Pilot Pages: Participatory
   Journalism and the Dilemma of Private Values as
   Public News   84
   BURTON ST. JOHN III

8 Citizen Journalism in the Community and the
   Classroom   99
   KIRSTEN A. JOHNSON

9 The Changing Face of News in a Major U.S. City:
   Hyper-Local Websites Try to Fill the Void in Chicago 113
   SUZANNE McBRIDE

   Open Source Interview: Online Dialogue, Public
   Life and Citizen Journalism   126
   TANNI HAAS

PART III
Looking Ahead: Public Journalism 2.0   133

10 Routinization of Charisma: The Institutionalization
    of Public Journalism Online   135
    JOYCE Y.M. NIP

11 Common Knowledge, Civic Engagement and Online
    News Organizations   149
    JACK ROSENBERRY

12 Madison Commons 2.0: A Platform for Tomorrow's
    Civic and Citizen Journalism   162
    SUE ROBINSON, CATHY DESHANO, NAKHO KIM AND
    LEWIS A. FRIEDLAND

    Open Source Interview: Civic and Citizen
    Journalism's Distinctions   176
    JAN SCHAFFER

Acknowledgments and Special Editor's Note

Acknowledgments

It takes a village to raise a child, according to a popular proverb. If that's the case, it takes something like the population of a small city to produce a work such as this with its many formal and informal collaborators.

First and foremost, we acknowledge the work of those who have contributed to this volume (in alphabetical order): Aaron Barlow, Serena Carpenter, Cathy DeShano, Lewis A. Friedland, Tanni Haas, Kirsten Johnson, Suzanne McBride, Donica Mensing, Davis "Buzz" Merritt, Kim Nakho, Joyce Nip, Sue Robinson, David Ryfe and Jan Schaffer. Their insights provide the real substance of this work, and we are exceedingly grateful that all of them agreed to be part of the project. All of them were wonderful collaborators who met deadlines promptly, accepted editing suggestions readily and made revisions willingly (often under even tighter deadlines than the original submissions). We could not have asked for a better team of contributors or a better experience working with them. (A few more details about each of them can be found at the back of the book.)

Special thanks go to Susanne Shaw of the University of Kansas for both tracking down and supplying a copy of Jim Batten's famous 1990 address at the school, and securing permission from the university and the William Allen White Foundation for it to be reprinted here.

We also would like to acknowledge and thank colleagues within the civic and citizen journalism research community, especially those from the Civic & Citizen Journalism Interest Group of AEJMC, who encouraged us with this project and who were instrumental in our meeting and recruiting several of the contributors. The anonymous initial manuscript reviewers provided several helpful suggestions toward shaping the manuscript. Matt Byrnie and Stan Spring from Routledge/Taylor & Francis supported us in the beginning and throughout the project.

For his part, Jack Rosenberry would like to acknowledge and thank colleagues at St. John Fisher College in Rochester, notably Communication/Journalism Department Chair Lauren Vicker and Dean of Arts & Sciences David Pate, for their support of a semester-long release from teaching to work on this project. He also thanks other Fisher colleagues who picked up the slack for teaching, advising and other work in his absence. Alex Halavais, Tom Jacobson and Junhao Hong deserve a belated thank you for helping him think through many of the ideas in this book, especially those in Chapter 11, when they were his dissertation advisers at the State University of New York at Buffalo a few years ago.

Burton St. John would like to acknowledge and thank colleagues at Old Dominion University who have provided valuable mentoring and insights, including Communication Chair Gary Edgerton, Tom Socha, Jeffrey Jones, Fran Hassencahl and Tancy Vandecar-Burdin. Numerous scholars have provided encouragement over the years that have helped him get to the point of making a book like this possible, especially Matt Mancini, Michael Murray and Philip Gaunt. Jay Rosen has also provided crucial observations that have been a vital source of momentum that led to this project. Also providing valuable assistance was Marian Anderfuren, former editor at the *Virginian-Pilot*. Finally, Melissa Baumann, Elizabeth Beaubien and Marina Evans were willing and enthusiastic coders for the study in Chapter 7.

Finally, we thank our families for their love and support, and willingness to put up with being ignored while we spent the hours necessary to complete the project. They are Missy, Sara, Sean and Erin Rosenberry, and Dana, Melissa and Aaron St. John (and the St. Johns' numerous household pets).

JR
BSJ
June 2009

Special Editor's Note

As this volume was going to press, too late to make any substantial changes to the material contained within it, situations changed regarding two of the online organizations discussed in Chapter 9. In August 2009, EveryBlock.com was acquired by MSNBC; financial terms were not disclosed. And in early September 2009, the Chi-Town Daily News announced it was ceasing operation as a non-profit organization and laying off its three paid journalists. But a statement from founder Geoff Dougherty also said the staff hoped to find investors to reconstitute it as a for-profit business. As of early October 2009, no further announcements about its future has been made.

Chapter 1

Introduction

Public Journalism Values in an Age of Media Fragmentation

Jack Rosenberry and Burton St. John III

Modern communication is defined by its fragmented nature. Blogs, tweets, Facebook postings, YouTube videos and literally billions of Web pages cover the media landscape. Content created and distributed by "the people formerly known as the audience" (to use Jay Rosen's particularly apt term) dwarfs information available from the one-time giants of mass communication such as daily newspapers, weekly magazines and network television. A.J. Liebling's sardonic quip that "freedom of the press is guaranteed only to those who own one" has been turned on its head as anyone with an Internet connection and some easy-to-use software can publish to the world.

But where does journalism fit in a landscape where people can – and frequently do – publish anything, all the way down to Twitter reports on the contents of their breakfast? What does such an environment mean for journalism's most important functions of supporting democracy and improving public life?

As Kovach and Rosenstiel put it, "Civilization has produced one idea more powerful than any other – the notion that people can govern themselves. And it has created a largely unarticulated theory of information to sustain that idea, called journalism" (2001, p. 193). The traditional view of this process held that journalists would report, citizens would read the reports, and some form of public opinion would develop that helped to connect the will of the people with public action. Election coverage helps citizens decide who should represent them, from City Hall to the floors of Congress and the county courthouse to the corridors of the White House. News reports about government activities or proposals, from local public works projects to national programs and policies, can translate into public support or opposition that affects policy outcomes. Reporting on scandal, abuse and incompetence can lead to reforms as journalists provide a crucial "watchdog" function. Thomas Jefferson's famous observation about preferring newspapers over government was rooted in these ideas of journalism as supporting democracy.

This approach reached its apotheosis in the early twentieth century, as the Progressive Movement sought to institutionalize journalism as the fourth estate, or even the "fourth branch of government." Here journalists served as the intermediaries between the public and the technocrats managing the state. But as the twentieth century ended, a more common view was the one expressed by journalist and press critic James Fallows that the news media were no longer contributing to a functional democratic system but undermining it. "Far from making it easier to cope with public challenges," he wrote, "the media often make it harder" (Fallows, 1996, p. 7).

A complete critique of problems with the late-twentieth-century political communication system is beyond the scope of this volume, but suffice to say that many observers in government, the media and academia saw it as dysfunctional and offered various ideas for improvements or repairs. One of those potential answers was public journalism, sometimes referred to as civic journalism, which attempted to encourage a more citizen-engaged press that would, in turn, facilitate improved citizen involvement with issues of public concern. In so doing, it drew on the ideas of educator and press critic John Dewey, who in the 1920s said newspapers needed to move beyond purely reporting events to become vehicles for public education, debate and structured discussion of public issues.

One of the bricks in the foundation of public journalism was laid by *Washington Post* columnist David Broder in the wake of the 1988 presidential campaign between George H.W. Bush and Michael Dukakis. The campaign was seen (then) as an all-time low point in American politics, with its most memorable images centered on superficialities – Dukakis looking silly riding in a tank and the "Willie Horton furlough" and "Pledge of Allegiance" themes from Bush's campaign. In the run-up to midterm elections two years later, Broder (1990) offered that journalists were largely to blame for the degrading level of campaign discourse because they did not demand better from the candidates on behalf of the public. His comments were echoed by scholars. James Carey remarked that the 1988 election revealed the extent to which journalists and elites concentrated on manipulating each other, relegating the public to the role of alienated spectators (1995, pp. 391–393). New York University professor Jay Rosen wrote that "A critique of press performance was brought forward by the depressing events of 1988. It saw the press as a player, caught up in a system that was making a mockery of politics" (Rosen, 1999, p. 54).

Correspondingly, the late 1980s brought the beginnings of the public journalism movement; newspapers began experiments in citizen-engaged coverage in places such as Columbus, GA; Charlotte, NC; Spokane, WA; and Wichita, KS. Several of the papers involved in these projects were from the Knight-Ridder group, and comments by Knight-Ridder CEO James Batten became a kind of manifesto for public journalism. In remarks in California in 1989, he called for "a fresh journalistic mindset rooted in the best of our past but shrewdly and tough-mindedly in touch with the realities awaiting us in the 1990s." A little later in the talk he continued:

> We can be more inventive than ever in making issues crackle in our news and editorial columns. We must drop our bland assumption that we have done our obligatory bit to stimulate debate by merely printing dull op-ed pieces that few bother to read. We can identify key issues and boldly assert them as never before in lively, readable formats.
>
> (Batten, 1989)

He followed up on those thoughts at a college address in early 1990 with a call for newspapers to re-connect with their readers in new and innovative ways, focusing on building communities and helping revitalize journalism at the same time. (That talk is reprinted as Chapter 2 of this volume and the publication of this book, in fact, coincides with the twentieth anniversary of the address.)

Citing declining voting participation over the previous quarter-century and particularly dismal levels in the 1988 presidential election, Batten observed that "These patterns, without question, are symptomatic of the sluggish state of civic health in many communities in the early 1990s." He then referred to several examples of newspapers' efforts to help rebuild the connections between the papers and their communities, emphasizing that

> Newspapers that immerse themselves in the lives of their communities, large or small, have the best prospects for success in the years ahead. And they have the best chance of drawing people in from the apathetic periphery to the vibrant center of community life.
>
> (Batten, 1990)

These statements struck a chord with many journalists who felt that if you're not part of the solution, you're part of the problem. Moreover, noted one scholar, more journalists and academics avowed that "if media are part of the problem, perhaps they can be redirected toward being part of the solution" (Meyer, 1998, p. 256). Early experiments in the field and philosophies such as those expressed by both industry representatives (such as Batten) and academics (such as Carey and Rosen) coalesced into a set of practices. These efforts centered on including citizen participation in news selection and encouraging dialogue about issues. Journalism's purpose, in this view, should be "addressing people in their capacity as citizens in the hope of strengthening that capacity. It [journalism] should try to make public life go well, in the sense of making good on democracy's promise" (Rosen, 1999, p. 50). The idea of "making public life go well" became perhaps the real theme of the public journalism movement, and over the next few years the experimentation expanded, by one tally reaching at least 600 discrete projects (Friedland and Nichols, 2002).

That's not to say what came to be called public journalism faced easy or universal acceptance; it drew criticism and opposition from many quarters inside and outside the industry. Consequently, within a few years much of the early energy, innovation and support from sources such as foundations and academics that gave the movement its momentum gradually declined. Additionally, several journalists brought forth alarms about public journalism: it drained newsroom resources, it was a marketing ploy, it was self-absorbed and self-righteous and even bordered on propaganda, they claimed (St. John, 2007). In 2004, Friedland noted that "public journalism is at a crossroads" (p. 36) because its bases of support "are not sufficient for a vital, continuing and innovative public journalism practice" and "do not counter the inertia of the journalism industries" (Friedland, 2004, p. 39).

To extend the crossroads metaphor, a vehicle coming down the intersecting highway was a bus – loaded with citizen journalists. Could they perhaps be the inheritors of the "democratizing" influences promulgated by public journalism and take up where it left off? It seemed a natural progression; what could be more democratic for journalism itself than coverage created by the people, for the people?

But in many respects, though for different reasons, citizen-created news was as flawed as the one-way, newsroom-centered model of traditional journalism. Neither served particularly well to create what Yankelovich (1991) called "public judgment." Yes, citizen journalism added more voices and perspectives to the mix. The Internet also made communication more fluid and gave news audiences access to a virtually unlimited information bank, literally at their fingertips, indexed and organized with hypertext links. "For utopian visionaries, the promise of nearly unlimited information delivered to your monitor in mere moments is the promise of a better democracy" (Hill and Hughes, 1998, p. 2). But because the network can make a more citizen-engaged press[1] possible does not mean it is inevitable. As a more citizen-initiated journalism unfolded, traditional notions of gatekeeping that for generations had confined the press to a narrow, proscribed model were swept aside. But the citizen-created coverage that emerged in its stead was all too often fragmented, incomplete, and in its own way even narrower, addressing private issues and concerns rather than anything related to building a more robust public sphere. Unalloyed citizen journalism didn't seem to be an automatic approach to making public life go better either.

Nonetheless, there are common threads between civic and citizen journalism. Public journalism sought to make journalists and citizens partners in driving the news agenda; citizen journalism does this in a direct fashion. The Internet – particularly so-called "Web 2.0" tools such as blogs and interactive websites – does offer a practical and efficient way for interactive communication to occur among citizens of a community grappling with a public issue. In fact, such communication was a central element of many traditional public journalism projects, though the movement generally employed "off-line" settings such as public meetings or discussion forums. Today, "cyber-democracy" holds the potential for greater deliberative efficacy, even if beneficial outcomes are not as automatic as its more utopian advocates believed they would be.

This book takes some of these common threads and weaves them into a tapestry that illustrates ways in which public journalism's principles and purposes can inform and build an improved citizen-engaged press. In computer lingo, this would be a version 2.0 upgrade; hence the title: *Public Journalism 2.0* – a new model built around improved technical capacities. But the need for an upgrade is embedded in the subtitle of the work: *The Promise and Reality of a Citizen-Engaged Press*. The *reality* is that citizen media production doesn't contribute much toward improving public life at present. The *promise* is that it could, if informed and guided by aspirations of public journalism and bolstered by professional journalists unafraid to engage more closely with their audiences using online tools.

This new fabric is woven through presentation of original research, case studies and essays (based on evidence in the existing literature of the field) that follow a rough pattern of public journalism's implications for the past, present and future. Part I examines root principles of public journalism and citizen journalism, and ends with an interview with Lew Friedland about the evolution of public journalism. Part II examines how news definitions differ for citizen journalists and their trained counterparts, and presents several case studies showing how these differences play out in print and online. An interview with Tanni Haas exploring the contemporary state of affairs regarding public journalism closes this section. Part III includes suggestions for where citizen and professional journalism might find synergies. It features a review of two different but somewhat overlapping "frameworks" for articulating the pro–am relationship and a final case study of how one citizen site has evolved to incorporate both more interactive tools and a greater sense of public engagement into its operation. Finally, Jan Schaffer – who has been deeply involved with citizen journalism's expansion as director of J-Lab: The Institute for Interactive Journalism – offers some thoughts about the common ground occupied by civic and citizen journalism.

A number of themes re-occur throughout the book, including how news is (or could be) defined, different perspectives on gatekeeping prerogatives, the different roles and orientations that citizen and professional journalists have, and the implications of those roles for collaborative work between them. Looming large behind all of this is an exploration of the dynamics of private versus public concerns. Without question the democratization of media forms puts more individual voices and perspectives within reach of public attention, which is beneficial. But is that the same as creating a news media ecology that enhances the public sphere by constructing a "space" where issues of common concern are addressed to the benefit of some greater public? If it's not, are there steps that professional journalists and citizens can take together to move things in that direction and help journalism sustain that powerful notion that people can govern themselves? This book attempts to address such questions. The ideas it provides will, we hope, point to ways journalism can critically examine its practices with an eye toward realizing a more citizen-engaged press.

Note

1. Using the word "press" in this context has a certain irony because the discussion centers almost entirely on Internet-based delivery; with the exception of the Virginian Pilot case study in Chapter 7 no presses (meaning ink-on-paper presentation) are involved in the type of citizen journalism referred to throughout the book. But after some consideration we have decided to use the word in selected instances (including the book's subtitle) in its traditional, holistic meaning when referring to institutions that provide news coverage, particularly of public affairs, even if that coverage is entirely online. Indeed, in some uses – e.g. "freedom of the press" – no other word is an adequate substitute.

References

Batten, J.K. (1989). America's Newspapers: What Are Our Prospects? Press-Enterprise Hays Lecture Series, No. 24, Riverside, CA, April 3.
Batten, J.K. (1990). Newspapers and Community: The Vital Link? William Allen White Address, University of Kansas, Lawrence, KS, February 8.
Broder, D. (1990). Democracy and the Press. *The Washington Post*, A15, January 3.
Carey, J. (1995). The press, public opinion, and public discourse: On the edge of the postmodern. In Glasser, Theodore and Salmson, Charles (eds.). *Public Opinion and the Communication of Consent* (pp. 373–402). New York: Guilford.
Fallows, J. (1996). *Breaking the News: How the Media Undermine Democracy*. New York: Pantheon Books.
Friedland, L. (2004). Public journalism and communities (excerpt). *National Civic Review* 93 (3), 36–43.
Friedland, L. and Nichols, S. (2002). *Measuring Civic Journalism's Progress: A Report Across a Decade of Activity*. Washington, D.C.: Pew Center for Civic Journalism.
Hill, K. and Hughes, J.E. (1998). *Cyberpolitics: Citizen Activism in the Age of the Internet*. Lanham: Rowman and Littlefield.

Kovach, B. and Rosenstiel, T. (2001). *The Elements of Journalism: What Newspeople Should Know and the Public Should Expect.* New York: Crown Publishers.

Meyer, P. (1998). If it works, how will we know? In Lambeth, E., Meyer, P., and Thorsen, E. (eds.). *Assessing Public Journalism* (pp. 250–274). Columbia: University of Missouri Press.

Rosen, J. (1999). *What Are Journalists For?* New Haven: Yale University Press.

St. John, B. (2007). Newspapers' struggles with civic engagement: The U.S. press and the rejection of public journalism as propagandistic. *The Communication Review* 10, 249–270.

Yankelovich, D. (1991). *Coming to Public Judgment: Making Democracy Work in a Complex World.* Syracuse: Syracuse University Press.

Part I

The Roots of Civic and Citizen Journalism

Where and when did public journalism start, and who can take credit for launching it? These are questions without discrete answers. Public journalism was, and is, an evolving set of practices, theories and attitudes that by all accounts began in the late 1980s. Public journalism scholars cite the public's disgust with the 1988 presidential campaign as a catalyst for ideas first to treat elections, and later coverage of other public affairs, in a different way. Early experiments in Charlotte, NC, Columbus, GA and Wichita, KS between 1988 and 1990 were among the first to implement innovative ideas designed to bring journalists and citizens together to formulate coverage. Later, scholars helped to elaborate on the theories behind public journalism, and external supporters – notably the Kettering Foundation, the Knight Foundation and the Pew Charitable Trusts – helped to pay for further research and practical applications of the emerging practice throughout the 1990s.

Reformist movements in the United States have bellwether moments that signify they are penetrating the public's consciousness. However, one must be careful about oversubscribing significance to isolated events. For example, it would be inaccurate to say that the environmental movement *began* with the publication of Rachel Carson's *Silent Spring* or that the push for African-American civil rights *began* with Rosa Parks' refusal to sit at the back of the bus. Yet these happenings are seen as signal events that inspired people and helped to spread isolated and episodic initiatives into coordinated causes that touched upon concerns of the wider population.

In similar fashion, it would be inexact to say that the public journalism movement *began* with the speeches given by Knight-Ridder CEO James Batten in the winter of 1989–90. In those speeches, Batten outlined his thoughts on the then-emerging public journalism practices and projects within his company and the industry that had been underway for a couple of years. But Batten's comments did help articulate the nascent impetus of public journalism, and the recognition his remarks received due to his prominence as an industry CEO spread the idea of public journalism to a wider audience. These talks included one he gave about newspapers and community-building in February 1990 at the University of Kansas on the occasion of the university honoring him with its William Allen White Award. The speech attracted attention at the time and has retained a high profile since. Batten's central theme was that the printed press could improve public life, benefiting both the communities and the newspapers that served them. Newspapers could do well by doing good, he said, but this meant seeking innovative ways to find and report news that built up their communities. This focus on making public life go well could help reverse the public apathy apparent in the 1988 election and, in the process, he said, make newspapers more relevant and important to their readership.

It's been 20 years since Batten, now deceased, gave this talk at the University of Kansas. But the timeless themes of this bellwether moment in the development of public journalism make it an appropriate beginning for this book, and so it appears as Chapter 2 of the volume.

Following immediately is a contribution from Batten's friend, Knight-Ridder colleague, and long-time commentator on public journalism, retired *Wichita Eagle* Editor Davis "Buzz" Merritt. Under Merritt, the *Eagle* became a paradigmatic example of "doing public journalism." He was truly one of the founders and innovators of the practice. An anecdote he relates in one of his books describes how when the Knight-Ridder corporate staff "was looking for a newspaper willing to try new approaches to election coverage" he told them: "You've come to the right place" (Merritt, 1998, p. 85). In his chapter, Merritt briefly retraces some of the historical roots of public journalism as "a theory in search of a practice" and compares its beginnings to citizen journalism's emergence as "a practice in search of a theory."

Continuing the historical perspective, David Ryfe and Donica Mensing pursue this theme of journalistic transformation. They examine citizen journalism websites for self-definitions of the practice. They find a strong tendency for citizen journalism sites to describe themselves in conjunction with traditional concepts of news (i.e. providing information) along with an under-developed sense of exactly what interactivity can mean for their presentations. They note an incomplete expression of citizen journalism, one that struggles to impose traditional notions of journalism upon emerging interactive technologies. Their findings offer the possibility that public journalism principles can fill the void. If so, public journalism's historical footings may well provide the theory Merritt says citizen journalism still struggles to articulate.

The notion of citizen journalists seeking to define what's appropriate for their coverage is further elaborated by Aaron Barlow's review of the evolving theory and practice of gatekeeping. He maintains that the emerging interactive platforms for defining and sharing news lead to new understandings of gatekeeping. Such an activity has gone from being closely managed by professional journalists to a more negotiated, peer-reviewed approach offered by other citizen contributors. By looking at citizens controlling both production and dissemination of news, he points to challenges to the idea that the professional newsroom determines the nature of a citizen-engaged press.

Part I ends with an interview with long-time public journalism scholar Lewis A. Friedland. This interview, and the other end-of-part interviews, are called "Open Source" because questions were developed with the help of the book's contributors. Then, the interviews were posted on a blog for comments by the civic and citizen journalism research community. Friedland offers some insightful, though not exactly optimistic, comments about the diminished state of public journalism, how it reached that point, and what the prospects might be for its reinvigoration.

Reference

Merritt, D. (1998). *Public Journalism and Public Life: Why Telling the News is Not Enough.* Mahwah: Lawrence Erlbaum Associates.

Chapter 2

Newspapers and Communities
The Vital Link

James K. Batten

Editors' note: This is the text of a talk that James Batten, who was chief executive officer of the Knight-Ridder newspaper group at the time, gave at the University of Kansas on February 9, 1990, when he was honored by the William Allen White Foundation with the William Allen White Award, for distinguished contributions to journalism. It is reprinted with permission of the University of Kansas and the William Allen White Foundation.

I begin with a faintly embarrassing confession. Unlike a number of your distinguished William Allen White recipients, I can claim no deep roots in the soil of Kansas. No graduate work at Lawrence. No newspapering in Coffeyville. Not even a brief Army stint at Fort Riley.

In fact, I never set foot in this proud state until the early 1970s, when I traveled to Manhattan for a couple of days' recruiting at Kansas State. I remember flying a big jet from Detroit to St. Louis, changing to another big jet to Kansas City, then hiking down to the gate for the flight to Manhattan. After a few minutes, a friendly fellow in coveralls strolled up and asked if I was headed for Manhattan. I said I was. There was a pause. I asked why he was interested. He grinned and replied, "I'm your pilot."

Soon we were winging over endless green fields of corn in a little two-engine propeller plane. I had the feeling of slipping away briefly from the fevers of urban America to a quieter, less contrived world that seemed somehow familiar, even though I'd never been there before. That feeling was underscored by the warm, open, unpretentious Kansans I had the good fortune to meet on my trip to your state almost two decades ago.

Those were the sort of unaffected people I grew up with in the peanut country of Tidewater, Virginia. Mine was a corner of America removed in time and place from William Allen White's Emporia – but it was a world he would have recognized and, I suspect, felt quickly at home in. The small-town South and the small-town Midwest of those years had much in common, and I'm sure they still do. People knew and cared about their neighbors. The sense of community was very real. Pride in one's town – or little country high school – was strong.

As I read up afresh on William Allen White in preparation for this trip, I must tell you I found myself mildly amused at the persistent images of him as a *small-town editor* – at least from the parochial vantage point of backwoods Virginia. In 1921, I discover, the population of Emporia was 20,610. Many of my neighbors in Holland, Virginia – population 300 – would have regarded a place as big as Emporia, Kansas, as dangerously overgrown, a place to buy new shoes for the kids and leave well before the afternoon traffic built up. The newspaper editor in such a teeming urban center would have been seen automatically as a towering man of affairs, whether he had any stature or not.

For reasons never fully understood, I have loved newspapers all my life. My first publishing venture came when I was in the second grade, bedridden for a few months from some never-diagnosed fever. Using a pan of funny-smelling jelly called a hectograph – a printing technology no longer on the cutting edge – I published the news of Holland, such as it was in the early 1940s. And for the first time – but not the last – I learned about the perils of advertising shortfalls. I remember solving that with a house ad featuring a hand-drawn P-38 fighter plane and a headline that said, JIM BATTEN SAYS BUY WAR BONDS.

That love affair with newspapers persists to this day. I have been blessed with a career that has been endlessly exciting and never dull – in a line of work that on its good days sends you home at night feeling you may have made at least a little difference.

Against that backdrop, you will understand my enormous sense of appreciation and honor as I receive the William Allen White Award. The 41 men and women who have been honored since James Reston led off in 1950 define much of what is best about American journalism. I am awestruck at joining such luminous company – and deeply grateful for the warmth of your welcome.

Four enormously eventful decades have rushed by since your first William Allen White citation. And by most measures, these have been halcyon years for American newspapering.

Despite the advent of television and a raft of other competitive sources of news and information, newspapers' prestige and influence have remained strong. Our employees are better educated and more professional than ever before. The quality of newspapers themselves is vastly improved. And at the bottom line over these 40 years, the publishing business has been one of our country's most prosperous. It still is.

But we all know the sky is not without a cloud here and there as we move into the final decade of this century. Circulation growth in most communities does not come easily. Readership – or at least willingness to read a newspaper *every day* – is under pressure from the escalating busyness of people's lives. And advertisers, while still quite dependent on newspapers, have proliferating alternatives for the delivery of their commercial messages.

If too many newspaper publishers and editors took their success for granted back in 1950 – or even as recently as 1980 – that dangerous complacency is rapidly disappearing at the outset of the 1990s. The old arrogance is receding, and we're inventing new ways to listen – really listen – to our customers. And we're learning how to act on what they're telling us about how to serve them better.

I want to focus for a few minutes on one of the most important elements of the challenge facing newspaper leaders in the 1990s. It is a factor some of us around the country haven't grasped fully – or acted upon with the energy and creativity it deserves.

I am talking about what William Allen White might have called community spirit, the willingness of people to care about where they live and to wade in to help solve its problems.

In the newspaper business, we have known for a long time – from common sense and increasingly from research – that people who feel strongly connected to their communities are much more likely to be good newspaper readers.

Last fall, in the most ambitious readership study in the history of our company, we surveyed more than 16,300 readers and non-readers in the 26 communities where we publish newspapers. We found that people who say they feel a real sense of connection to the places they live are *almost twice as likely* to be regular readers of our newspapers than are those who say they lack such ties.

Mario Garcia, the noted designer and newspaper strategist based at the Poynter Institute, told me the other day that our research simply confirms what he has seen again and again at the newspapers big and small all over the country. "I cannot overemphasize," Mario says, "the importance of 'community' as perhaps the most influential area affecting readership. It is this community attachment that precedes reader expectations, and loyalty to a newspaper."

None of this is terribly astonishing, but the insights coming out of this massive research have direct, real-world usefulness. If we can find ways to enhance these feelings of community connectedness, that may help produce at least part of the readership and circulation growth American newspapers are pushing for.

That's the good news: We're beginning to see more clearly the value of this weapon in the crusade to assure newspapers' healthy future into the twenty-first century.

The bad news is that in fact, the community-connectedness issue in many places is cutting against us. Less so in Kansas, I suspect, but in much of America. There is abundant evidence that growing millions of our fellow citizens feel little interest in – or responsibility for – their communities. They are increasingly consumed by their own narrow, personal concerns, with no time for even a nod to the needs of their neighbors.

And as you might expect, these people feel that they have no time for newspaper stories about what's going on at city hall, or the school board, or in local politics, or even on the presidential campaign trail.

Consider, for example, the record of voter participation itself, surely the lowest common denominator of civic involvement. If you don't care enough to bother to vote, you're unlikely to be engaged outside your own self-contained, self-indulgent world in any more demanding way.

So what's the story on voting? Our record is poor, as you know, and getting worse. Among the democracies of the world, our country's level of voter participation is among the very lowest. Turnout in presidential elections has been dropping ever since the Kennedy–Nixon campaign of 1960. Participation in the Bush–Dukakis election 15 months ago was the lowest since 1924. Fully half of the voting-age population stayed home.

These patterns, without question, are symptomatic of the sluggish state of civic health in many communities in the early 1990s.

John Gardner is a long-time personal hero of mine. He is the founder of Common Cause, author of the book *Excellence*, the wonderful little classic that's been selling well ever since it was published in 1961, and one of this country's most thoughtful citizens.

In a note a few months ago, John Gardner had this to say:

> Communities have been disintegrating for a long time, and the *sense* of community is increasingly rare. A steadily increasing proportion of our people do not belong to *any* community; they float around like unconnected atoms; they have no sense of *any* common venture. So why vote? Why read the newspaper? The newspaper is an instrument of community, but they have torn free of all that.

If John Gardner is right – and I believe he is – then there are powerful lessons here for us. If communities continue to erode, how can we expect newspapers to continue to prosper, over the long term?

All of this, it seems to me, adds up to a wonderful opportunity for good newspaper people at the beginning of the 1990s. If we can help revitalize our communities by cracking through the apathy and indifference, we keep faith with the Founding Fathers and, at the same time, look after our own important interests.

How do we do that? The answers will vary from town to town. They will come from wise and caring newspaper people who know their communities and have good ideas about how to make them more vibrant.

One of the best examples I know comes from the *Columbus Ledger-Enquirer* in Georgia. Columbus was a town awash in civic problems, yet nothing was being done. The town was starved for leadership. Its citizens didn't know where to turn, except perhaps to their newspaper.

Executive Editor Jack Swift decided something must be done. The newspaper paid for a survey to determine just what Columbus citizens were thinking and what they felt their community needed. The *Ledger-Enquirer* published the results in a series called "Columbus Beyond 2000," then initiated a series of town meetings to let people talk about the survey's findings. Jack then invited politicians and key community leaders to his home for a barbecue to decide what to do next.

The story has been developing over the last year, but it boils down to this: An apathetic town now has adopted its newspaper's "Beyond 2000" slogan and has developed a five-year plan of improvement. New civic organizations and fresh government initiatives are springing up to deal with the issues. The community is alive with activity, and the newspaper – initially criticized by some for its bold and direct approach – has been embraced for its effective leadership.

Now, even surrounding communities have invited the *Ledger-Enquirer* to come in and help ignite similar civic revolutions.

"What we have done has made a difference in the way the paper is viewed," publisher Billy Watson told me this week. "You can sense a feeling about the newspaper when you're out in the community – a degree of respect that's beyond the ordinary."

The Columbus success story was possible because the *Ledger-Enquirer* and its leaders were determined to build closer relations between the town's citizens, its government, and its newspaper.

But too many newspapers are poorly positioned to encourage community-connectedness among readers because they themselves are basically *disconnected* from their communities.

Newsrooms too often are over-stocked with journalistic transients who care little about the town of the moment. Their eyes are on the next (and bigger) town, the next rung up the ladder. They know little about their community's past and make no effort to learn. Worse, nobody insists that they do. And there is always the temptation to make their byline files a little more glittering at the expense of people and institutions they will never see again. It happens, unfortunately.

Some of our problems flow from our own folkways, based on the purest of journalistic intentions. Out of our manic concern about being compromised, we sometimes piously keep the community at arm's length, determined not to be in anybody's pocket. So we come off as distant – and unfeeling, better at criticizing than celebrating, better at attacking than healing.

My old friend Rolfe Neill, the publisher of *The Charlotte Observer*, the paper that gave me my start, puts it this way:

> Newspapers are preoccupied with the auditing function. You can audit your communities, but it needs to be done in sort of a motherly fashion. You can audit your children, but they need to know they will be loved, nurtured and guided. A newspaper should not be afraid to put its arms around a community and say, "I love you." Yet we live in mortal fear of being caught *approving* of our communities!

Rolfe is right, of course. Loving our communities, warts and all, is not something most of us were taught growing up in this business. To show affection was somehow soft-headed and un-journalistic. We were the clear-eyed monitors, the keepers of civic rectitude, the bane of the bad guys. All essential qualities, surely, but far from enough. Getting close to your community and your readers is also an essential part of the job.

I suspect the Sage of Emporia would be a little bewildered by these kinds of concerns. He knew his town and loved it, and certainly had no hesitation about saying so. That didn't keep him from taking Emporia to the woodshed when circumstances required it.

In his introduction on one of those occasions a few years ago, Buzz Merritt reminded us that the window by Mr. White's desk looked out on Main Street – the post office, the Masonic Hall, the comings and goings of the town. *The Gazette* and its editor were in the mainstream of community life, and the newspaper showed it.

Newspapers that immerse themselves in the lives of their communities, large or small, have the best prospects for success in the years ahead. And they have the best chance of drawing people in from the apathetic periphery to the vibrant center of community life. That will be good for the communities, and good for the newspapers.

There are, happily, a long list of newspapers around the country excelling at precisely that assignment.

In suburban Chicago, for example, there seems to be an unusually intense rapport between the 19 Pioneer Press newspapers and the communities they serve. Newsroom staffers, I'm told, are required to live in the communities they report on. Reporters are rarely in the newsroom. Armed with portable phones, they spend most of their time out in their towns, talking with readers and gathering news – including lots of names. There are few, if any, of what Mario Garcia calls "executive journalists," sealed-off folks who never poke their noses out into the communities they supposedly serve.

One night last fall, I flew up to Tallahassee for a dinner honoring a wonderful old newspaper editor named Malcolm Johnson, who was dying of cancer.

Malcolm had been retired from the editorship of the *Tallahassee Democrat* for a full ten years. But here were 400 folks from the community, eager to pay tribute to him and all he had done for their town. We almost never got home that night, there were so many people who wanted to tell stories about Malcolm and his love for Tallahassee.

For years Malcolm, a bush-browed, plump little man built much along the lines of William Allen White, wrote a page-one column called "I Declare!" Day after day, he celebrated Tallahassee's successes and raised hell about what he regarded as its wrongheaded failures. He was a part of the landscape.

His community-building brainstorms were almost endless:

- When construction threatened to destroy acres of native trees and shrubs, Malcolm mobilized "plant digs" – not to stop the bulldozers but to save the native flora and plant it elsewhere around town. The beauty of Tallahassee today is in part a testimonial to his success.
- When Malcolm was talked into doing a column about raising money to send disadvantaged kids to camp, his heart was touched. He organized a permanent program that has sent 7,000 children to camp since the early 1970s.
- Much as he loved Tallahassee's small-town flavor, he understood the need for economic growth. So he encouraged and founded Innovation Park out near the airport. Today 22 businesses employing almost 400 people are located in Malcolm's park.

Just as William Allen White chose to spend most of his working life in Emporia, Malcolm Johnson chose to spend most of his in Tallahassee. With his talent and heart, he could have had a successful career in a much bigger place. But he chose to stay in Tallahassee. He lived there for more than 40 years.

In this age of hyper-mobility, there are invaluable contributions to be made to newspapers and communities by those who, like Malcolm Johnson, choose to sink their roots deep in a single place.

One of my favorite examples is Jack Claiborne, the long-time associate editor of *The Charlotte Observer*. Jack, now 58 years old, moved to Charlotte when he was four. He was among the most gifted of a high-powered generation of young journalists at *The Observer* in the 1950s and 1960s. Most of the others left, never to return. Jack stayed, to the enormous good fortune of the newspaper and its readers.

In 1972, *The Observer* had just moved into a huge new building that covered a city block. It bore no resemblance to the modest plant the paper had occupied on the same site since 1927. There was concern that the community might feel something had been lost in the move. So Jack Claiborne launched a Saturday editorial-page column called "This Time and Place."

Still running with strong readership 18 years later, "This Time and Place" beautifully weaves today's events into the fabric of Charlotte's history. Jack helps readers see things in context, not as disembodied events with no connection to the past. I know of no newspaper that does this sort of job as well. Jack is a treasure to his paper and to his community.

The point of the Johnson and Claiborne stories is clear. By staying put, they proved exceptions to the rule. The rule is mobility – too often a degree of mobility that chews at the ties that knit good newspapers to their communities.

Companies like mine face a real dilemma on this subject. On one hand, we are nurturing the careers of gifted and ambitious professionals. They understandably want and deserve more responsibility. Often that means pulling up stakes and moving on to the next assignment in the next town. Yet their departures can bring pain and resentment in the communities they leave behind.

There is no simple answer. In our company, we have worked over the years, not always successfully, to avoid too-frequent turnover. We are determined never to let our newspapers be seen as branch offices of a distant, impersonal corporation. Strangers can't be leaders – or community builders.

My plea, I suppose, is to remember the wear and tear that excessive coming and going inflicts on the bonds between newspapers and their communities. And to be on the lookout for the Malcolm Johnsons and Jack Claibornes, and encourage them to put their roots down where they are. Kansas newspapering has a long list of these happy journalistic stories, many represented in this room today – and your newspapers and your communities are better for it.

Let me conclude with a final quote from John Garner's penetrating letter on the linkage between the fortunes of newspapers and the communities they serve:

> I don't think that newspaper readership will recover an upward trend if communities continue their *downward* trend. Newspapers might prove to be a splendid instrument for the regeneration of communities. If this country is to regain its strength, vitality and values, the recovery will begin at the grassroots. And that's where you operate.

That *is* where we operate. If we are looking for bracing new challenges for newspapering in the 1990s, it occurs to me that I have not yet heard a better one.

Chapter 3

What Citizen Journalism Can Learn from Public Journalism

Davis "Buzz" Merritt

The ideas that became known as public journalism emerged in the late 1980s as a theory in search of a practice. The thinking of a few widely dispersed journalists and academics began to coalesce around the proposition that public life – the way democracy is expressed and experienced – was in trouble and that journalism was implicated in the decline.

The rationale was as follows: Journalism and democracy are fully interdependent; one cannot exist without the other. Democracy works best when it is a continuing conversation among citizens aimed at deciding "What shall we do?" A healthy civic conversation requires shared information (which is what journalism theoretically provides) and a way to discuss the implications of that information. Participation in that conversation was waning, as evidenced by declining voter participation and high levels of distrust in institutions – pointedly including politics and the press. People increasingly withdrew into private niches and away from public life, and problems went unsolved because of an increasingly polarized ideological divide.

If democracy was thus threatened, so was its symbiotic mate journalism. Therefore an idea emerged that journalists, in the interest of democracy and in their own self-interest, must learn to do their work in ways that help sustain rather than discourage that essential conversation. Merely telling news, said some journalists and academics, is not enough; journalism must actively nurture the conversation that healthy public life requires. It can do that in many large and small ways, and these observers set out to identify those ways without abandoning journalism's core principle of objectivity.

As a result, deep into the 1990s the profession of journalism, not historically inclined to introspection, found itself doing a bit of it. The discussion, sometimes civil and insightful and other times not, was spurred by what sociologist Michael Schudson (1999, p. 118) called "the best organized social movement inside journalism in the history of the American press."

Not coincidentally, the business side of journalism was also in trouble during that decade, a decline that continues. As a result, the primary focus of journalism in its print and broadcast forms has narrowed from professional performance and reform to economic survival, leaving to conjecture the question of whether public journalism will ever fulfill its promise.

What is coming to be called citizen journalism, in contrast to public journalism's beginnings, is emerging as a practice in search of a theory. The ever-expanding Internet provides virtually everyone unfettered access to information and a way to publish to the world. Operating in that vastness are an undetermined number of people who share an interest in public life going well. They are telling other people about events they believe are important and exchanging thoughts about the meaning of those events (e.g. ibrattleboro.com, tcdailyplanet.net and portions of OhmyNews [english.ohmynews.com]). As traditional journalism institutions struggle to maintain their reach and relevance, this array of people and interests may provide the seeds for the emergence of a new kind of journalism. But as was the case with public journalism two decades ago, this new journalism is fragmented, not easily defined, and highly experimental. Its future as a sustainable practice and, eventually, as a viable business model is unshaped and uncertain. In their most ambitious forms, public journalism and citizen journalism share an interest in public life (and thus democracy) going well, but their evolutionary arcs separate at that point.

Given the fragmentation imposed by its origins in technology, citizen journalism unavoidably lacks both an architecture and a unifying theory. If it is to play journalism's traditional role in symbiosis with democracy, it will need both. Thus it is important that those interested in its potential consider, at the earliest possible stage, what its future structure and philosophy should look like. As they do so, these questions, among others, will arise: What can citizen journalism learn from public journalism? How can a philosophy that emerged from the concerns of career journalists be articulated to and adopted by non-professionals? What structure will reliably nourish and protect citizen journalism's fiscal and philosophical ambitions?

Then: Public Journalism

In the mid-1980s, what New York University professor Jay Rosen later catalogued as "alarm bells" (Rosen, 1996, pp. 18–33) were going off in the largely self-satisfied and somnambulant world of newspaper journalism, which constituted most of America's serious journalism. Daily readership was plummeting toward 50 percent of Americans, and alternative advertising possibilities were multiplying even as civic life was showing severe cracks.

A few journalists and academics worried about the alarm bells they could hear, though not all heard the same ones in the same way. Outside of a limited number of associations and institutions with varying agendas, resources and reach, no broad platform existed for the profession to seek consensus about either the nature and extent of the problems or possible solutions.

From my perspective as the editor of *The Wichita Eagle*, the presidential campaign of 1988 set off a distressing jangle. Barely more than one-half of eligible American voters had bothered to go to the polls after a campaign centered on images of a skulking Willie Horton, of George H.W. Bush in a flag factory, and Michael Dukakis grinning goofily under an out-sized military helmet. Substantive discussion of issues was sparse, particularly of those issues that most concerned citizens rather than the incestuously intertwined political–news-media establishments. In an op-ed column the week after the election, I wrote:

> The campaign just concluded showed at its worst the mutual bond of expediency that has formed over the years between campaigns and the media. . . . Together they have learned that feeding the lowest common appetite among the voters is safer, cheaper, and less demanding than running the risk . . . of providing in-depth information.

Campaign managers have no interest in breaking that bond of expediency, I wrote, because they value control, "so changing the contract is up to the media" (Merritt, 1988).

As the 1990s arrived, alarm bells continued going off in many places and were being heard by more people. In Miami, James K. Batten, the new CEO of the *Wichita Eagle's* corporate parent, Knight-Ridder Inc., was concerned about the twin declines of his profession and public life and his 37 newspapers' apparent disconnect from the communities in which they operated. He articulated those concerns during the 1989 Press-Enterprise Lecture Series in Riverside, CA. His newspapers' authority and credibility were being endangered

> by the very same forces that seem to erode the civic health of our cities and our nation: an inclination to withdraw into narrow, personal concerns and behave with indifference to our neighbors today and our communities tomorrow. . . . One wonders some days who is really caring about the public's business. And who is willing to read about it. And act on what they read.
>
> (Batten, 1989)

In Washington, DC, David Broder, dean of the nation's political commentators, wrote in his *Washington Post* column:

> We [meaning political journalists] cannot allow the [upcoming 1990 midterm] elections to be another exercise in public disillusionment and

political cynicism. . . . It is time for those of us in the world's freest press to become activists, not on behalf of a particular party or politician, but on behalf of the process of self-government.

(Broder, 1990)

In Dayton, OH, David Mathews of the Kettering Foundation, a think-tank devoted to improving democracy and civic engagement, acted on the premise that democracy exists to answer the question "What shall we do?" as a society. He put together discussions about how that question could be answered and concluded that the essential ingredients are shared information and civic deliberation. Clearly, journalism had a place in that equation.

In New York City, Rosen, a disciple of John Dewey and student of James Carey and Neil Postman with a background in philosophy and a deep interest in the workings of democracy, realized "that the press had a problem: how to puzzle through the evidence of civic withdrawal and its many implications for their work." He later wrote, "This was not something journalists could easily address from within. They were accustomed to covering the news, not rebuilding the logic on which the news was based" (Rosen, 1999, p. 25).

The thinking of those people and others across the country would be informed and expanded in the early 1990s by growing interest in the research and writing about the problems of the public, the press and politics by Jurgen Habermas, Daniel Yankelovich, Robert Putnam, E.J. Dionne Jr., Michael Schudson, Richard Harwood, Carey, Postman and others. Those thinkers' analysis of the dynamics of the public sphere was drawn, in turn, on the writings of philosophers such as Alexis de Tocqueville, John Dewey and Walter Lippmann.

And back in Wichita, as the 1990 gubernatorial election approached, I decided that the *Eagle* would move purposefully to "break the mutual bond of expediency" between journalists and political campaigns by re-directing our efforts. We would focus most of our resources and energy on covering the job voters faced – electing – rather than the task politicians faced – campaigning. That fundamental shift resulted in "The Voter Project," one of the first organized, conscious journalistic response to some of the alarm bells. It was not thought of as "public journalism," because the term did not yet exist, only the impetus. The name would not emerge publicly until 1994 and became almost immediately a matter of some contention that persists to this day. It arose out of necessity – a term for a rethinking of both journalistic theory and practice.

While some of us in journalism, typically more inclined to action than rumination, were stewing in our separate pots of concern and frustration, Rosen, the philosopher more inclined to rumination than action, was gearing up to address the politics–press–public concerns. His thought, he later wrote, was to mix Batten and Broder and Dewey and Carey, add Merritt's reflections to my own, find a language that isn't airy or obscure, fashion with it a story, or a sequence of arguments, add illustrations from the field, and take the whole thing public, bring it out into the open in as many forums as you can find.

(Rosen, 1999, p. 71)

With the backing of the Kettering Foundation, Rosen in 1992 acquired a multi-year grant from the John S. and James L. Knight Foundation to form the Project on Public Life and the Press. The first step in taking the idea public was to articulate the theory that was in search of a practice. We had a method; the Kettering Foundation would publish a pamphlet to which Rosen and I would contribute from our different perspectives (Rosen and Merritt, 1994). But in order to write about it, we needed to call "it" something, a matter of no small consequence. We settled on "public journalism" because the thrust of the idea was to make a positive impact on public life and because its practitioners would be public – that is, open and unselfconscious – about what they were doing and why.

We recognized that a name was also a label and we would thereby risk putting the ideas into a box when our strong intention was that the ideas would remain free-flowing and nurture broad experimentation. As Jay had put it, we wanted journalists

to ask themselves . . . how can I find a way of doing journalism that helps reconnect people to public life...? There could be no copyright on the idea, no official version. No right way to do it, only better or worse attempts to explain and experiment. Public journalism would have to be owned by all who felt the possibilities in it, and it existed only to give direction to those possibilities.

(Rosen, 1999, p. 73)

Naming it was necessary, but we recognized that the long-term goal was for it to lose its name, to become simply the way journalism is done.

What some observers began to call "the public journalism movement" reached its concrete stage in 1993 with the first in a three-year series of seminars mounted by Rosen's Project on Public Life and the Press, bringing together journalists to kick around their ideas and hear from thought leaders in the related fields of public life and politics. The invited journalists all shared at least a vague feeling that something was amiss in the press–public life equation; they could not deny that both were in trouble and that the press was somehow implicated because it was largely disconnected from the public it thought it served. The journalists left the seminars encouraged that they might be able to do something about the deteriorating situation, or at least willing to risk the effort.

There were at least two immediate results. One was dozens of very public experiments, some brilliant, some ill-conceived and dull, some memorable, some quickly forgotten. Another key development was foment within the profession, evident in arguments that were often loud and ill-tempered. Journalism has never been very good at covering itself or accepting challenges to its traditional principles, and this was no exception. The idea of public journalism was incubating outside the realm of the elite newspapers and journals, so the "not invented here" syndrome arose in some potentially important and influential places. Not surprisingly, some early coverage was cynical and portrayed public journalism's proponents as fevered evangelists, while some critics incorrectly read into it a pandering retreat from objectivity. Few of its detractors took the time to understand the underlying theory, dismissing it out of hand.

Even some journalists who were instinctively attracted to the idea were more inclined to action than theory. Traditional newsrooms tend to be more habituating environments than learning environments, so "Just tell us how to do it," they said. "Skip the philosophy." That approach could not work, because understanding the need for public journalism was a prerequisite for doing it well.

But other, positive forces were stirring. Batten knew Rebecca Rimel, president of the Pew Charitable Trusts, whose many interests included safeguarding and renewing civic life. Their discussions over time led to Rimel asking Edward Fouhy, a former news executive at several national networks, to think about the twin problems of journalism and public life and suggest how Pew could be involved. The upshot, announced in 1993, was the Pew Center for Civic Journalism, which Fouhy would direct. Armed with $4.5 million from Pew, he and his top assistant, Jan Schaffer, expanded the idea of public journalism into broadcast news and provided grants to newspapers and stations for experimentation and research. While their decision to use the adjective "civic" rather than "public" led to some confusion over time, the objectives of that program and Rosen's were essentially the same, so the number and reach of the experiments grew rapidly.

By 1995, the first of dozens of books on public journalism was published (my own *Public Journalism and Public Life: Why Telling the News is Not Enough*) and the theory began to solidify, as least as much as a theory can or should solidify. Its fundamentals were:

- Public life – that is, democracy – is in trouble and so is journalism.
- They are fully interdependent; one cannot exist without the other.
- Some of journalism's habits and mores are implicated in the problems of public life and in the disconnect between citizens and the press.
- It is in both the public interest and journalism's self interest to figure out how to fulfill journalism's historic role in ways that repair those disconnects.

- Doing this requires a fundamental mental shift for journalists; it calls for moving away from detachment toward becoming a fair-minded participant in public life while maintaining professional objectivity.

(Merritt and McCombs, 2004, pp. 70–71)

But even as these tenets developed, the public corporations supporting most of journalism faced a growing and even more immediate threat than the separation from readers. They encountered the tipping point in the evolutionary shift from long-term value investing by individual shareholders to a short-term focus for ever-rising profit margins demanded by the institutional investors and mutual funds that now dominated Wall Street.

The rules of financial score-keeping had changed from annual earnings per share to quarterly, monthly and even weekly operating margins. As circulation leaked away, taking advertising with it, the companies met the demand for ever-rising profits only by reducing costs, which in journalism meant reducing staffing and coverage. By the end of the century, few journalism organizations could indulge in the expense and risk of the experimentation that public journalism required; newsrooms were frantically bailing just to stay afloat, jettisoning great chunks of their resources and, in the process, their core reason for existing.

Stripped of much of their musculature on the financial side, these news-owning companies entered the new century totally unprepared to deal with the even more devastating effect of the loss of audience and revenue streams to the explosion of the Internet. The issue quickly became not whether public journalism would fulfill its potential, but whether even the most basic coverage of public affairs – government, politics, civic life – would survive in any meaningful form.

And Now, Citizen Journalism

The Internet, as is now well understood, restructured the architecture of information flow including, among many other things, the conversation upon which democracy depends. Virtually everyone is within reach of information and a way to publish to the world and can re-package the information within the bounds of their personal predilections, motives, biases and level of intellectual honesty. In the long scheme, the Big Bang of the Internet has only recently occurred, and within its roiling and rapidly expanding cloud of energy, countless ideas are swirling around other, similar ideas, with the potential to form into galaxies, star clusters and solar systems bound together by mutual interests.

It is helpful to think of citizen journalism in that context. It is too early in an emerging dynamic environment to locate citizen journalism precisely, and its ultimate attachment to the broad concept of traditional journalism is uncertain.

Citizen journalism's core exists in people motivated to tell other people about facts and events they believe are important and exchange thoughts about the meaning of the facts and events. That's undoubtedly a form of journalism, but also a form of public life, the way democracy is expressed and experienced. If people interested in the phenomenon of citizen journalism want to articulate a useful theory on which to guide its growth, what can they draw from the experience of public journalism?

The first step would be to understand fully why helping public life go well is an important mission and what barriers must be overcome to fulfill it. That means replicating the intellectual journey of public journalism, through primary and secondary sources. (An appendix to this book lists a sampling of key philosophers and researchers.) The intellectual journey is essential because accomplishing public journalism's aims requires more than a grasp of techniques; it requires full understanding of the "whys," not just the "hows." Simply mimicking the "hows" restricts the possibilities for experimentation and growth.

Citizen journalism, even in its infancy, has avoided at least one of the large hurdles originally encountered by public journalism – it is clearly in practice, and its origins are individual and spontaneous. Its practitioners readily accept, even relish, the fact that they are involved in public life. In contrast, public journalism advocates faced the problem of trying to convince news professionals steeped in the mistaken credo of detachment that not only should they be involved in public life but that they unavoidably already were. Another advantage for citizen journalism is that it has the ability to operate from multiple platforms at minimal fiscal cost to either the creator or the consumer, unlike the revenue-driven models of traditional journalism institutions.

Barriers do exist, however:

- The fragmentation of the Internet, while providing some fiscal and technological advantages for citizen journalists, is at the same time a challenge to cohesive action. Public journalists for the most part operated within defined information structures – newspapers and broadcast outlets dealing in comprehensiveness as opposed to narrow areas of interest. A cohesive, institutionalized platform already existed to which public journalism theory could be applied; meanwhile, the Internet tends toward decentralization and diffusiveness.
- Implicit in this fragmentation is the fact that many people practicing citizen journalism begin with concerns about individualized problems, events or causes, and not the generalized concern about democracy that animated public journalism. People interested in a form of citizen journalism that can reinforce civic conversation will have to figure out how to meld those individualized agendas into a broad philosophy.

- Central to the idea of a viable civic conversation is an agora, a place or mechanism for the conversation to occur, whether physical or virtual. The Internet has the potential for the formation of agoras, but just as public journalism needed a few like-minded people to organize around the theory they shared, citizen journalism will need like-minded people to organize the practice they share. Citizen journalism needs to pull together a useful mass of mutual interests from the individualized bits whirling around in cyberspace's Big Bang's aftermath.
- To adopt and pursue a shared goal such as helping public life go well, citizen journalism practitioners at some point will need or want to organize and even monetize their efforts, and that is the point at which a cohesive theory, philosophy and practice will be mandatory.

Carrying out a group mission and monetizing it requires the development of a recognized, credible brand. Operating under a brand, in turn, requires the development of standards, which are the natural offspring of a cogent theory of existence. Adopting standards requires determining who decides if standards are being met, a point of fact that aims right at the heart of the concept of citizen journalism as a free-flowing, spontaneous, individualized pursuit. Would structure and control be toxic to the very core of citizen journalism?

The End Game

At some point, traditional newspapers will disappear. Newspaper companies are scrambling to catch up after their failure to comprehend the implications of the Internet's Big Bang. They may be able to transfer remnants of their business to digital platforms, but the question is whether they will do it in time to preserve the level of journalism they have traditionally provided. While newspapers may soon no longer provide shared information and an agora traditionally associated with them, citizen journalism must come to terms with both for the healthy public life that our democracy requires. Citizen-generated journalism based on public journalism principles can help both our public life and the press go well, but only through deliberate, dedicated effort. It is unlikely to happen on its own, and, without such an effort, journalism would be taking the unacceptable risk of leaving the maintenance of democracy to chance.

Summary

Theoretical Implications

- Public journalism emerged in the 1980s as a theory in search of a practice. A few journalists and academics, concerned about the health of public life

and of journalism, with help from several foundations, began to think about
and experiment with ways to attack the intertwined problems.

- The movement spurred a vigorous debate within the profession of journalism because it represented generational and cultural change in a tradition-
bound profession.
- Wrenching changes in the economics of journalism around the turn of the
twenty-first century limited the resources and attention that public journalism required if it were to be widely and permanently adopted.
- About the same time, the Internet explosion fundamentally changed the
structure of information flow. Out of that explosion, citizen journalism
began to emerge as a practice in search of an underlying theory. Whether
public journalism theory will help citizen journalism define its philosophical base is an open question at this point.

Practical Implications

- Public journalism and some citizen journalism practitioners share an interest in public life going well, that is, solving problems and sustaining democracy through sharing information and ideas.
- Public journalists began with concerns about the viability of public life and
their profession. They attempted to act on that generalized concern through
specific changes in the practice of journalism. Citizen journalists are animated by individualized concerns and attempt to act on them directly.
- The public journalism movement was initially driven by a group of journalists and academics who came together in an organized way and set out to
incorporate others. Citizen journalism consists of individuals pursuing specific interests and to this point no core group has come together to organize
it into a movement.

Reflection Questions

- How can citizen journalism respond to the problem of the conscientious
citizen who wants to "keep up" with events and discussions in a community
or a nation but is faced with the fragmentation of that information over
countless narrowly based, limited-subject websites?
- What can be learned about the motivations of people who consider themselves citizen journalists? How can this data be marshaled to help the development of associations or other cooperative entities that can address the
dilemma in the previous question?
- If such associations develop, what decision-making mechanisms would be
necessary to ensure that standards and elements of the association's "brand"

were followed? If they strive to be comprehensive in order to meet the needs of the conscientious citizen seeking information, how should such entities be structured and, if necessary, monetized?

- Would such associations by their very nature contradict the origins and character of citizen journalism?
- If citizen journalism remains fine-grained and resistant to organization and standards, what educational and informational methods can be developed to help citizen journalists understand their role in the crucial connection between their journalism and democracy?

References

Batten, J.K. (1989). America's newspapers: What are our prospects? Press-Enterprise Hays Lecture Series, No. 24.

Broder, D. (1990, January 3). Democracy and the Press. *The Washington Post*, A15.

Merritt, D. (1988, November 13). A new political contract must restore meaning to election campaigns. *Wichita Eagle*, 3B.

Merritt, D. and McCombs, M. (2004). *The two W's of journalism: The why and what of public affairs reporting.* Mahwah: Lawrence Erlbaum Associates.

Rosen, J. (1996). *Getting the connections right: Public journalism and the troubles in the press.* New York: The Twentieth Century Fund.

Rosen, J. (1999). *What are journalists for?* New Haven: Yale University Press.

Rosen, J. and Merritt, D. (1994). *Public journalism: Theory and practice.* Dayton: The Kettering Foundation.

Schudson, M. (1999). What public journalism knows about journalism but doesn't know about "public." In Glasser, T.L. (ed.). *The Idea of Public Journalism* (pp. 118–133). New York: The Guilford Press.

Chapter 4

Citizen Journalism in a Historical Frame

David M. Ryfe and Donica Mensing

Is citizen journalism – blogging, open-source newsgathering, wikis, informational "mash-ups" and citizen journalism sites – transforming the nature of news? Many observers believe so. Carr (2007) refers to open-source journalism as nothing short of a "revolution" in newsgathering. Lemann (2006) wonders if citizen journalists aren't in the process of "stripping away" the possibility of professional journalism entirely. Bowman and Willis summarize the prevailing wisdom: the "profession of journalism finds itself at a rare moment in history when, for the first time, its hegemony as a gatekeeper of news is threatened by not just new technologies and competitors but, potentially, the audience it serves" (2003, p. 7).

Drawing on an analysis of 21 citizen journalism sites accessed from November 1–7, 2007, this chapter assesses this conventional wisdom by placing the potential for a transformation of journalism in a historical context that includes public journalism. Citizen journalists describe their work in ways similar to traditional journalism, except for the significance they place on interactivity. The relation between interactivity and traditional norms has not been worked out by citizen journalists – at least as reflected by the evidence available from their sites – but the intellectual work of public journalism may be of some help in this regard.

For this study, transformation is defined in terms of journalism's avowed purposes. A focus on journalism's aims rather than practice lends a historical dimension to assessments of citizen journalism. Historians (Kaplan, 2002; McGerr, 1986; Schudson, 1978, 1998) tell us that fundamental changes in the purpose of news are relatively rare. In a review of 300 years of news, Schudson (1998) detects only two such shifts: the move from a journalism of affiliation to a journalism of association in the 1830s, and the transition from a journalism of association to a journalism of information at the turn of the twentieth century. On these occasions, journalism was put to fundamentally new purposes, and justified by new goals.

Does citizen journalism signal such a shift? This review suggests that it at least has planted the seeds of such a change. Citizens who contribute to these sites remain committed to a longstanding journalistic purpose; namely, to inform a public. As professional journalists have done since the Progressive period, citizen journalists describe their mission as disseminating information in the form of facts, descriptions and analyses. To this extent, they share a conception of journalism's purpose that is deeply engrained in the profession of news. At the same time, the evidence presented here indicates that citizen journalists embrace much more strongly the benefits of interaction around the news. Unlike their professional brethren, citizen journalists insist that the value of news lies in the opportunity it affords to interact and engage with other citizens.

This conception of journalism-as-interactivity remains largely undeveloped by citizen journalists. Most importantly, they have failed to address the critical question of interactivity's purposes. Is it intended to entertain? Is it designed to inform citizens? Or does it have some other rationale? Nip (2006) is correct to note that as they address these questions, citizen journalists might profit from a careful assessment of public journalism. Today, public journalism, as practiced in traditional newsrooms of the 1980s and 1990s, is dead (Nip, 2008). However, its interest in making the news more transparent and interactive lends it an affinity with citizen journalism. Further, more than any other journalistic movement since the Progressive period, public journalism sought to reorient journalism's central purpose. Specifically, public journalists shared a sense that journalism's mission was to catalyze citizens toward the solution of public problems (Haas, 2007). Our review indicates that citizen journalists find themselves in something of an intellectual cul-de-sac, essentially using the new tools at their disposal primarily for the old purposes of disseminating information. Perhaps public journalism's emphasis on public problem-solving represents a way for citizen journalists to flesh out interactivity's potential in ways that will make it truly transformational.

What is Citizen Journalism For?

Within a historical frame, citizen journalism is only the latest chapter in a nearly 400-year conversation about journalism's purposes. Much of this conversation has orbited around journalism's relationship to democratic community. As Kovach and Rosenstiel (2001) note, since its emergence in seventeenth-century Europe, "the concept of journalism" always has been related to the "concept of community and later democracy" (p. 18). Put more precisely, conversations about journalism's significance have been linked to the relationship between democratic community and modernity. Consider, for instance, Hegel's famous quote regarding early modern newspapers:

> Reading the newspaper in early morning is a kind of realistic morning prayer. One orients one's attitude against the world and toward God [in one case], or toward that which the world is [in the other]. The former gives the same security as the latter, in that one knows where one stands.[1]

Hegel's thought is set in the context of a rapidly secularizing society, one in which religion no longer seemed able to bind individuals to one another and to their communities as it had once done. How were these communal ties to be sustained in a modern world? In the eighteenth century and beyond, versions of this question have been asked again and again (Tönnies, 1957; Delantey, 2003). Hegel provides one answer: journalism. In his view, the purpose of news is to offer public rituals out of which new communal attachments might form. Some formulation of this idea has reappeared in conversations about journalism's purpose ever since (Carey, 1989; Dewey, 1927; de Tocqueville, 1969). Much of this conversation has centered on the importance of journalism to the formation of public opinion. As Habermas (1989) argues, in helping to forge common political sentiments, journalism allows modern societies to fuse the morality of community to the rationality of the state (Kant, 1983).

In the American context, since the 1920s the relationship of journalism to public opinion, and by extension to democracy, has been understood in Progressive terms. More than 50 years ago, Hoftstadter observed "the Progressive mind is characteristically a journalistic mind" (1955, p. 185). He meant by this that Progressives equated social progress with rigorous inquiry and publicity. In so doing, they placed their faith in two ideas: first, that getting the right information could reveal the inner workings of modern society; and second, that a public exposed to such information could acquire correct opinions about what ought to be done. For Progressives, then, political community was grounded in information rightly understood. As Hofstadter argues, this conception of public life made journalism central to the functioning of democratic society. Gans (1979) writes that Progressive "values enhance[d] the professionalism of journalism ... giving it a respected social role" (p. 205). Not surprisingly, the professional identity of mainstream news workers has been shaped by this conception ever since (Schudson, 1998). Mainstream journalists imagine themselves as "trustees" of the public, representing their interests and concerns in the corridors of political power. They see their primary purpose as delivering accurate, timely, relevant information to the public. They hold to this self-conception because they also believe that the ultimate safeguard of democracy is a well-informed citizenry.

A close reading of their mission statements indicates that citizen journalists, ironically enough, see their role in similar terms. During the first week of November 2007, data were obtained from 21 citizen journalism websites located across the United States Canada, and South Korea. This sample was created from lists of citizen journalism sites developed by the Knight Citizen News Network (www.kcnn.org/citmedia_sites/full_list) and cyberjournalist. net (http://wiki.cyberjournalist.net/citmedia-independent). From the original 30 websites located in this manner, all professionally run sites or sites that relied mostly on content from professional journalists were excluded, leaving 21 sites. For analysis, the "About Us," "Statement of Purpose" and "Mission Statement" pages for each site were printed. Google and Lexis/Nexis searches for every site also were conducted to find references to these sites in other popular media. Finally, the editors of these sites were contacted directly. Only a few responded, but where appropriate their comments are included.

Many of the sites reviewed are very direct about their intention to inform the public. The creators of CitizenShift, for example, describe their site as providing users a "chance to become informed . . ." The Muncie Free Press adopts nearly all of the mission statement of the American Society of News Editors (ASNE), including its first principle: that journalists can contribute to the social welfare "by informing the people and enabling them to make judgments on the issues of the time." Assignment Zero's principal editor, David Cohn, says that the ultimate goal of his project, as he saw it, was to "help journalism fulfill its important function [of] informing people" (personal communication, August 2, 2007).

On other sites, the Progressive conception of news is more muted, but nonetheless apparent. Many, for instance, highlight their interest in distributing information:

- The Great Lakes Wiki explores new ways of speeding the flow of information, knowledge and news about one of the world's greatest natural resources (Great Lakes Wiki).
- Knox and Waldo VillageSoup, locally dubbed TheSoup, is an extraordinary experiment bringing immediate information . . . to weekly newspaper markets . . . (Village Soup).
- WestportNow is Westport, Connecticut's 24/7 news and information source . . . (WestportNow).

And, in line with Progressive conceptions of news, many equate information with facts, and facts with truth. The first of Oh Yeon-ho's (the founder of OhmyNews) ten principles for successful participatory journalism is, for example: "To deliver correct and non-manipulated facts" (Oh, 2007). Similarly, in an interview with Michael Tippett, co-founder of Nowpublic.com, Maurice Cardinal – citizen journalist for AssignmentZero – prefaces one of his questions this way: "Crowdsource networks break down walls and provide transparency. When you do that, truth comes out."[2]

The interest expressed by these sites in publicizing truthful facts places them firmly within the traditional Progressive conception of the news. In line with the views of professional newsworkers, they believe that the ultimate purpose of journalism is to inform citizens, and that good effects in public life can be obtained only when this information is accurate and truthful. Another way of putting the point is to say that citizen journalists place great faith in the power of information to animate political community – an information-dissemination paradigm that is a hallmark of the mainstream news media. One wonders why editors of these sites feel compelled to create them; aren't journalists, after all, already informing citizens?

For citizen journalists, the answer to this question is largely "no." Indeed, most of the sites reviewed justify their existence by noting that professional journalism is not doing its job. For example, Gordon Joseloff, publisher of WestportNow, notes that two local newspapers and three neighboring dailies cover Westport. But, he observes, the two local newspapers publish only two days per week. Moreover, "staff cutbacks [and] declining circulation" mean that "Westporters can instantly find out what's happening in the streets of Baghdad but not in their own community" (personal communication, December 12, 2007). Other citizen journalists express similar sentiments. In a blog posting on Jay Rosen's PressThink site, Lisa Williams of H₂oTown notes that her community has a local newspaper – the *Watertown* (MA) *TAB* – but "by cutting costs on things like staff, office, and production costs . . ." the paper had ceased to cover much of its community (Williams, 2005). And Vivian Martin, one of the "pro" editors for AssignmentZero, says that in her community the local paper has stopped covering neighborhoods, and that this has "opened an opportunity for citizens to fill in the gaps" (personal communication, August 26, 2007). The implication of these statements is that local journalists simply are not doing enough to cover their communities, and that citizen journalism is necessary to fill this gap.

Citizen journalists feel compelled to practice journalism not because they see the ethos of professional journalism as illegitimate, or because they wish to invent a new form of journalism. Rather, they feel compelled to do journalism because they believe that professional journalists are not doing their jobs. They note that since there are no longer enough journalists, the information contained in newspapers is too thin to bind people to their communities. Additionally, they argue that conventional journalists too often focus on the wrong topics or are too biased, and this makes it difficult for citizens to form common judgments. To the extent that citizen journalists are animated by such concerns, their efforts are more recuperative than transformational; citizen journalists appear motivated to recover a kind of journalism (and therefore a political community) that, they fear, is being lost. They intend to resuscitate the Progressive vision of news rather than offer journalism a new mission.

Having said this, citizen journalists deviate from professional norms in at least one crucial respect: much more than their professional brethren, citizen journalists extol the benefits of interactivity. For purposes of this study, interactivity is defined simply as the process by which two entities (in this case, persons) have an influence on one another (Bucy, 2004). Throughout their sites, citizen journalists encourage users to post, comment, debate and argue over shared information. It is true that professional journalists also embrace interactivity of a kind, but theirs is mostly a one-way conception in which the news influences the views of citizens, with very little citizen feedback to journalists. By contrast, citizen journalists encourage and even celebrate two-way interactivity, in which producers and consumers of news mutually influence one another.

This sensibility is evident in several ways. It is quite common, for instance, for editors to emphasize that their users ought to make contributions to these sites. The mission statement of Coastsider stresses that readers are encouraged to "post stories that they have a personal interest in, whether they think they can add something new to the conversation, or want to ask a question" (About Coastsider, 2003). PhillyFuture proclaims its goal to "empower people" by providing access to "news YOU write, for the city and the world" (About Philly Future, n.d.). Editors at Seaside.com describe their site as one in which "you take the lead in telling your own story" (About Seaside-Sun.com, n.d.). At Universal Hub, users are told that for the site to be successful, "YOU [must] report the news – or post your reactions to the news" (About Universal Hub, n.d.). In one way or another, all of these sites define success not in terms of the accuracy of the information they provide, but in terms of the amount of interactivity they can stimulate. We "promote the idea of participatory journalism," the editors of Wikinews state, "because of the belief that citizens know what is news like no others. You are invited to join this effort, and share news that is of interest to you" (Wikinews Mission statement, n.d.).

It is not enough, however, for people to post information on these sites. As some of the comments above suggest, editors also wish to stimulate conversation around this information. Village Soup advertises itself as a "place for community based discourse, debate and commerce" (About Village Soup, n.d.). Lisa Williams of H_2oTown describes her site as one in which people can "participate in the local conversation" (About H2otown/Contact H2otown, n.d.). And the creators of ToledoTalk define their site as a place "to discuss the news and events in Northwest Ohio and southeast Michigan" (About Toledo Talk, n.d.). The sense one gets from these sites is, as the editors of Arbor Update put it, that "[their] true value . . . is not in the posts themselves but in the discussion" (About this site, 2005).

This embrace of interactivity plants a seed through which citizen journalism might grow in a different direction than mainstream news. And ultimately, its growth may signal a fundamental transformation of news. But for this to happen, citizen journalists must develop a more substantive theory of their purpose. In the Progressive model, news is primarily intended to inform citizens, and particular news organizations distinguish themselves by how well they fulfill this purpose. By comparison, at least on the evidence we have gathered, it is unclear what citizen journalists hope to achieve by fostering interactivity. Users are asked to comment, for instance, on the work of others, but editors do little to nothing with these comments, and indeed, when stories are archived the associated comments simply disappear. The same is true for most of the interactivity that takes place on these sites. In their mission statements, a few editors make an implicit connection to the goal of informing citizens. Editors at Great Lakes Wiki, for instance, describe their site as a place that "speed[s] the flow of information" and, in the same paragraph, as a site where "you can collaborate in telling the Great Lakes story" (Great Lakes Wiki: About, n.d.). Similarly, Wikinews tells its users that they are "invited to contribute reports" within a framework of "open decision-making" to produce more accurate, relevant and immediate information than when professional journalists act as gatekeepers (Wikinews Mission Statement, n.d.). But most give no clear sense of the purpose of prompting interactivity on their sites. The result is that citizen journalism remains yoked, if only implicitly, to a Progressive, informational model of news.[3]

This observation may seem abstract, but it has real consequences for citizen journalists. Most notably, it has had the ironic result of sending citizen journalists off to prove that they can do the things professional journalists do — only better. If professional journalists maintain they serve as watchdogs over government, then citizens can do it better. If professional journalists produce long investigations of political or corporate malfeasance, then citizens can do the same, only with more insight and accuracy. However, as other chapters in this volume attest, citizen journalists do not come out very well in these comparisons. Moreover, the exercise largely avoids the question of how interactivity might make a unique contribution to journalism and democracy. Citizen journalists, then, find themselves in something of an intellectual rut. Compared to traditional journalism, their work is found wanting, yet they appear unable to imagine their journalism outside the purposes and conventions of mainstream news. If citizen journalism is to be a truly transformational moment in the history of journalism, then the issue of purpose must be addressed.

The Contribution of Public Journalism

Perhaps public journalism might be of some assistance. Public journalism emerged in the late 1980s and expanded through the mid-1990s, mostly in small and mid-sized daily newspapers along with a smattering of TV and radio stations. By 2002 it had sprouted more than 600 journalistic experiments in the United States and abroad (Friedland and Nichols, 2002), a dozen or more books advocating its practice, and more than 70 academic studies investigating its results. It is no wonder that one scholar (Schudson, 1999) dubs public journalism the "most impressive critique of journalistic practice inside journalism in a generation" (p. 118).

Haas (2007) correctly notes that in all this activity public journalists never developed a coherent public philosophy. However, one of public journalism's central legacies is the notion that journalists ought to interact with their communities. Many news outlets that experimented with public journalism focused on the benefits of conversation for journalism and democracy. Friedland and Nichols (2002) report, for instance, that more than half of the 600 public-journalism projects conducted since 1988 included some form of public deliberation. The Minneapolis *Star Tribune* initiated a series of "Minnesota's Talking" roundtables. In collaboration with Wisconsin Public Radio and Television, the Wisconsin *State Journal* organized a "We the People" project that involved citizens in televised deliberations. And the *Dayton Daily News* organized 300 citizen roundtables in 1994 on the subject of juvenile violence. Newsrooms designed these exercises to create situations in which citizens and journalists could interact with each other.

Given their shared interest in interactivity, citizen journalism and public journalism seem to have a natural affinity. However, much more than citizen journalists, public journalists sought to separate themselves from a Progressive conception of news. To do so, they worked very hard to describe journalism's purpose in different terms. Specifically, they argued that the purpose of interactivity was to help citizens solve public problems. For instance, thinking about what he had come to believe about journalism after 20 years in the business, Cole Campbell (1999) lists as his first belief: "journalism is in the problem-solving business, not the truth business" (p. xiv). Among public journalists, this sentiment was an article of faith. Nearly every summary of public journalism begins with the idea that journalism's overall mission is to recreate a vibrant, participatory democracy. As Rosen (1999a) puts it, public journalism was intended to "help the community act upon, rather than just learn about, its problems" (p. 22). This problem-solving orientation stemmed from the movement's philosophical roots in the pragmatic tradition of John Dewey (Perry, 2003; Rosen, 1999b). It was also a natural consequence of public journalism's view of the public sphere. If journalists were responsible for stimulating public conversation, the next natural question was, "To what end?" The answer was deceptively simple: to help citizens act on shared public problems. This is, to play off the title of Rosen's book, "what journalism is for." It is this sense of journalism's mission that led public journalists to advocate not just any kind of public conversation, but a deliberative one. "To deliberate," Merritt notes, "is not just to 'talk about' problems. To deliberate means to weigh carefully both the consequences of various options for action and the views of others" (quoted in Nip, 2006, p. 215).

And it is this sense of purpose that served as public journalism's central critique of the Progressive tradition within mainstream journalism. As we have noted, traditionally journalists have held that reporters fulfilled their purpose when they provided citizens with the information they needed to be free and self-governing (Kovach and Rosenstiel, 2001). Public journalists argued that this was not enough. In their view, American public life was broken. For this reason, journalists needed to move beyond merely informing the public; journalists also had to catalyze public action – literally to reinvent public life. For public journalists, this was journalism's ultimate purpose.

Critics of public journalism are correct to note that, in practice, public journalists often fell short of this ideal (Schudson, 1999). Their initiatives were often one-shot affairs. Reporters sometimes resisted experiments in their newsrooms, and some of the efforts simply failed. But research has shown that in communities where a news organization practiced public journalism, civic life benefited (Haas, 2007). People voted in larger numbers, and talked about politics with one another more often. Citizens and public officials expressed greater trust. A few public problems actually got solved. Moreover, the overall failure of the movement should not diminish its signal accomplishment. For the first time in 100 years, public journalists imagined a new purpose for the news. The purpose of news was not, as in the nineteenth-century party press, to prompt association, nor was it, as in Progressive news, to inform citizens. Instead, the mission was to provoke, facilitate and amplify public work; that is, to prompt public discourse and deliberation that led to improvements in civic life. This was, to their mind, journalism's best contribution to democratic community.

Citizen Journalism as Public Work

What would a citizen journalism imbued with this new purpose look like? The 600-plus experiments in public journalism give some indication: it would focus discussion on public issues; it would prompt citizens to adopt an experimental attitude toward these issues; it would facilitate public deliberation; it would strive to create thicker relationships between citizens and public officials. But a citizen journalism-as-public work would not simply morph into public journalism. Even if citizen journalists had this ambition, it would be impossible. Public journalism took place in the context of traditional newspaper newsrooms, and was distributed through traditional news media. Citizen journalism websites are not traditional newsrooms, and the Internet is a network, not a mass medium in the traditional sense. Such differences mean that the practice of citizen journalism will be very different from that of public journalism. It is not the purpose of this chapter to describe these differences. Other chapters in this volume highlight many of them. Here, it is enough to end with this thought: today, citizen journalists typically put their new practices to old purposes. Were they to embrace a vision of journalism as public work, they would put their new practices to new purposes. The result might be a true revolution in news.

Summary

Theoretical Implications

- Public journalism, and now citizen journalism, represent the latest chapters in a 400-year conversation about journalism's role in democratic community.
- Public journalism signified a potentially significant shift in the fundamental purpose of journalism, moving from the Progressive goal of informing citizens, to a Deweyean conception of journalism as a form of public problem-solving. Citizen journalism, however, has been framed largely in terms of the Progressive role of informing citizens. This frame makes citizen journalism a recuperative rather than revolutionary exercise.
- Public journalism's problem-solving approach to the news could provide the transformative purpose that would enable citizen journalists to distinguish and define their work.

Practical Implications

- A journalism-as-public-work approach to news means that citizen journalists will think closely about how to catalyze and facilitate public problem-solving.
- Citizen journalism imbued with a public-work purpose will not duplicate public journalism. Rather, it will experiment with ways of applying this approach to journalism to the networked platform of the Internet.
- Citizen journalism practiced in a public journalism vein might invent new practices for new purposes, and thereby truly revolutionize the news.

Reflection Questions

- How can citizen journalists build on the successes of public journalism and apply these lessons to the networked nature of the Internet?
- Should it be successful, will citizen journalism-as-public-work transform the entire practice of journalism, or will it become one way of practicing journalism in a broader, more diverse ecology of journalism?

Notes

1. Although often referenced, the exact provenance of this quote is difficult to track down. A reference in Andersen (1983, p. 35) traces back to Eisenstein's (1968, p. 42) essay. But although Eisenstein makes the observation, she does not attribute it to Hegel. More recently, Buck-Morss (2000, p. 844) traces the reference to a German-language biography of Hegel by Rosenkranz (1977, p. 543) who apparently takes it from a note made by Hegel in his notebooks sometime in the years 1803–5.
2. According to Jeff Howe, an expert on the practice, crowdsourcing is the act of "taking a job traditionally performed by a designated agent (usually an employee) and outsourcing it to an undefined, generally large group of people in the form of an open call" (this definition appears on Howe's website: http://crowdsourcing.typepad. com/). Retrieved on April 6, 2009. The entire interview with Cardinal can be found at http://zero.newassignment.net/filed/nowpublic_michael_tippett. Retrieved on August 8, 2007.
3. It is worth asking why citizen journalists remain tied to a Progressive conception of journalism's purpose. The primary data collected for this chapter – statements of purpose, mission statements and "about us" pages – shed little light on this question. Moreover, data drawn from our conversations with editors were too thin to warrant conclusive answers. But two sorts of answers seem sensible. The first arises from an observation made by Jan Schaffer in her interview with the editors of this volume. Schaffer notes that citizen journalists often come to the practice more out of an interest in building community than in journalistic innovation. With this orientation, citizen journalists quite naturally attend more closely to issues of community than of journalism, and so accept standards of the practice – which largely arise from a Progressive conception of news – as normal and expected. A second answer is suggested by Bourdieu's "field theory" of journalism (Benson and Neveu, 2005). Bourdieu argues that the "field of journalism" is held together by shared practices and values. Individual journalists conform to these practices and values so that their activities can be recognized as journalism by other journalists. Something like this process may be at work in citizen journalism. Given that their status as journalists is in doubt, citizen journalists may embrace the values and practices of the profession as, or even more tightly than, professional journalists, just so that they can secure status in the field. Obviously, more research into this question is in order.

References

About Coastsider. (2003, Nov. 19). Retrieved June 10, 2009 from http://coastsider. com/index.php/site/news/about_coastsider.

About H2otown/Contact H2otown. (n.d.). Retrieved November 2, 2007 from http:// h2otown.info/book/export/html/2400.

About Philly Future. (n.d.). Retrieved November 3, 2007 from www.phillyfuture. org/about.

About Seaside-Sun.com. (n.d.). Retrieved November 2, 2007 from http://seaside-sun.com/main.asp?SectionID=12&SubSectionID=12&ArticleID=124&TM=78687.

About this site. (2005, May 22). Retrieved November 3, 2007 from www.arbor
    update.com/meta/7/about-this-site.
About Toledo Talk. (n.d.). Retrieved November 3, 2007 from www.toledotalk.com/
    cgi-bin/about.pl.
About Universal Hub. (n.d.). Retrieved November 4, 2007 from www.universalhub.
    com/node/142.
About Village Soup. (n.d.). Retrieved November 1, 2007 from www.villagesoup.
    com/about/index.cfm.
Anderson, B. (1983). *Imagined communities: Reflections on the origin and spread of national-
    ism.* London: Verso.
Benson, R. and Neveu, E. (eds.) (2005). *Bourdieu and the journalistic field.* Cambridge:
    Polity Press.
Bowman, S. and Willis, C. (2003). *We media: How audiences are shaping the future of news
    and information.* Reston: American Press Institute.
Buck-Morss, S. (2000). Hegel and Haiti. *Critical Inquiry*, 26, 821–865.
Bucy, E. (2004). Interactivity in society: Locating an elusive concept. *The Information
    Society*, 20, 377–383.
Campbell, C. (1999). Foreword: Journalism as a democratic art. In T. Glasser (ed.).
    The idea of public journalism (pp. xiii–xxx). New York: Guilford Press.
Carey, J. (1989). *Communication as culture: Essays on media and society.* Boston: Unwin
    Hyman.
Carr, D. (2007). All the world's a story. *New York Times*, March 19, C1.
Delantey, G. (2003). *Community.* London: Routledge.
De Tocqueville, A. (1969 [1835]). *Democracy in America* (J.P. Mayer, ed., G. Lawrence,
    trans.). Garden City: Doubleday & Co.
Dewey, J. (1927). *The public and its problems.* New York: Henry Holt.
Eisenstein, E. (1968). Some conjectures about the impact of printing on western society
    and thought: A preliminary report. *The Journal of Modern History*, 40, 1–56.
Friedland, L. and Nichols, S. (2002). Measuring civic journalism's progress: A report
    across a decade of activity. Washington, D.C.: Pew Center for Civic Journalism.
Gans, H. (1979). *Deciding what's news: A study of CBS Evening News, NBC Nightly News,
    Newsweek, and Time.* New York: Pantheon Books.
Great Lakes Wiki: About (n.d.). Retrieved November 4, 2007 from http://great-
    lakeswiki.org/index.php/Great_Lakes_Wiki_:About.
Haas, T. (2007). *The pursuit of public journalism: Theory, practice and criticism.* London:
    Routledge.
Habermas, J. (1989). *The structural transformation of the public sphere: An inquiry into a
    category of bourgeois society* (T. Burger, trans.). Cambridge: MIT Press.
Hoftstadter, R. (1955). *The age of reform: From Bryan to F.D.R.* New York: Knopf.
Kant, I. (1983). An answer to the question: What is enlightenment? In *I. Kant, Perpetual
    peace and other essays on politics, history, and morals* (T. Humphrey, trans.). Indianapolis:
    Hackett Publishing.
Kaplan, R. (2002). *Politics and the American press: The rise of objectivity, 1865–1920.* Cam-
    bridge: Cambridge University Press.

Kovach, B. and Rosenstiel, T. (2001). *The elements of journalism: What newspeople should know and the public should expect.* New York: Crown Publishers.

Lemann, N. (2006). Amateur hour: The wayward press. *New Yorker*, 82 (24) August 7, 44.

McGerr, M. (1986). *The decline of popular politics: The American North, 1865–1928.* New York: Oxford University Press.

Nip, J. (2006). Exploring the second phase of public journalism. *Journalism Studies*, 7, 212–236.

Nip, J. (2008). The last days of civic journalism: The case of the Savannah Morning News. *Journalism Practice*, 2, 179–186.

Oh, Y. (2007, February 26). 10 Preconditions for the Value of User-generated Content. Retrieved November 3, 2007 from http://english.ohmynews.com/articleview/article_view.asp?article_class=8&no=347268&rel_no=1.

Perry, D.K. (2003). *The roots of civic journalism: Darwin, Dewey, and Mead.* Lanham: University Press of America.

Rosen, J. (1999a). The action of the idea: Public journalism in built form. In T. Glasser (ed.) *The idea of public journalism* (pp. 21–48). New York: Guilford.

Rosen, J. (1999b). *What are journalists for?* New Haven: Yale University Press.

Rosenkranz, K. (1977). *Georg Wilhelm Friedrich Hegels Leben.* Darmstadt.

Schudson, M. (1978). *Discovering the news: A social history of American newspapers.* New York: Basic Books.

Schudson, M. (1998). *The good citizen: A history of American civic life.* New York: Martin Kessler Books.

Schudson, M. (1999). What public journalism knows about journalism but doesn't know about "public." In Glasser, T. (ed.). *The idea of public journalism* (pp. 118–134). New York: Guilford Press.

Tönnies, F. (1957 [1887]). *Community and society* (C.P. Loomis, trans.). East Lansing: Michigan State University Press.

Wikinews Mission statement. (n.d.). Retrieved November 4, 2007 from http://en.wikinews.org/wiki/Wikinews:Mission_statement.

Williams, L. (2005, November 14). If I didn't build it, they wouldn't come: citizen journalism is discovered (alive) in Watertown, MA. Retrieved November 2, 2007 from http://journalism.nyu.edu/pubzone/weblogs/pressthink/2005/11/14/lw_h2tn.html.

Chapter 5

The Citizen Journalist as Gatekeeper

A Critical Evolution

Aaron Barlow

The evolution of Internet gatekeeping in relation to blogging and citizen journalism has yet to reach stasis. Questions still revolve around who should do the
gatekeeping and under which standards it should operate. Fortunately, movement is apparent; journalists and citizen journalists are beginning to work out
means for keeping order in the news-related part of the blogosphere. After
general discussion here of traditional views of gatekeeping and of how some
journalists are trying to approach the question, this chapter explores how group
blogs try to "police" themselves in what is still an undefined and, often, unsuc-
cessful manner. This examination ends with a discussion of why it is important
in the new technological milieu to recognize that gatekeeping today needs to be
understood in ways far beyond its more traditional definition.

In his 1731 *Apology for Printers*, an early exploration of gatekeeping through
necessity, Benjamin Franklin tried to divorce responsibility for the act of printing from responsibility for content. He failed: "I my self have constantly refused
to print any thing that might countenance Vice, or promote Immorality; tho' by
complying in such Cases with the corrupt Taste of the Majority, I might have
got much Money" (Franklin reproduction, originally published 1731). By refus-
ing to relinquish all control over content, he maintained control over all content.
Franklin argued that no middle route could be safely or effectively trod, for the
placing of that route between "hands off" and "hands on" is extraordinarily
subjective.

Where Franklin did succeed, however, was in clearly laying out a dilemma
faced by the controllers of media production and distribution, one that continues even in the twenty-first century. At what point do community standards
relieve the "printer" of responsibility for refusal to print? Or, turning it around,
what are the limits of the printer's options? Community standards are often
poorly defined and if the printer defaults to such guidelines too loosely, the
printer faces consequences. If, on the other hand, the printer interprets community standards too strictly, the printer still faces consequences. Ultimately,

for Franklin, questions of gatekeeping came down to skill in negotiating between community standards and the need to disseminate information. Over the next two centuries, another point was added: as journalists gained skill in sorting and prioritizing information, gatekeeping came to include decision-making based on that skill. Though questioning the value of this was not a central concern of the public journalism movement of the 1990s, it has become critical in the years since as new types of entities have appeared, and confidence in the "journalist" to fulfill this role has eroded.

Journalists as Gatekeepers

During the second half of the twentieth century, theories of gatekeeping began to appear, generally extending the work of Kurt Lewin (1947) whose explorations of leadership and group dynamics provided a starting point and initially were applied to journalism by David Manning White (1950). Examinations of gatekeeping continue today in the work of Pamela Shoemaker, whose most recent book (with Timothy Vos) is *Gatekeeping Theory* (2008). Shoemaker has provided the framework for study of gatekeeping on a theoretical level since the 1980s, with her 1991 work (written with Stephen Reese), *Mediating the message: Theories of influences on mass media content*, examining the gap between experienced and mediated versions of events.

Prior to the work of Lewin, White *et al.*, little attention was paid to any theory of gatekeeping (if it was perceived at all) with emphasis instead on practice as it affected a developing profession. Following Franklin's own example, nineteenth-century producers of news-media content cemented their position as its distributors, developing certain senses of their unique position of professionalism and responsibility by World War I. The movement toward professionalism was gradual, in part a growing response to what many journalists saw as the excesses of the older penny presses and the ensuing "yellow" journalism of the early 1900s. Throughout the twentieth century, the journalistic professionalism that had recently reached maturity endured, unfortunately obscuring the dilemma between publishers' decisions and standards the community would find acceptable that Franklin (almost accidentally) pointed out. Even advocates for public journalism, such as Davis "Buzz" Merritt (1998), discussed journalism only in relationship to its professional orientation: "In the dynamic of people, public life, politics, and journalism, only journalism has the combination of complete freedom and potential power to define its role, to set its own goals, to act – within reason – as it wishes" (p. 143). Because the line marking the end of responsibility ("within reason") is so ephemeral, only the professionals, the assumption goes, have the background necessary for handling the task of moderating debate within the media, of acting as gatekeepers. The journalists might even style themselves as the protectors of dissent, keeping at bay the incipient tyranny of the majority and marking the profession as a distinct "fourth estate" with unshared rights and responsibilities. This line of thinking, and the special status associated with it, eventually gained the status of assumed wisdom, as Merritt's comment showed, at least up to the time when blogs and Internet journalism began to break the hold that the controllers of older media had on efficient and effective distribution.

In many respects, questions of gatekeeping become questions of cultural stewardship, something that journalists, starting with Franklin, had found themselves forced to accept for their own survival. In Franklin's case, as his "Apology" revealed, the gatekeepers could not appear to contravene public morality. This necessity has, as White (1957) pointed out, led to a complicity with those who saw themselves, in circumstances well beyond (but including) journalism, as cultural guardians protecting against growth and change, a collusion carrying with it nostalgia for simpler times and a greater sense of control:

> One gets the impression that those who find the mass media anathema would feel more secure if we could go back to a period that had no radios or television sets, no motion pictures, an era in which books were the possessions of the few and the newspapers were priced beyond the means of all but the elite whose class interests were catered to. Short of going back to this pre-media era, which is palpably impossible, they would remove from the "average" man's leisure anything that didn't meet their self-styled standards of high culture.
>
> (p. 17)

Not even going back would help: White, of course, is participating in a dialectic at least as old as the United States, a discussion that also helped in the formation of the first American political parties, reflecting the differing attitudes toward the public held by Thomas Jefferson and Alexander Hamilton. In the twentieth century, the debate between elite and popular sovereignty was furthered by Walter Lippmann in *Public Opinion* (1922) and John Dewey in *The Public and Its Problems* (1927).

According to Philip Meyer (2004), one "of the less admirable things that [journalism] professionals do is exercise their social control to resist the development of new and threatening technologies and value systems" (p. 233). Still, by 2009, resistance to Internet-enabled journalism, with its implicit embrace of amateurism, waned as journalists began to come to terms with a new paradigm, one in which gatekeeping needs and possibilities cannot be imagined simply as the responsibilities of professionals.

The Gates Come Down

Yet the resistance to change had a point: information today has become more readily available than ever before. The problem with this, as professional journalists are absolutely aware, is that information alone isn't sufficient. It can, said N. Katherine Hayles (1999), "become free-floating, unaffected by changes in context" (p. 19) and effectively useless as a result. The journalistic gatekeeper not only sorts information (through rejection of much of it) but tethers it to contexts both within the world of information and the world of physical presence. When he or she is gone, the value of information (in the arena of journalism, at least) becomes problematic. As Simon Waldman (2005) points out in writing on coverage of the tsunami in the Indian Ocean in 2004, "There is a fundamental difference between reading hundreds of people's stories and understanding the 'real' story" (p. 78). He defends traditional journalistic practices: "Without the order they impose, it's much, much harder to make sense of what's happening in the world" (p. 78). This is at the heart of one older definition of "professional": all of what happens within your chosen field happens to you and is then synthesized through you. The journalistic profession, through its own notions of standards, ethics and peer pressure, thereby makes shared responsibility a reality. And that reality, for journalists, provides a check on flights of fancy, tethering to the ground the information finally presented for public viewing.

In contrast, with their unconscious and often amateur attempts to organize information, blogs have become contributors to disorganization. When there are millions of active, independent blogs, the information they try to present becomes, as Hayles (1999) said, cacophony. This would be the case even were each and every blog carefully vetted and constructed because (to quote Franklin again), "the Opinions of Men are almost as various as their Faces." Therefore, it is impossible to both accent significant stories and trace every opinion back to its root, to the truths (if there be any) underlying the pieces. Though there are myriad attempts to aggregate blogs, the sorting attempts, so far, have merely added to the available information while doing very little to organize and evaluate entries in an efficient and elegant fashion.

Writing almost a century ago, Walter Lippmann (1922) pointed out that:

> News and truth are not the same thing, and must be clearly distinguished. The function of news is to signalize an event, the function of truth is to bring to light the hidden facts, to set them into relation with each other, and make a picture of reality on which men can act. Only at those points, where social conditions take recognizable and measurable shape, do the body of truth and the body of news collide.
>
> (p. 358)

Blogs and other venues for citizen journalism on the Internet are contemporary points for collision of news and truth, so it is here that the question of Internet gatekeeping relating to the news media generally becomes most important. Whatever the venue, the problem remains: no one seems interested in letting signalization and truth into the intersection in an unfettered manner. Yet no one (including journalism professionals) has provided an adequate argument for their own unique ability to apply filters. As Lippmann said:

> There is no defense ... for stating six times that Lenin is dead, when the only information the paper possesses is a report ... shown to be unreliable. ... If there is one subject on which editors are most responsible it is in their judgment of the reliability of the source. ... The absence of [an] exact [test] accounts, I think, for the character of the profession, as no other explanation does. There is a very small body of exact knowledge, which it requires no outstanding ability or training to deal with. The rest is in the journalist's own discretion.
>
> (1922, p. 359)

Gatekeeping, as we have seen, comes down to discretion and expertise. One problem for citizen journalists lies in finding a way (outside of standing aside for the professional) of showing a consistency in judgment powerful enough to slow the deterioration of the news from information to assumption. Not surprisingly, Lippmann decides in favor of the professional and not the amateur. Ultimately, as Jay Rosen (1999) wrote:

> [Lippmann] ... reminded readers of the limitations of the average citizen, the stubborn realities of human nature, the daunting complexities of modern life, and the prosaic facts of manipulation. He put his faith elsewhere, in well-informed experts, who might provide leaders with better and better facts on which to base their decisions. Not popular opinion but a more reliable and relied-upon social science would have recommending force. The public "must be put in its place," he wrote. An exceedingly modest place it was.
>
> (p. 65)

Rosen, critical of Lippmann's view, would later become involved in the development of "crowdsourcing," an attempt to radically expand the place of the public in journalism through combining the bits of knowledge held by the many into one whole. The role of the amateur, in Rosen's projects, lies in simultaneously signalizing and fact-finding. Meanwhile, the role of the journalist moves toward truth-finding through information vetting and final presentation. In essence, in Rosen's view, the journalist is holding on to a reduced gatekeeping role that continues to focus on being a protector of community standards and provider of on-call expertise.

Through his attempts to yoke the interests of amateurs and the skills of professionals, Rosen has been exploring new models that could retain a role for the professional without placing him or her on a par with the amateur – yet without restricting either one. Few amateurs are in a position to signalize anything effectively. Yet one of the consequences of real crowdsourcing is the striking out of "few" and replacing it with "many" and the creation of a momentum beyond the purview of most journalists. With collective knowledge brought to bear on it, the story "takes on a life of its own."

In 2006, Rosen established NewAssignment.net with a mission

> to spark innovation in "open platform" journalism, distributed reporting and what's now called crowdsourcing. These are forms made possible by the Web and by the falling costs for large numbers of people to locate each other, share information, and collaborate across distance.
>
> (About NewAssignment.net, n.d.)

One of the offshoots of Rosen's NewAssignment.net is journalist David Cohn's Spot.Us,

> an open source project, to pioneer community-funded reporting. Through Spot.Us the public can commission journalists to do investigations on important and perhaps overlooked stories. . . . It's a marketplace where independent reporters, community members and news organizations can come together and collaborate.
>
> (What Is Spot.Us About?, n.d.)

Cohn recognized that he could not coordinate an unregulated marketplace:

> Spot.Us does have types of pitches that it will reject. We only support civic journalism (topics like education, public health, etc.). And if we ever got a pitch that was overtly racist, I wouldn't hesitate to take it down. I suppose that does fall under "gatekeeping" but I would never characterize it that way. I consider that more "civil-keeping." If you want to build a community site, of any nature, you must define your own sense of good/bad taste and stick to it. Gatekeeping around that is more to create a strong sense of community that keeps things functional – otherwise, even the best of people end up in screaming matches.
>
> (Personal communication, January 17, 2009)

Spot.Us could afford to keep such "civil-keeping" in the background, much as Franklin did. Still, Cohn's warning about providing a framework for avoiding "screaming matches" is extremely important to any successful gatekeeping attempt on blogs or citizen-journalism sites.

Few have gone quite as far as Rosen or Cohn in promoting the role of the amateur as partner to the professional. Efforts like NewAssignment and Spot. Us put the amateur volunteer into a subsidiary position that many do not accept, for they can set up shop for themselves and act as their own "boss." They move to their own blogs, or to group blogs run by people they generally see as their equals.

These group blogs, especially those with relatively open access for posters and commenters, have found that they have to be more explicit than, for example, Spot.Us when it comes to keeping things civil. Daily Kos, a widely read liberal political blog in the United States, provides "guidelines" designed to push contributors toward writing factual accounts and avoiding defamatory and inflammatory postings. Most online blogging, citizen journalism, or other discussion and investigative forums on the Web have standards of some sort, and people designated to enforce them – along with a community of users who often take it upon themselves to act as gatekeepers for the sites they have come to care about. In this way, they make "community standards" less an abstract concept whose impact is almost unseen and make active gatekeeping a prominent element of the forum.

However, as Siegel (2008) said, paraphrasing Kenneth Tynan's distinction between the artist and the critic: "the critic knows the way, but the artist knows how to drive the car." To Siegel, the critic is the signalizer and the artist the truth-finder. That formula, however, leaves no place for the audience. Therefore, his signalizer/truth-finder dichotomy is problematic today when the audience has muscled into almost every online communications venue, including journalism – demanding an active role and pushing aside those who try to insist that it remain passive. Siegel's argument is ultimately reduced to an insistence that his writing exhibits artistic skill and knowledge greater than that found within his readers, giving him greater authority (the audience be damned) – something that today's readers object to strenuously.

No longer can the story easily be controlled from above – not by superior knowledge, ability, access to media, or even political power – as the situation of the 2008 elections in Kenya showed and as the Mumbai terrorist attack revealed later that same year. News of these events spanned both the domestic and international spheres, with initial and ongoing coverage supplied by citizen journalists using the Internet or cell phones. In *Born Digital: Understanding the First Generation of Digital Natives*, John Palfrey and Urs Gasser (2008) said this was an example of a:

new mode of activism, made possible by the use of networked digital tools, [that] leads to benefits for citizens of established democracies, countries in transition, and authoritarian regimes alike. First, as the Kenyan example demonstrates, it is possible to harness the Internet's power to render more transparent the actions of a specific government. This transparency matters both in times of crisis – in an unruly election, for example – and in times of orderly governance. Second, the Internet can provide a means for ordinary citizens to participate in ways that public events are told to others, set into context, understood by people far and near, and remembered for posterity. The traditional hierarchies of control of news and information are crumbling, with new dynamics replacing the old.

(p. 256)

New means of controlling news and information, at least from a "civil-keeping" standpoint, are forming – as are new paradigms for both evaluating information and providing the gatekeeping duties that are necessary in the evolving news-media world.

Community Standards Revisited

What blogs have not successfully addressed for themselves is how to deal effectively with conflict in a manner that deters dysfunctional interactions escalating among users without the "admins" having to step in and ban someone from the site. However, some group blogs are moving toward an understanding of the volatility of a "world" that can seem, at first glance, divorced from the off-line daily reality we also inhabit. There is a need, within any online community, for a certain amount of gatekeeping. People are making up the process as they go along, as they discover the differences between online discourse and face-to-face situations.

A number of citizen-journalism groups have begun to experiment with various formats for gatekeeping that avoid the problems of hierarchical gatekeeping, yet also manage to keep order. Among these is ePluribus Media (ePMedia), a group that the author of this chapter, a charter member, knows well. Bloggers created the ePMedia site in the aftermath of the "Jeff Gannon" affair, when a man named James Guckert posed as journalist Jeff Gannon and appeared at White House news briefings for more than a year without a single professional White House correspondent publicly questioning his presence. It was bloggers, founders of ePMedia among them, who first questioned Guckert's presence and discovered his true identity. Having worked together on this story, some of those bloggers decided to develop a media venue that could, they hoped, house amateur journalism and present it in a professional fashion.

The goal would be for the group together rather than single individuals to provide gatekeeping functions. According to one ePMedia administrator, who uses the pseudonym "GreyHawk," one of the most important distinctions the group makes regarding unsolicited postings on the open portion of the site is "unpublishing" vs. deletion. An item that is "unpublished" is no longer publically visible but available to the author for revision or clarification. He said:

> We try to unpublish items rather than delete when there could be questions or issues arising, or to ensure that the pieces were properly reviewed. After enough time has passed to ensure that the piece won't be revised, revisited or otherwise defended, it can then be deleted.
>
> (Personal communication, May 25, 2009)

"GreyHawk" continued:

> We take our community quality very seriously. . . . Anything well-written and referenced has a chance of hitting the front page, regardless of whether a particular editor or site monitor agrees with it. But our past history . . . has shown us that there are many ways that publicly accessible forums can be co-opted toward political ends that aren't necessarily in line with open and transparent government, and most certainly violate the concept of getting news and information out to the people in an easily accessed, community-vetted and well-referenced way.

As any discussion of gatekeeping on the Web is likely to demonstrate, one of the most interesting ironies about the Internet age is that the more influential blogs often seem, ultimately, to obscure as much as they reveal. They may attempt to present information, but they are also venues for almost incomprehensible (to an outsider) tug-of-war battles and nearly invisible machinations over what they publish. They create virtual communities and norms that spill over into the "real" world – and not simply in terms of understanding "real"-world information. Though much of the fear-mongering about the dangers of the Internet are probably overblown, expansion of one's world is always going to include the unexpected and the potentially harmful.

In addition to the concerns raised by Franklin of balancing the public's need for information against "community standards," the contemporary gatekeeper has to deal with questions of motivation. Are there hidden agendas – political, commercial or otherwise, such as creating a fictional online personality for purposes of a personal vendetta – behind a particular Web presentation? Like questions of "community standards," this cannot be answered through skills training in information sorting, vetting and ranking. Rather, beyond any individual effort, successful attempts to find answers will come only through community actions, and through a non-hierarchical framework at odds with the rigid structures of the journalism profession as they have developed over the past centuries.

The question remains, however, as to how successfully blogs and citizen-journalism sites will be able to police themselves over the long run. Certainly, professional journalists will craft a new gatekeeping role for themselves, perhaps following models of the type that Jay Rosen and David Cohn have experimented with, models based on the skill of information management rather than the information control that has long been implicit in the profession. It will remain for the bloggers and citizen journalists themselves, however, to develop a means of keeping their own houses in order. The journalists will not likely be involved.

Summary

Theoretical Implications

- Two groups, trained journalists and bloggers/citizen journalists, claim some degree of responsibility for journalistic gatekeeping on the Web.
- News-media gatekeeping operates at two initial levels, one of community standards and the other of standards developed within the profession of journalism.
- Gatekeeping for citizen journalism adds a third level on the Internet – that is, gatekeeping specific to the discourse within each particular community and not gatekeeping drawn from professional status.

Practical Implications

- Professional journalists are finding that they can take on new roles in relation to citizen journalism, those of shepherd (gatekeeping of a sort), specialist, trainer or (more generally) information specialist. These new roles, however, are not yet accepted by citizen journalists/bloggers who have yet to be convinced that the professional has something to offer that the blogger cannot accomplish alone.
- The citizen journalist is, today, in a process of discovery and development of a new sort of grassroots, lateral gatekeeping – but the process is experiencing growing pains and lacks clear definition.

Reflection Questions

- Should gatekeeping be left to those with the greatest experience and tradition in journalistic gatekeeping, the professional journalists themselves? Or

should gatekeeping responsibilities now rest with the community of users, the bloggers and citizen journalists, to work out for themselves?
- What should the role of the professional journalist become in relation to the new citizen journalism of the Web and gatekeeping?
- How should citizen journalists view members of the professional journalism community in terms of gatekeeping?

References

About NewAssignment.net. (2009). Retrieved February 2, 2009 from http://new-assignment.net/about_newassignment_net.

Dewey, J. (1927). *The Public and its Problems*. New York: Henry Holt and Company.

Franklin, B. (1731, June 10). Apology for Printers. *The Pennsylvania Gazette*. Reproduction of original work retrieved June 1, 2009 from www.historycarper.com/resources/twobf2/pg1731.htm.

Hayles, N.K. (1999). *How We Became Posthuman: Virtual Bodies in Cybernetics, Literature, and Informatics*. Chicago: University of Chicago Press.

Lewin, K. (1947). Frontiers in group dynamics II: Channels of group life; social planning and action research. *Human Relations*, 1 (2), 143–153.

Lippmann, W. (1922). *Public Opinion*. New York: Harcourt, Brace and Company.

Merritt, D. (1998). *Public Journalism and Public Life: Why Telling the News Is Not Enough*, 2nd edition. Mahwah: Lawrence Erlbaum Associates.

Meyer, P. (2004). *The Vanishing Newspaper: Saving Journalism in the Information Age*. Columbia: The University of Missouri Press.

Palfrey, J. and Gasser, U. (2008). *Born Digital: Understanding the First Generation of Digital Natives*. New York: Basic Books.

Rosen, J. (1999). *What Are Journalists For?* New Haven: Yale University Press.

Shoemaker, P.J. and Reese, S.D. (1991). *Mediating the Message: Theories of Influences on Mass Media Content*. New York: Longman.

Shoemaker, P.J. and Vos, T. (2008). *Gatekeeping Theory*. London: Routledge.

Siegel, L. (2008, May 27). Truth and Consequences. *Guardian*. Retrieved May 27, 2008 from www.guardian.co.uk/artanddesign/2008/may/27/art.culture.

What Is Spot.Us About? (2009). Retrieved February 2, 2009 from http://spot.us/pages/about.

Waldman, S. (2005). Arriving at the Digital News Age. *Nieman Reports*, 59 (1), 78–79.

White, D.M. (1950). The gate keeper: A case study in the selection of news. *Journalism Quarterly*, 27, 383–390.

White, D.M. (1957). Mass culture in America: another point of view. In Rosenberg, B. and White, D.M. (eds.). *Mass Culture: the Popular Arts in America*, 13–21. Glencoe: The Free Press and The Falcon's Wing Press.

Open Source Interview

The Evolution of Public Journalism

Lewis A. Friedland

We're calling these interviews Open Source, and asked our contributors to come up with some questions. That's what was in the question list I sent you, and I think it worked out pretty well.

It's a great project that you're doing; I think the book itself is going to be good. This will come out in the questions better than anything I'll say right now but it's a tough question for me whether there is such a thing as "public journalism 2.0." I don't see it as a given, for a bunch of reasons that we'll probably be discussing, just because the world has changed so much.

That's probably a good segue into the first question in the set I sent you and where I did want to start, which is to say that in your article in *National Civic Review* that was excerpted from your Kettering Foundation book, you said it was hard to be optimistic about the future of public journalism. But that was several years ago, around 2003–4. So what's changed in the landscape since then to either make you more optimistic if you are, or more pessimistic, if that's the way you have gone?

I think one of the hard questions that we have to think about in answering this first question is what public journalism is; the "pivot" of the answer really depends upon how we define it. I don't necessarily want to go into a long definition at this point but I think I at least need to address it. To me, public journalism was a movement. It was a series of experiments that were largely newspaper based that ran for roughly 10 years, from 1990 or a little earlier, depending on how you're counting, through about 2002 or 2003. It's not as if when the Pew Center for Civic Journalism ended that all of a sudden public journalism ended. But what did, I think, change radically around that time was the beginning of the challenge of the Internet to newspapers. The experiments that happened before were for the most part newspaper experiments and, more specifically, they were local newspaper experiments, with some significant exceptions. There were some TV stations, there were some national news organizations – *USA Today,* for example – but for the most part this was a local-newspaper movement.

That means part of the answer to the question for me is intimately bound up with the answer to the question: what is the fate of local newspapers? How much experimentation is there likely to be in local journalism in the next period of, let's say, ten years? To me, the answer to that is "precious little." In fact, what even a few years ago would have seemed to me a somewhat hyperbolic way of framing the question – are there even going to be local newspapers? – now is actually a legitimate way of framing the question. So when I think about whether public journalism will continue and how, whether I'm still pessimistic, the short answer would be: yes, I'm very pessimistic because I'm very pessimistic about the short-/medium-term fate of local journalism in the United States.

Reader Comments

I think Lew is right to be pessimistic about the fate of public journalism as practiced by newspapers. It is true that some public journalism techniques have been adopted as standard practices in these newsrooms, but I know of no large-scale experiment in public journalism under way at a metropolitan newspaper of any size.

(David Ryfe)

If public journalism is defined as a movement propelled by local newspapers, then I agree it is over for all practical purposes. But if public journalism is defined as a vision and aspiration for journalism, then it still has value and could provide a practical framework for online experiments.

It has value to the degree that it stands for an alternative conception of journalism, one that moves from journalism-as-information, to journalism-as-public-engagement.

Both conceptions of journalism are alive and well online. "Public journalism" as a vision provides a way to understand the differences between the traditional model of top-down, authority driven journalism and journalism that works from the point of view of a community.

If the idea of "public journalism 2.0" could be better theorized than the first iteration, if it could be shaped and discussed, it could provide a powerful model for shaping and evaluating the many experiments taking place online.

(Donica Mensing)

Breaking there is a good segue into the question that Joyce Nip has, which is whether traditional news operations should strive to have as a goal this notion of involving citizens in deliberation. And in addition to asking whether they *should* have that as a goal – building off what you were just saying – *can* they have that as a goal?

There really are two or even three parts to the answer. First of all, should newspapers strive to involve citizens, more generally, and I think the answer to that fairly obviously is: yes, by any means necessary and through every medium possible. And we are seeing that. My colleague Sue Robinson and a number of other folks write about the opening up of the newspaper, changes in journalistic authority, the use of blogs by journalists and certainly the incorporation of various forms of citizen journalism into local Internet versions of newspapers. Clearly there is a rise in citizen involvement and to my mind that's a good thing, an unabashed good.

The second question is: is that deliberation? And I think that's a much more difficult question that many people who are involved in advocating for citizen journalism haven't really answered very well or haven't thought through as well as perhaps they might have.

The third part of the question concerns deliberation itself and whether that is possible and desirable. In the best of circumstances there was some very deep and rich deliberation conducted by and sponsored by civic and public journalists, particularly for example the Norfolk *Virginian Pilot*'s efforts that were just very rich and very well prepared. The [Wichita] *Eagle* did that, too, extremely well, in the beginning. There were other papers obviously that did that quite well; I don't want to suggest that only those papers [Norfolk and Wichita] did this, but they were particularly good at it.

So there was deliberation conducted by these papers. It required a huge amount of work, a lot of time, and a lot of preparation. There were very skilled public-life editors or heads of public life teams that went out and organized them. They often involved various kinds of citizen surveys or focus groups. There was a lot of time and effort and of course money, which pays for time and effort, put into them. I don't see that happening again in almost any local news organization or newspaper that I can think of any time soon. The *Philadelphia Inquirer*, which just declared bankruptcy, did some experiments under Chris Satullo in urban planning several years ago. So, it has happened in the period since I wrote that piece. But it's been very rare, it's been fairly expensive, it's usually involved some kind of broader civic partnership along with the newspaper – somebody has to organize and convene it and that's a whole other set of questions. Right now newspapers are barely equipped to put out the daily news much less organize and convene public deliberations. So, I'm not very sanguine about what I would call genuine deliberation continuing through the auspices of local newspapers. I just don't think that the personnel in terms of the skill or the time and money is there to do it.

Some people might argue that online citizen journalism is a substitute for deliberation – essentially that the wisdom of crowds that emerges in the context of an ongoing discussion is one possible and a sufficient substitute for that kind of intensive deliberative local experiment. I myself don't think that it is for a variety of reasons, known to most people who have observed the overall quality of discussion that goes on in most responses to local online newspapers. The quality of that discussion, while sometimes interesting and often lively, is rarely deliberative. I don't see that kind of deliberation happening anywhere. Again, some advocates of a kind of wisdom-of-crowds approach might say: well, it need not happen because it's more distributed over space and time, there are more open voices, we don't need to have that same intensive discussion like we used to. Well, either way I don't think that it is occurring and I'm not sanguine about it occurring.

Having said that, do I think it should and could occur? Yes, I do. There are now a number of new ways of doing online deliberation that are truly deliberative – experiments that have been conducted by America Speaks and others in using online deliberative modalities that are pretty rich and quite good. But they involve, like I think all real deliberation does, some form of moderated discussion. They don't do away with the need for an organizer, they don't do away with the need for a moderator. It's just that they take place online rather than face-to-face, and that still requires a convener and the money to do that convening. So while I think that the capacity for the kind of deliberation that was done in the heyday of public journalism is there, I think that the will and the resources to do it are not.

Reader Comments

One thing to think about with respect to the question of deliberation is that people deliberate when they confront a choice: should we go to the movies or dinner? Should we turn this land into a public park or a parking lot? Deliberation is bound up with choice-work. So the question of whether news organizations can/will/ought to engage citizens in deliberation begs a prior question: will public issues be framed in such a way that citizens are given choices, and will their choices have an effect on ultimate outcomes? If the political sphere of a community is not set up in such a way as to open choices to citizens, then news organizations will have little ability to engage people in deliberation.

(David Ryfe)

Conversely, to pick up where David left off, if public journalism 2.0 draws attention to the need for journalism that encourages genuine consideration of public choices, then the result of that shift in focus would imply more attention to serving as the convener of deliberative conversations.

Given the need for local newspapers (print and online) to distinguish themselves in ever more crowded competitive markets, it is conceivable that these news organizations could again choose to become more integral to their communities by shifting the emphasis of their work. They have to find a competitive advantage to be viable. Could public journalism and accompanying deliberation be that distinguishing characteristic? Perhaps it will be for a few.

(Donica Mensing)

Moving on and talking about how the media system has fragmented, what David Ryfe in his question calls a more diverse media ecology developing and the mainstream news media no longer serving as the gatekeepers and filters: what's your view of what's being gained and what's being lost as this happens?

In some ways what's being gained is fairly obvious, which is a breakdown of one set of institutions and one set of actors, namely editors and reporters as the primary gatekeepers of what people read. I'm going to qualify that in a moment, but we are seeing, among other things a plurality of news sources for anyone who wants to essentially know anything that's going on in the world. If I want to know what's going on in Pakistan, I can read an English-language Pakistani paper or I can read the *Times of India* or I can read the *Guardian*. I can read the *New York Times*, I can read the *Washington Post* and dozens if not hundreds of other supplementary blog sites, independent journalists and so on. So clearly on a global scale the number of perspectives that are open to people is growing rapidly – but not exponentially. The sense of exponential growth is that more and more sources will come online fed by the doubling or tripling of those numbers every year and that somehow there will just literally be an infinite number of sources of reportage on world events. While at some level that's true and that's the promise of citizen journalism, that essentially every person can be a reporter, so everyone with an opinion, everyone with some bit of knowledge no matter how small about any issue or event is a possible contributor. Well, that's formally true now and that's an achievement that I think we need to acknowledge and not bemoan.

But, on the other hand, there are unanswered questions about the organization of that material, the refining of that material, the development of that material according to a multiplicity of points of view that go beyond the one-off reporting of events done with crowdsourcing. I think that even on the global scale or on the large metropolitan scale there's still this issue and this problem of how much reporting is going to be done. Colleagues like my friend and longtime colleague Jay Rosen are adamant about the need for support for a so-called pro–am model. At the same time these proponents – Dan Gillmor, Jay Rosen, Jeff Jarvis, to some extent – are NOT saying that somehow citizen reporting is going to replace the role of the professional; it's important to be clear that they are resolutely not saying that. Nonetheless, there is a lack of answers to how the reporting institutions are going to sustain themselves.

At times I think there's an assumption that because we have this plurality of points of view that somehow it's going to keep developing and growing, whereas I actually think that if we turn to the ecology model and we take it seriously it's possible that we're about to see the collapse of a niche rather than the continued growth of a set of niches – by which I mean an ecology starts to die when the population can't actually be supported by the resources available, and I think that we're starting to enter into a period where not just local papers but even the *Wall Street Journal* and the *New York Times* and the *Washington Post* are starting to feel the pinch of the rapid shift of the news ecology. And so, I'm not so sanguine that the "pro" part of the pro–am is going to be sustainable. If it's not, then I think that the media ecology is not actually a richer, more vital one. I think that were the pros to disappear, which is happening already, or if they were to scale back, which they certainly and absolutely will at least for the next seven to ten years of some form of transition . . .

Look at what Detroit is doing...[1]

Exactly. Detroit, and you could go on and on and on . . . the *Chronicle* in San Francisco, the *Philadelphia Inquirer*, and this is just in the last week. So we don't have to look very hard or very far to see the – if not implosion; I don't want to use that word because it's hyperbolic – but the radical scaling back of journalism in the United States. European papers, although they're funded somewhat differently, are under similar kinds of pressures. It's not clear to me that a new, robust, networked media ecology is going to remain as robust as it appears to be right now.

Now, everything that I've said about the global scale is even more true at the local scale and that's what I think is the largest blind spot of a lot of this discussion. A lot of the pro–am models that have been relatively successful have been things like the collaborative Sunlight Foundation project that Jay [Rosen] helped convene. The thing that people don't want to acknowledge is that that's on a national scale and it's able to draw on a critical mass of national users who are paying attention to a national problem.

When you scale that back to local community, most local communities don't have anything like that scale and they don't have anything like that critical mass. It's fine to say, "We're going to get two or three people in every congressional district to keep an eye on earmarks." I think that's a good thing, even a great thing. Only a fool would say that it's not. But it's much more difficult to say that here in Madison we're going to get someone in every school district to pay attention to report on the workings of the school board. That's not a substitute in a local community in a way that it's at least a plausible substitute on a national scale. And that's where I think that in a federal democracy, which is what we live in here in the United States – where so much political and economic power is vested in the local, county and state level – to have to rely upon citizen journalism even in the main to report on many of the stories that are now reported on by daily metros I think is delusional.

Reader Comment

Perhaps one of the characteristics of public journalism 2.0 will be a scaling down of the large, cross-media, mega projects of the past, to more focused, smaller projects produced by much smaller journalistic institutions. The networks of online journalism provide alternative ways of identifying issues, reporting, organizing community and publishing, which could enable much smaller organizations to produce work of measurable impact. Funding for journalism has not disappeared entirely; it's not sufficient to sustain large metros, but a not-insignificant number of small organizations in the U.S. are finding ways to provide credible journalism about public issues in local communities.

(Donica Mensing)

You've started to answer this, but let me bore in on it a little more specifically. What role might citizen media play in relation to mainstream media in enhancing public life? You seem to be saying there's maybe a small role there but we maybe are valorizing citizen media a little too much as to what's possible?
One of the problems is that there is a tendency at times to make a virtue out of necessity – to say that because newspapers are scaling back or even disappearing that citizen journalism can or should take their place or play that role. I want to stress that people like Jay Rosen and Dan Gillmor do not say that. But there are people who are less connected with journalism who have somewhat suggested that a lot of what was important and necessary – a lot of what people actually want to read that was being supplied by the local newspapers – can be supplied by various bloggers and citizen contributors at the local level. I think that's just not the case. So I think that public life will definitely suffer. There may be more formal transparency, but the problem is that formal transparency and reporting are not the same thing. I think that formal transparency without reporting is not strong enough to sustain a democratic public life. It's necessary but it's not sufficient.

Shifting gears to discuss notions of citizen and civic journalism: what do you see are the principal differences between those?
I see really huge differences between them and I really don't like the aligning of the distinctions. I think that it was done almost out of convenience when civic journalism started to decline around 2003 and not coincidentally with the sunsetting of the Pew Center for Civic Journalism. There were some people who basically thought, for reasons of good will, that citizen journalism was going to be a continuation of what civic journalism was and in fact even an expansion. If civic journalism's goal was to involve citizens in the newsgathering process, then certainly the Web was going to open that up even further and to make that process even easier.

For some of the reasons that we've just talked about, certainly the Web and Web 2.0 in particular have opened up journalism to more voices. There have been some places like the Spokane *Spokesman-Review* up until about a year ago under Steve Smith and Ken Sands, where they actually were making a mixed model of citizen and civic journalism work extremely well. But again, that required not just citizens but editors and reporters. There are three legs to that stool and what we've seen, I think, since then is fewer editors, fewer reporters, more citizen voices less well-edited and less well-organized. I know that there are supporters of citizen journalism who would say "well, that's fine." Essentially the Web is self-organizing, that we don't really need editors and reporters to organize that discussion, that the discussion people spontaneously engage in tends to organize itself.

Again, I don't want to contest that there is a great benefit there; I think that's an important moment to understand. We need to be able to hold two sides of a contradiction in our minds at once. It is positive that citizens are able to in fact both write and report but also contest and question and dispute the accounts of the traditional press. I think that's a good thing. But I also think that in the absence of the journalistic function, which does involve editing and reporting at a moderate to high level of professionalism, that we are actually missing an important element that adds significant value to citizen journalism as well.

Reader Comment

Lew makes a good point about the distinction between civic/public journalism and citizen journalism. A more detailed elucidation of those differences would be useful. Writing in 2006, Cole Campbell suggested: "We should take care to discern which kinds of citizen journalism build civic capacity and create publics or public relationships and which kinds serve other functions."

Building civic capacity implies an important role for editors and reporters to organize the discussion, as Lew notes. I can imagine an environment where a journalist's primary role is facilitator of public conversation, editing, verifying and organizing the ongoing reporting going on in a community. Building civic capacity, creating publics from disparate groups, serving as a connecting tissue between those doing public work could all be useful journalistic functions in the future.

(Donica Mensing)

Is there a way that citizen journalism can be made more civic minded in light of all the limitations you were just talking about?

I think there are ways. I think that there are new models that are emerging; there certainly are experiments going on that are worth watching and in some cases emulating. Voice of San Diego is one such model that people point to as a Web-based, online journal; the MinnPost and Twin Cities Daily Planet in Minneapolis-St. Paul point toward a new model. I think that there are experiments that are taking place locally. Of course, Walter Isaacson recently pointed toward the possibility of micropayments,[2] and that would follow the OhmyNews model of South Korea to some extent.

People also have raised the question of philanthropic support. Paul Starr recently wrote an important piece in the *New Republic* that said we might have to and perhaps we ought to be looking not simply at non-profit models but large philanthropies as a model for sustaining more traditional journalism and reporting. I think there's validity, potentially, to all of those models and almost certainly ones that we haven't thought about yet. I probably would throw our own Madison Commons model into the mix as well, where there's an active effort to go out and organize the community to report on itself, to supplement the reporting of the mainstream news organizations. We had to train people to do that. So there are if not a thousand, at least dozens of flowers blooming as potential alternatives.

Having said that, and I hate to be very pessimistic but I think I am realistic in saying that all of those are very fragile. I am not convinced that the philanthropic sector, which of course is under significant economic pressure right now like every other institution, is going to step up to the degree necessary to replace something like the role of robust local journalism in the United States. The Voice of San Diego model is working at some levels; it's having some significant success. But it's also having some trouble sustaining itself economically. They're also relying on philanthropy and the public radio model; that is part of their business model. But, they're struggling. Madison Commons struggles because people work [at other jobs], for example, and journalism is real work. People don't necessarily want to do the work of journalists. So it's hard to have citizen reporters replace professional reporters on any kind of scale. I'm not that sanguine that any of these experiments that are being tried are necessarily going to succeed. I don't think there's enough money there. I don't think that micropayments are going to be sufficient to support local newsrooms, although that could change.

Ironically, this goes with a question about the future, if and I think unfortunately when newspapers actually start to collapse in the United States as opposed to limp along so that – to go back to my ecological metaphor we have the actual death of a population as opposed to simply the war of each against all for a more limited resource pool – once we've cleared the field we might see new ways of combining display ad revenue, micropayments, various public–private subsidies and so on, that might support a new kind of local journalism. But we don't know what those are yet. Some of the models that we've seen are very creative and important experiments. By no means am I putting them down because they are not economically sustainable – but they aren't economically sustainable. I'm not sure what will happen. It's possible that – and I think this goes to another question – but it's not clear to me that the structure of civic life that we have in the United States at this point demands or will support local journalism. It may be that we've just moved on from there historically.

Notes

1. Editor's note: The interview took place on February 26, 2009, about two months after the Detroit newspapers had announced cutbacks in home delivery four days of the week that were implemented in late March 2009. Three days before the interview, the Philadelphia newspapers had declared bankruptcy, and just the day before the Hearst Corp. had announced it was considering closing the *San Francisco Chronicle* because of tens of millions of dollars in losses. The *Rocky Mountain News* in Denver published its final edition the day after the interview.
2. In a story in *Time* magazine, February 5, 2009.

Part II

Contemporary Civic and Citizen Journalism

Getting a snapshot of anything involving the Internet requires aiming at a moving target, and making a current assessment of citizen-engaged journalism on the Web is no different. Both journalism and interactive technologies are in their own respective states of flux.

However, a prominent aspect of contemporary appraisals of citizen journalism is the ongoing negotiation of the boundaries between traditional journalism and citizen efforts, a theme touched on by David Ryfe/Donica Mensing and Aaron Barlow in Part I and elaborated on in Part II. Should "news" be defined by traditional criteria even if it is produced by members of the public? Or is there room for greater latitude in the definition? What sort of editing or direction should citizen contributors receive, and who should provide it? How much time, effort and commitment can be expected from unpaid contributors in comparison with professionals? How should the roles of professionals adjust to a more collaborative interactive environment? Finally, what can the ideals and aspirations of public journalism offer as guideposts toward answering these questions?

This contemporary situation is explored with one piece featuring empirical research and three case studies shedding light on these questions. Assuming that professional journalists and citizens will approach news definitions and news values differently, Serena Carpenter explores the outcomes of those decisions by looking at the actual news produced and evaluating it with traditional measures of journalistic quality. Citizen-produced content does differ on measures such as sourcing and viewpoint-inclusion, areas in which public journalism also has departed from more traditional approaches. Her work suggests that public journalism could provide ideas for building up the quality of citizen journalism.

Other authors in this Part review examples of citizen journalism practice in an assortment of settings: in print (in a mid-sized metro paper), online in a small town, and online hyper-local efforts in one of the largest cities in the

United States. The first of these, by book co-editor Burton St. John III, reviews the short-lived Co-Pilot project of the Norfolk (VA) *Virginian-Pilot* newspaper. This was a thrice-weekly in-print section within the paper that editors had hoped would be a catalyst for discussion of civic issues. But it turned into a forum for essays of a more personal nature, leading managers of the paper to end it after just a few months because, in the words of its editor, the contributions "weren't taking [the readers] anywhere interesting." Kirsten Johnson supplies a developer's view of a citizen-journalism project created by faculty and students of a local college to serve the small Pennsylvania community of Elizabethtown. The chapter reviews other "town-gown" citizen journalism efforts and goes on to describe the struggles and successes, and decisions that were made, in creating such an effort from scratch in Elizabethtown. Suzanne McBride then examines more than a half-dozen citizen-journalism sites that seek to provide neighborhood-level news in Chicago and their sometimes similar, sometimes different, approaches to defining news and working through professional–citizen collaboration.

Each of these pieces has unique aspects, but they describe recurring dilemmas for today's citizen-engaged journalism – uncertainty in defining news values, shifting standards and responsibilities for gatekeeping, and difficulties negotiating the professional–amateur relationship. In total, they provide new insights into the challenges that come with blurring the boundaries between traditional concepts of journalism and emerging citizen-focused ideas. Finally, the Open Source interview with Tanni Haas offers further perspective into many of these same contemporary concerns as they involve a citizen-engaged press.

Chapter 6

News Quality Differences in Online Newspaper and Citizen Journalism Sites

Serena Carpenter

The traditional news media's position as the primary provider of information in the United States is being challenged because the ease of publishing content online has increased the number of people producing content. The people who publish information with little to no professional training are sometimes referred to as online citizen journalists. Controversy exists because it is assumed that some citizen journalists produce content without traditional journalistic values in mind (Glaser, 2006; Merrill, 1974). Some citizen journalists are not aware of such principles or they value the independence of creating articles that are not based on traditional principles (Gladney *et al.*, 2007; Johnstone *et al.*, 1976; J-Lab: The Institute for Interactive Journalism, 2007). Nonetheless, a study by J-Lab: The Institute for Interactive Journalism (2007) found the majority (79 percent) of citizen journalists surveyed felt they were producing "journalism."

Principles are, among other attributes, considered a set of standards for achieving news quality. This research addresses whether online citizen journalists are producing "quality" journalism as defined by scholars and traditional journalists by comparing their work to the content of online newspapers.

For purposes of this study, an online citizen journalist will be defined as "an individual who intends to publish information meant to benefit a community." This means citizen journalists and traditional journalists fall under the definition of a journalist. Not every person is a journalist, but any citizen can become one. While the word "community" often refers to individuals who are bounded by common interests, this research is limited to journalists reporting on a geographic community.

The definition of a citizen journalist can be dissected into several parts. The First Amendment protects a citizen's right to *publish*, and infringements on that right go against the ideals of the First Amendment. "Freedom to publish means freedom for all and not for some. Freedom to publish is guaranteed by the Constitution" (*Associated Press* v. *United States*, 1945, p. 20). *Intent to publish* is important because the rights of journalists must be protected not only with regard to publishing content, but even as they gather information. Journalistic information also should be intended *to benefit* the public; content that does not meet this standard should not be classified as journalism. Most traditional news organizations utilize geography to link themselves with their advertisers and news users (Lacy and Simon, 1993). However, in an online setting, many people don't use geography to define themselves (Chyi and Sylvie, 2001) but articulate their connectedness through common interests.

The Citizen Journalism Debate

Since the 1920s, news organizations and academic institutions have taught journalists principles that guide them as they gather news (Johnstone *et al.*, 1976; Weaver *et al.*, 2007). Despite a lack of specified credentials for entering the field, most news employers prefer journalists to have at least a bachelor's degree before they will employ them (Johnstone *et al.*, 1976; Weaver *et al.*, 2007). However, online citizen journalists prove that formal newsroom training is an unnecessary attribute to produce content online.

There is tension between those who consider themselves online citizen journalists and those who work as journalists for news organizations. One leading reason is that many citizen journalists are not trained to subscribe to the traditional journalistic standards (e.g. objectivity, fairness, accuracy, etc.) found in news organizations. Many citizen journalists value the freedom to create stories not based on those traditional principles (Gladney *et al.*, 2007; Johnstone *et al.*, 1976; J-Lab: The Institute for Interactive Journalism, 2007). Despite the criticism that journalistic principles can constrain news workers, these standards, in large part, have come to define journalism, and thus concern arises when citizen journalists produce content without these traditional norms in mind (Glaser, 2006; Merrill, 1974).

News Quality

The debate over how to define news quality has historically plagued journalism (Bogart, 2004; Johnstone *et al.*, 1976; Soloski, 1997). Many principles have stood the test of time; accuracy and depth are examples (Burgoon *et al.*, 1982). The Hutchins Commission's report is regarded as a broad indicator of what is considered quality journalism. The commission called for journalism to be more comprehensive, offer forums for compromise and criticism, present a representative picture, communicate the day's intelligence, and feature the goals and values of society (Commission on Freedom of the Press, 1947).

Quantitatively operationalizing and measuring adherence to broad principles of journalism is challenging because operational measures can be categorized under more than one principle. For example, the inclusion of a large number of sources in stories could be classified as a measure of accuracy, thoroughness, independence or fairness. Due to this challenge, this research has focused on defining story attributes that have historically represented quality in news, such as the use of transparent sources, rather than defining subjective principles such as fairness.

Although various organizations and researchers have attempted to quantify quality, no rigorous operational definition of journalistic quality exists (Gladney, 1996; Lacy and Fico, 1991; McManus, 1992; Picard, 1998; Commission on Freedom of the Press, 1947). Most research focuses on the analysis of quality at the publication level, based on newspaper editors' opinions of perceived journalistic quality, rather than based on the perceptions of consumers. Other research has defined quality based on the proportion of staff-written to wire-service stories and non-advertising content, the ratio of illustrations to text, the length of average front-page news stories, the use of interpretative pieces versus spot news, the number of letters to the editor, and the diversity of political columnists per issue (Bogart, 1989; Lacy and Fico, 1990, 1991). A survey of editors based on criteria from Bogart's research identified five factors that define media quality at the publication level: (1) ease of use, (2) localism, (3) editorial vigor, (4) quantity of news and (5) interpretation (Koang-Hyub and Meyer, 2005).

Gladney found larger and smaller newspaper editors define news quality differently. He identified 17 standards of excellence and found that circulation size was a factor in determining how editors assess quality. Larger newspapers tend to value staff enterprise, staff professionalism, comprehensive news coverage and interpretation, while smaller newspapers favor local news, community values and community leadership (Gladney, 1990). More recent research by Gladney and others (2007) revealed online editors and other news employees identified 38 indicators of online quality, 12 of which are related to general content quality. Although the majority of Gladney's indicators of news quality lack the precision necessary to evaluate whether news outlets are adhering to high standards, his research does support that differences exist regarding the definition of quality between smaller and larger newspapers. Reader's (2006) research also supports that differences exist between smaller and larger publications. He found editors of larger newspapers were more concerned about their professional reputation, while those at smaller papers were more concerned about adhering to community values.

Academic research on online citizen journalism publications is limited; however, research conducted on smaller publications such as alternative, neighborhood, weekly, urban, dissident and community-oriented publications can shed light on citizen journalism publications. Citizen-generated content is more likely published for smaller, more homogenized audiences, which will result in content that is dissimilar from that of daily newspaper journalists (Johnstone *et al.*, 1976; Tichenor *et al.*, 1980). Carpenter (2008) found that online citizen journalists were less likely than newspaper journalists to rely on media routines; they produced content that contained more opinion from sources and journalists and fewer organizational and official sources. Carpenter (2009) also found that online citizen journalists, by providing commenting opportunities and a profile, were more likely to be transparent than online newspaper journalists.

The Project for Excellence in Journalism (PEJ) defined quality local television news in the late 1990s based on input from television news professionals and academics. The PEJ identified quantifiable features that were considered hallmarks of local television news. Features representing quality included the use of enterprise stories, multiple viewpoints, a large number of sources, expert sources and stories that reflect the community (Rosenstiel *et al.*, 1999, 2000a, 2000b; PEJ, 2001). The PEJ's *State of the News Media* reports (2004, 2005, 2006, 2007) also assessed whether news media in America were producing journalism of high caliber by identifying quantifiable traits via a content analysis of one single day's publication. A team of researchers analyzed variables such as the use and number of sources, topics, multiple viewpoints, geographic focus, story tone and story origination across multiple publication types.

The goal of this study was to identify objective standards of quality that could be applied across all publication types, assessing quality at the story level. The PEJ's definition of a "good" local television newscast (Rosenstiel *et al.*, 1999, 2000a, 2000b; PEJ, 2001), *State of the News Media* research (PEJ, 2004, 2005, 2006, 2007) and other past research have been utilized to identify features considered hallmarks of "quality journalism." Elements used in this research to define "news quality" are: (1) a large number of sources, (2) a diversity of viewpoints, (3) the use of identifiable sources and (4) the use of local information.

While this research draws on this body of literature for its attributes of news quality, some of the previously mentioned categories were not used for three reasons:

- The element should not be included in every text story. (For example, the use of multimedia is a debatable attribute in defining quality because not every story is best told visually due to the nature of the story or because, based on the limited-capacity theory, users can only absorb so much information (Lang, 2000.))
- The incorporation of the story element collided with other journalistic principles; or
- The inclusion of the element is considered a debatable attribute. (For example, the inclusion of "mobilizing information" in stories can demon-

strate the news outlet's desire to civically engage its community, a tenet considered important by smaller news outlets (Gladney, 1990). However, the incorporation of this information can be uncomfortable for journalists because its inclusion may create the appearance of bias (Lemert, 1984).)

Attributes of News Quality

Number of Sources

To ensure diversity and accuracy, a journalist must obtain information from a number of sources to ensure representativeness, according to the PEJ (Rosenstiel et al., 1999, 2000a, 2000b; PEJ, 2001). The greater the number of sources used by the journalist, the more likely the story will reflect the issue accurately. State of the News Media research by PEJ has shown national online sites were more likely to contain a greater number of sources per story than weekly alternative newspapers or metro daily newspapers, which are smaller publications (PEJ, 2006).

Multiple Viewpoints

For journalists, it is important to check with more than one source to ensure the completeness of a story. Deadlines loom hourly for traditional journalists who work in an online environment, leaving many of them with little time to thoroughly cover an issue. Due to continual deadlines, journalists have learned to skim the surface of issues by relying heavily on media-planned events and official sources (Cunningham, 2003). This reliance shapes content, which is why the PEJ studies argued that journalists should include varying viewpoints from multiple sources because the incorporation of one or only a few perspectives limits how a person understands an issue (Rosenstiel et al., 1999, 2000a, 2000b; PEJ, 2001).

Anonymous Sources

The use of anonymous or unnamed sources undermines the credibility of information presented to the public and fuels a loss of confidence in journalism, according to the Nieman Reports (2005). The Pew Research Center for the People and the Press (2005) revealed that a little more than half (52 percent) of the public believed that the reliance on unnamed sources could lead to faulty or unreliable information. Riffe (1980) argued that the use of veiled sources sacrifices the believability of news stories. For the most part, U.S. newspaper publications do not contain a proportionately high number of anonymous sources

(Zoch and Turk, 1998). This may be because traditional journalists are trained to fully identify a source. Research has shown that U.S. national publications are more likely to cite anonymous sources than smaller publications (Culbertson, 1975, 1978; PEJ, 2006).

Geographical Focus

News stories that focus on local concerns can address people's need to connect. Local content can encourage citizens to become more involved in public affairs because they feel as though they have some knowledge and control over issues that affect them. The Federal Communications Commission (2007) and the PEJ (1999) stressed the importance of covering issues that reflect one's community; accordingly, the availability of local content is considered an indicator of quality (Bogart, 1989). Additionally, proximity is a strong factor traditional journalists rely on to determine newsworthiness as it positively affects readers' news awareness and recall (Graber, 2006; Donnelly, 2005). The more local the publication is, the more likely it will resonate with readers because local journalists tend to speak the language of their audience (Hindman, 1998).

Assessing Differences in News Quality

This research examined the extent to which online newspapers and citizen journalists differed in their adherence to traditional definitions of news quality. To assess news quality, this study used a quantitative content analysis of articles from English-language daily newspaper and citizen journalism websites in the United States. Data points centered on number of sources, use of multiple viewpoints, presence of anonymous sources and presence of local information. The unit of analysis was the individual text article located on the home page of the news website for one day's time.

Online Citizen Journalism Sample

A purposive sample of online citizen journalism sites was selected because no master online citizen journalism site list existed from which a probability sample could be drawn. To begin the selection process, Cyberjournalist.net was consulted. Cyberjournalist.net is a site that is dedicated to examining how technology affects the news media (Dube, 2005). In early spring of 2007, Cyberjournalist.net listed 77 U.S. "citizen media initiatives." Each site from this list was placed in one of two categories based on the size of the publication's home city. The goal was to find 100 representative citizen journalism websites nationwide: one "small" and one "large" community from each state in the United States based on size categories defined in previous research (Demers, 1994). To accomplish this task, one site from a given state was selected because it covered a city with a total resident population greater than 100,000, and the other because it covered a city with fewer than 100,000 people.

However, the Cyberjournalist.net list of 77 sites did not provide a diverse or large enough number of sites to represent all 50 states. To supplement that list, Placeblogger.com was used. Placeblogs are sites devoted to covering a particular neighborhood, city or region, according to the site (Williams, 2006).

Online Newspaper Sample

After the online citizen journalism list was complete, a matching technique was used to populate the online newspaper list. For example, in Alabama, The Birmingham Blog online citizen site's counterpart was *The Birmingham News* online newspaper. An online daily newspaper was not included in the final sample if one could not be found to represent the home community of the citizen journalism site. A total of 50 online daily newspapers were found to match the online citizen journalism publications' home cities.

Sampling Procedure

Once the online citizen journalism and online newspaper lists were complete, the sampling procedure was determined. This study utilized two different sampling techniques because of the likelihood there would be an over-representation of online daily newspaper content due to different news cycles (Greer and Mensing, 2006). To compensate for the expected smaller number of new articles available daily, online citizen journalism content was captured every day for one month (March, 2007), while online newspaper articles were captured every day for one constructed week during that same month.

Online Newspaper and Citizen Journalism Article Sample

This sampling procedure produced a total of 6,485 articles. To make the study more manageable while maintaining the meaningfulness of the data, articles were randomly reduced because of the large number of online citizen journalism ($n = 2,221$) and online newspaper ($n = 4,264$) articles retrieved. Articles were randomly reduced to 500 for online citizen journalism sites and 500 for online newspaper sites. From the available 1,000 articles selected from the 72 online citizen journalism sites and 50 online newspaper sites, some articles were discarded because they featured sports, wire articles or other excluding factors. After removing the unusable articles from the 1,000 article sample, 962 articles were available for analysis (480 online newspaper articles and 482 online citizen journalism articles).

Coding Categories

For the *number of sources* coders recorded the number of sources used within each article, including document sources. *Source anonymity* was noted if the source identity was impossible to establish (e.g. "sources said"). The presence of *multiple viewpoints* was measured in controversial stories. Controversy included physical, intellectual and ideological conflicts. Factual articles such as crime stories that relay only what happened were excluded from this particular analysis. Coders examined the presence of assertions addressing different viewpoints. Viewpoints were categorized as (1) all one opinion, (2) mostly one opinion (at least 66 percent of all assertions), (3) two views (no one view dominated more than 65 percent of the quotes), (4) more than two views or (5) not applicable or not controversial. The *geographical focus* was defined based on the geographic proximity of the story to the home city of the publication. Geographical focus was categorized based on whether the majority of the story reflected metro/city, state, national or international coverage. Local was defined as metro/city if the article focused on the home city of the publication or on cities located within 30 miles of the home city.

Coding Reliability

To establish intercoder reliability, two graduate students coded an overlapping 9 percent ($n = 91$) of the total sample. Intercoder reliability for ratio level variables measured with Pearson's r ranged from 0.82 to 1.0 and reliability of nominal level variables using Scott's pi ranged from 0.85 to 1.0.

Findings

An independent t-test was used to determine which publication type was most likely to cite more sources. The analysis revealed significant differences existed in the average number of sources cited ($p < 0.001$). Online newspaper articles ($n = 480$) averaged 3.64 sources per article, while citizen journalism articles ($n = 482$) averaged 1.37 sources per article. A goal of many traditional news publications is to maintain or gain readership. Larger publications may include a greater number of sources to attract a larger reader pool.

A Chi-square test was used to determine whether publication type was related to the presence of multiple viewpoints in controversial articles. The results were significant ($p < 0.001$). About one-third (29.5 percent) of the analyzed articles were considered controversial (see Table 6.1). Among this subset of controversial articles ($n = 139$ for online papers, $n = 145$ for citizen journalism sites), more than two-thirds (67 percent) of the citizen journalism ones were from a single viewpoint compared with slightly more than one-quarter (27 percent) of those from online papers. About 17 percent of citizen journalism articles on controversial topics came from *mostly* one viewpoint while 41 percent of articles in online newspapers were framed that way.

Previous research indicates online publications provide a greater opportunity to increase the number of viewpoints available to the public (PEJ, 2006); however, both publication types fared poorly by featuring *mostly or entirely one viewpoint* in a majority of the articles considered controversial. Online newspapers performed better at featuring articles with *two views or more*, with 31 percent of the controversial articles having this characteristic, while only 16 percent of citizen journalism articles on controversial issues did this.

The purpose of each publication type may explain why online newspapers are more likely to incorporate more viewpoints. Online citizen journalists may utilize their articles during times of controversy to promote viewpoints that reflect their community's values. Research indicates that smaller publications tend to omit outside viewpoints. The exclusion of viewpoints is one approach to promoting community consensus (Donahue *et al.*, 1972; Haas, 2007; Janowitz, 1952).

This research also addressed whether these publication types differed in their use of anonymous sources. Based on a difference in proportions test, 21.0 percent of 480 online newspaper articles contained an anonymous source, while 16.6 percent of the 482 online citizen journalism articles included an anonymous source; however, there was not a significant difference between each publication type.

This research also addressed the extent to which the content was local, used in past research as a measure of news quality. Table 6.2 reflects the findings.

Table 6.1 Presence of multiple viewpoints in controversial articles

Viewpoints	Online newspaper	Online citizen journalism
	($n = 480$) (%)	($n = 482$) (%)
All one viewpoint	8	20
Mostly one viewpoint	12	5
Two views	7	4
More than two views	2	1
No controversy present	71	70

Note
$X^2 = 40.86$, d.f. $= 4$, $p < 0.001$.

Table 6.2 Geographical focus of articles

Geographical focus	Online newspaper	Online citizen journalism
	(n = 480) (%)	(n = 482) (%)
City/Metro	47	69
State	21	13
U.S.	18	11
International	9	5
No geographical focus	6	2

Note
$X^2 = 49.9$, df = 4, $p < 0.001$.

The majority (68.9 percent) of citizen journalism articles were local, while 46.9 percent of the online newspaper stories were local ($X^2 = 49.9$, df $= 4$, $p < 0.001$).

Online newspaper journalists unite the public at the state and national level, while online citizen journalism publications concentrate their efforts at the community level. This research found both publication types devoted the majority of their coverage to local issues; online citizen publications were more proportionately local. However, a different sampling method that compared numbers may have produced different results because online citizen journalism publications publish fewer stories daily compared with online newspapers, and thus online newspapers may produce more local accounts because they offer more stories.

Conclusion

Smaller news publications differ from larger publications (Hindman, 1998; Reader, 2006), and the present research has demonstrated that in a similar fashion, significant differences exist between online citizen journalism (smaller) and online newspaper (larger) publications. This research revealed that online newspapers performed better at featuring a greater number of sources and a diversity of viewpoints in articles, while online citizen journalists offered proportionately more local information. This research found no significant differences existing in this sample related to the use of anonymous sources by each publication type.

The premise of the First Amendment is that everyone has the right to act as a journalist. This does not necessarily mean everyone who publishes content is creating "journalism." This study does not argue journalism should be defined solely on the measurements of quality assessed in this study. This research instead seeks to detour the conversation from identifying what is or is not "journalism" toward identifying traits that define "quality journalism." This research identified historical definitions of quality to encourage others in the field to identify and define quality themselves in order to encourage citizens' ability to recognize and create superior journalism.

To build user trust and loyalty, an information site must focus on quality (Kim and Han, 2009; Rieh and Belkin, 1998). However, journalists must consider what constitutes excellence from the user's perspective as well. Public trust in the news media has declined over the past two decades (PEJ, 2006). Online users typically seek information of interest to them, and that content needs to be perceived as believable. It is not considered believable if the content contradicts personal experiences (Cozzens and Contractor, 1987; Kim and Han, 2009). Information should not only be accurate, but it must also be useful. If it is not useful, readers may abandon the site. Users choose one information source over another because of perceived value. If content is perceived as "good" and "useful," it is considered of high information quality (Rieh, 2002). Thus, content should reflect more than regurgitation of information from sources; rather it must be deciphered and applicable to the site user's everyday life.

The news industry has been primarily responsible for defining standards; however, research has shown that other content creators disagree with the current definitions of quality (Gladney, 1990; Gladney et. al., 2007). This research shows online citizen journalists do not meet some of the traditional news media's definition of excellence; however, research needs to be conducted to determine whether they define quality differently. It is important to identify how all parties (news media, citizen journalists and consumers) evaluate quality to determine what each party has in common in how quality is perceived. Still, a broad definition of quality may not exist. A group's definition of quality may be an approach to maintaining jurisdictional control of its work (Lowrey and Mackay, 2008), and thus differences in the definition of quality may continue to exist because providers will always try to differentiate themselves from their competition. But it is still important to identify the factors, values and rituals that influence variations in content among different publication types, especially as citizen journalism sites play a more prominent role in providing communities with information about themselves.

Summary

Theoretical Implications

- Research on smaller news publications can be applied to online citizen journalism sites. Smaller publications are more likely to emphasize community consensus, be more trusted as a source, and prefer interpretative reporting.

- Information quality is a multidimensional concept that varies among news producers in both the traditional and online news arenas. News consumers also differ in how it is defined. However, the field of journalism has focused on quality from the provider prospective.
- Quality is important to identify to help users recognize and create reliable content.

Practical Implications

- Online citizen journalists do not perform as well as professionals when measured against some of traditional journalism's standards of news quality. Online citizen journalists were more likely to use fewer sources and include less diversity of viewpoints in articles. However, they were more likely to use proportionately more local information than online newspaper journalists.
- Content should not only be accurate, transparent and diverse, but also meaningful. Geographically focused content is not enough to make content meaningful to users. Future research could extend the definition of quality to include benevolence or helpfulness.
- Smaller publications are guided more by community standards, while larger publications are guided more by professional standards.

Reflection Questions

- Should a standard definition of news quality exist for the field of journalism? Or should each publication define its standards to ensure access to diversity of information? Alternatively, should the focus be on establishing trust with the user?
- Can citizen publications engage the public and create meaningful content while adhering to traditional journalistic standards such as fairness and objectivity?
- What are the implications if communities come to rely on citizen journalists for significant amounts of content, but information from those sources doesn't match traditional journalistic quality standards?
- What is the likelihood that as citizen journalism matures the quality of the work (as measured by traditional standards) will improve over time?

References

Associated Press v. *United States*, 57 (Supreme Court of the United States 1945).

Bogart, L. (1989). *Press and public: Who reads what, when, where, and why in American newspapers* (2nd edn). Hillsdale: Lawrence Erlbaum Associates.

Bogart, L. (2004). Reflection on content quality in newspapers. *Newspaper Research Journal*, 25(1), 40–53.

Burgoon, J.K., Burgoon, M. and Atkin, C. (1982). *The world of the working journalist*. New York: Newspaper Advertising Bureau.

Carpenter, S. (2008). How online citizen journalism publications and online newspapers utilize the objectivity standard and rely on external sources. *Journalism & Mass Communication Quarterly*, 85(3), 533–550.

Carpenter, S. (2009). A study of journalistic and source transparency in U.S. online newspaper and online citizen journalism publications. In Monaghan, G. and Tunney, S. (eds.), *Web journalism: A new form of citizenship?* Eastbourne: Sussex Academic Press.

Chyi, I.H. and Sylvie, G. (2001). The medium is global; the content is not: The role of geography in online newspaper markets. *Journal of Media Economics*, 14(4), 231–248.

Commission on the Freedom of the Press, The. (1947). *A free and responsible press*. Chicago: The University of Chicago Press.

Cozzens, M.D. and Contractor, N.D. (1987). The effect of conflicting information on media skepticism. *Communication Research*, 14(4), 437–451.

Culbertson, H.M. (1975, May). Veiled news sources – Who and what are they? *American Newspaper Publishers Association News Research Bulletin*, 3–23.

Culbertson, H.M. (1978). Veiled attribution: An element of style? *Journalism Quarterly* 55(3), 456–465.

Cunningham, B. (2003, July/August). Re-thinking objectivity. *Columbia Journalism Review*, 42 (2) 24–32.

Demers, D.P. (1994). Effects of organizational size on job satisfaction of top editors at U.S. dailies. *Journalism Quarterly*, 71(4), 914–925.

Donahue, G.A., Tichenor, P.J. and Olien, C.N. (1972). Gatekeeping: Mass media systems and information control. In Kline, G.F. and Tichenor, P.J. (eds.), *Current perspectives in mass communication research*. Beverly Hills: Sage.

Donnelly, L. (2005). Proximity, not story format, improves news awareness among readers. *Newspaper Research Journal*, 26(1), 59–65.

Dube, J. (2005, March 20). Citizen media initiatives list. Cyberjournalist.net. Retrieved January 11, 2007 from www.cyberjournalist.net/news/002226.php.

Federal Communications Commission. (2007, April 12). Localism task force. Retrieved June 20, 2007 from www.fcc.gov/localism/.

Gladney, G.A. (1990). Newspaper excellence: How editors of small & large papers judge quality. *Newspaper Research Journal*, 11(2), 58–72.

Gladney, G.A. (1996). How editors and readers rank and rate the importance of eighteen traditional standards of newspaper excellence. *Journalism & Mass Communication Quarterly*, 73(2), 319–331.

Gladney, G.A., Shapiro, I. and Castaldo, J. (2007). Online editors rate web news quality criteria. *Newspaper Research Journal*, 28(1), 55–69.

Glaser, M. (2006, September 27). Your guide to citizen journalism. Retrieved March 25, 2007 from htp://www.pbs.org/mediashift/2006/09/your-guide-to-citizen-journalism270.html/. *Mediashift* (pp. 1).

Graber, D. (2006). *Mass media & American politics* (7th edn.). Washington, DC: CQ Press.

Greer, J.D. and Mensing, D. (2006). The evolution of online newspapers: A longitudinal content analysis, 1997–2003. In Li, X. (ed.), *Internet newspapers. The making of a mainstream medium* (pp. 13–32). Mahwah: Lawrence Erlbaum Associates, Inc.

Haas, T. (2007). *The pursuit of public journalism.* New York: Routledge.

Hindman, E.B. (1998). "Spectacles of the poor": Conventions of alternative news. *Journalism & Mass Communication Quarterly*, 75(1), 177–193.

J-Lab: The Institute for Interactive Journalism. (2007, February). *Citizen media: Fad or the future of news?* Retrieved February 28, 2007 from www.kcnn.org/research/citizen_media_report/.

Janowitz, M. (1952). *The community press in an urban setting.* Glencoe: Free Press.

Johnstone, J.W.C., Slawski, E.J. and Bowman, W.W. (1976). *The news people: A sociological portrait of American journalists and their work.* Urbana: University of Illinois Press.

Kim, B. and Han, I. (2009). The role of trust belief and its antecedents in a community-driven knowledge environment. *Journal of the American Society for Information Science and Technology*, 60(5), 1012–1026.

Koang-Hyub, K. and Meyer, P. (2005). Survey yields five factors of newspaper quality. *Newspaper Research Journal*, 26(1), 6–16.

Lacy, S. and Fico, F. (1990). Newspaper quality & ownership: Rating the groups. *Newspaper Research Journal*, 11(2), 42–56.

Lacy, S. and Fico, F. (1991). The link between newspaper content quality and circulation. *Newspaper Research Journal*, 12(2), 46–57.

Lacy, S. and Simon, T.F. (1993). *The economics & regulation of United States newspapers.* Norwood: Ablex.

Lang, A. (2000). The limited capacity model of mediated message processing. *Journal of Communication*, 50, 46–70.

Lemert, J.B. (1984). News context and the elimination of mobilizing information: An experiment. *Journalism Quarterly*, 61(2), 243–249, 259–262.

Lowrey, W. and Mackay, B. (2008). Journalism and blogging. A test of a model of occupational competition. *Journalism Practice*, 2(1), 64–81.

McManus, J.H. (1992). What kind of commodity is news? *Communication Research*, 19(6), 787–805.

Merrill, J.C. (1974). *The imperative of freedom: A philosophy of journalistic autonomy.* New York: Hastings House.

Nieman Reports. (2005, summer). Offering anonymity too easily to sources. *Neiman Reports.* Retrieved March 25, 2007 from www.nieman.harvard.edu/reportsitem. aspx?id=101110.

Pew Research Center for the People and the Press. (2005). *Public more critical of press, but goodwill persists.* Pew Research Center for the People and the Press. Retrieved March 25, 2007 from http://people-press.org/report/248/public-more-critical-of-press-but-goodwill-persists.

Picard, R.G. (1998). Measuring and interpreting productivity of journalists. *Newspaper Research Journal*, 19(4), 71–80.

Project for Excellence in Journalism. (2001, November 1). *Local TV news project 2001. Gambling with the future. What is a "good" newscast?* Retrieved March 15, 2007 from www.journalism.org/node/238.

Project for Excellence in Journalism. (2004). *The state of the news media 2004*.Retrieved March 25, 2007 from www.stateofthemedia.org/2004/.

Project for Excellence in Journalism. (2005). *The state of the news media 2005*. Retrieved March 25, 2007 from www.stateofthemedia.org/2005/.

Project for Excellence in Journalism. (2006). *The state of the news media 2006*. Retrieved March 25, 2007 from www.stateofthemedia.org/2006/.

Project for Excellence in Journalism. (2007). *The state of the news media 2007*. Retrieved March 25, 2007 from www.stateofthenewsmedia.com/2007/.

Reader, B. (2006). Distinctions that matter: Ethical differences at small and large newspapers. *Journalism & Mass Communication Quarterly*, 83(4), 851–864.

Rieh, S.Y. (2002). Judgment of information quality cognitive authority in the web. *Journal of the American for Information Science and Technology*, 53(2), 145–161.

Rieh, S.Y. and Belkin, N.J. (1998, October). Understanding judgment of information quality and cognitive authority in the WWW. Paper presented at the Proceedings of the 61st ASIS annual meeting, Pittsburgh, PA.

Riffe, D. (1980). Relative credibility revisited: How 18 unnamed sources are rated. *Journalism Quarterly*, 57(4), 618–623.

Rosenstiel, T., Gottlieb, C. and Brady, L.A. (1999, March 1). *Local TV news project 1998. What works, what flops, and why. What is a "good" newscast?* Project for Excellence in Journalism. Retrieved March 15, 2007 from www.journalism.org/node/377.

Rosenstiel, T., Gottlieb, C. and Brady, L.A. (2000a, March 1). *Local TV news project 1999. Quality brings higher ratings, but enterprise is disappearing. What is a "good" newscast?* Project for Excellence in Journalism. Retrieved March 15, 2007 from www.journalism.org/node/387.

Rosenstiel, T., Gottlieb, C. and Brady, L.A. (2000b, October 1). *Local TV news project 2000. Time of peril for TV news. What is a "good" newscast?* Project for Excellence in Journalism. Retrieved March 15, 2007 from www.journalism.org/node/265.

Soloski, J. (1997). News reporting and professionalism. In Berkowitz, Dan (ed.), *Social meaning of news*. Thousand Oaks: Sage Publications.

Tichenor, P.J., Donahue, G.A. and Olien, C.N. (1980). *Community conflict & the press*. Beverly Hills: Sage Publications.

Weaver, D.H., Beam, R.A., Brownlee, B.J., Voakes, P.S. and Wilhoit, G.C. (2007). *The American journalist in the 21st century. U.S. news people at the dawn of a new millennium*. Mahwah: Lawrence Erlbaum Associates.

Williams, L. (2006, October 25). What's going on around here? Placeblogger. Retrieved March 15, 2007 from www.placeblogger.com/location/directory.

Zoch, L.M. and Turk, J.V. (1998). Women making news: Gender as a variable in source selection and use. *Journalism & Mass Communication Quarterly*, 75(4), 762–775.

Chapter 7

The *Virginian-Pilot's* Co-Pilot Pages

Participatory Journalism and the Dilemma of Private Values as Public News

Burton St. John III

In June 2007, Norfolk's *Virginian-Pilot* newspaper began an effort to incorporate citizens' voices into its printed pages with "Co-Pilot," a page that appeared in the paper's front section three times a week (see Figure 7.1). Billed as an area where "you pilot the *Pilot*," on the day the page was introduced reader editor Marian Anderfuren wrote that it "provides many avenues for your participation, from writing a personal essay to sharing newsy photos to covering events." She cautioned "this isn't a soapbox or a place to grind an ax," since Co-Pilot was a vehicle for "sharing and connecting" (Anderfuren, 2007).

Co-Pilot arose from discussions between Anderfuren and *Virginian-Pilot* management in early 2006, conversations that centered on finding ways to integrate more citizen perspectives within the newspaper. In fact, the *Pilot* had some institutional knowledge concerning citizen-engaged efforts; the paper had been an early proponent of public journalism in the 1990s (Charity, 1995). By 2006, however, renewed conversations about citizen stories in the paper's pages took on added momentum. The paper was working on a redesign that would offer the *Pilot* a page where "we can ask readers to cover things that we don't get to," said Anderfuren (personal communication, July 30, 2008). By November 2006, the paper sent Anderfuren to Spain to see how the newspaper *El Correo* used its daily citizen-contribution page Enlace (or "Link"). She noted how that section had communicated readers' knowledge and experiences, especially through opinion pieces and photos that sparked community discussion within Enlace. By the middle of 2007, the *Pilot*'s redesign was finished and Publisher Bruce Bradley committed to the Co-Pilot experiment for one year. The first page appeared on June 6, 2007. However, by mutual agreement, Anderfuren and Bradley terminated Co-Pilot on March 24, 2008. Designed with reader contributions in mind, Anderfuren indicated that Co-Pilot folded before that one-year commitment was up due to a lack of quality submissions (personal communication, July 30, 2008).

Figure 7.1 The Co-Pilot's inaugural appearance (*Virginian-Pilot*, June 6, 2007).

Public Journalism and Community Dialogue

Co-Pilot's intent to bring citizen perspectives and information into the pages of the newspaper echoed the impetus of the public journalism movement that had arisen in the United States circa 1990 (Merritt, 1998; Rosen, 1999). After the United States' national elections in 1988, several American journalists and academics voiced concern about traditional journalism's news-gathering and reporting practices (Broder, 1990; Carey, 1995; Merritt, 1998; Rosen, 1999). These observers noted that the news media's focus on political spectacle revealed a dangerously entrenched newsroom preference for expert sources. Elite actors commanded the press's attention, they cautioned, while the issues that mattered to communities were pushed to the background. Scholar James Carey noted that, after that 1988 election cycle, Americans increasingly did not trust the press, seeing it as an obstacle to more meaningful citizen participation in the political process (1995). Philosophically, the public journalism movement renewed a debate about framing of news accounts. Where traditional journalism had long privileged Walter Lippmann's perspective of a detached, objective reportorial style that favored using elite actors and experts, public journalism reinvigorated John Dewey's view that accurate accounts of reality are best achieved by delving into the dialogue within communities (Rosen, 1999; Haas, 2007).

Succinctly put, public journalism attempted to re-connect news coverage to the concerns of local communities by integrating citizen viewpoints into the construction and reporting of stories and using the influence of news outlets to facilitate public deliberation on civic issues. Most recently, Haas (2007) pointed out that public journalism's fullest potential rests in its capacity to empower marginalized groups through reporting their particular concerns and following up to ascertain that politicians and other influential actors are responding to the interests of the disadvantaged. Of particular relevance to this study was his observation that the movement toward a hyper-local emphasis within newspaper websites often led to content that represented communities as "unified sites, bounded by shared values and goals." Consequently, voices from disparate citizen viewpoints were often not included on hyper-local sites (Haas, 2007, p. 154). His observations, however, were mostly confined to online construction of news. Since the Co-Pilot was a print vehicle for community connection and dialogue, it provided an opportunity to examine how a traditional news outlet attempted a similar hyper-local approach for conveyancing a range of citizen viewpoints.

The Co-Pilot as Participatory Journalism

The Co-Pilot effort fit within Nip's (2006) description of a second phase of public journalism. She maintained that new interactive technologies helped morph public journalism into three broad categories: interactive journalism, citizen journalism and participatory journalism. In this second phase, she said, interactive journalism was rooted closely to the newsroom and featured journalists using emails, online chats and reader postings to provide further content options (pp. 216–217). On the other extreme, citizen journalism emphasized a detachment from the newsroom: citizens placed their own reporting or analysis on a "news blog, news website or newspaper" without any professional journalist involvement (p. 218). Her discussion of the third category, participatory journalism, described it as having more potential for a fuller embrace of public journalism on both a technical and theoretical level. In participatory journalism, news users generated content for a professional news organization's operation. These citizen contributors do it "more or less independently of the professionals," she said, "whereas the professionals generate some other content, and also produce, publish and market the whole news product" (p. 217). Co-Pilot more clearly fell within the participatory journalism framework – citizen contributions were not complemented by additional professional reporting and they were subject only to reviews for relevance and copy-editing.

However, as this study describes, participatory journalism's emphasis on building a public space through a news medium can be woefully insufficient for encouraging citizen-generated content that successfully bridges public and private life. Indeed, if a news site features only the proscriptive hand of the journalist (e.g. gatekeeper of potentially "ax-grinding" contributions; copy-editor, fact-checker, etc.) then citizen contributions can understandably trend toward the purely personal. Such stories, without the facilitative hand of the professional journalist, cannot be readily situated as accounts that more readily engage the fuller spectrum of the community.

Method

This study pursued a close examination of the stories within Co-Pilot with two aims: (1) to determine what kinds of citizen values appeared within the stories and (2) to critically assess participatory journalism's potential as regards furthering coverage of local news and promotion of civic discourse regarding community concerns. In this way, this chapter explores how this particular use of participatory journalism engages citizens' perspectives into creating news that can help public life go well.

This study used a content analysis of the themes of citizen-contributed pieces in Co-Pilot from its inception on June 6, 2007 through December 10, 2007. An a priori reading of the Co-Pilot revealed that the section concentrated exclusively on individuals providing pro-social stories, photos and artwork from their personal lives. There were no stories that were more clearly situated in the public realm – for example, accounts of local city meetings or citizen involvement in social action groups. Instead, true to Anderfuren's guidelines that individuals should not submit anything bordering on polemical, citizens provided pieces that reflected their perspectives of daily life.

Not surprisingly, when individuals choose to provide to others a glimpse of their daily experiences, their accounts will normally be framed by values that positively reflect on their lives. Accordingly, this study applied theme categories – curiosity, kindness, citizenship, love of learning, creativity and humor – from the 2004 book *Character Strengths and Virtues: A Handbook and Classification*, by Christopher Peterson and Martin Seligman. These categories not only fit well with the a priori reading but they also aligned suitably with how citizens used the page to communicate their values. The *Pilot* encouraged individuals to trumpet aspects of their daily lives; Peterson and Seligman's categories apply to a range of "signature strengths" that a person "owns, celebrates and frequently exercises" (2004, p. 18). In essence, the categories allowed for describing and measuring how citizens used the section to affirm their private sphere ideals.

Three trained coders evaluated 313 units of analysis – stories, photos and artwork – and achieved a reliability of 0.796 on Cronbach's Alpha reliability test, just slightly below the recommended level of 0.800 (Riffe *et al.*, 2005, p. 147). Three themes predominated – curiosity, citizenship and kindness.[1]

Curiosity is defined as an "interest, novelty-seeking and openness to experience" that is "associated with desirable psychosocial outcomes" such as better interpersonal relationships, greater learning and engagement, and willingness to put oneself in challenging situations (Peterson and Seligman, 2004, pp. 134–135). Individuals display citizenship as "social responsibility, loyalty and teamwork," operating out of a sense of duty to a common good that goes beyond one's self-interest (p. 370). Kindness is an altruistic state toward others that demonstrates "the assertion of a common humanity in which others are worthy of attention and affirmation for no utilitarian reasons" (p. 326). Kindness consists of acts that normally appear as more individualistic and, at times, random. In contrast, citizenship is an orientation toward helping others within the structure of community-focused, organized activities (p. 380).

Findings

Curiosity Values in Co-Pilot Contributions

Many curiosity pieces within Co-Pilot were constructed more like reminiscences of an unusual event with no clear discernible pro-social value connected with the seeking of novel experiences. For example, many contributions centered on how citizens sought out novelty through travel or attending unusual one-time occurrences such as a costume party surrounding the release of a new book. However, other pieces contained clear indicators that curiosity could be the spark to action that would benefit the individual both in skill-acquisition and in fostering a confidence in engaging others. For example, within its first month, Co-Pilot ran a submission by Katrina Manikad, a 32-year-old shareholder services associate from Virginia Beach. She began with a description of her sense of dread as she sat in a car outside a building:

> I was feeling the things people feel when they haven't done something before: fear and anticipation. It started to rain and the little voice of fear told me, "Look, you don't have an umbrella, and you should turn around and go home." But, for once, I didn't listen.
>
> (Manikad, 2007)

Manikad followed through on her curiosity and made her first-ever visit to the monthly meeting of Virginia Beach Toastmasters Club 3267. She found at the meeting that speakers received "positive and constructive feedback," something that she found startling as she had formerly associated the notion of evaluation with "a lecture on what you did wrong." Her initial curiosity paid off, she said, because she continued coming to the meetings and after every one, she left "feeling like I can conquer the world" (Manikad, 2007).

In September 2007, Co-Pilot ran a lengthy piece from high-school student Ryan Warren, 14, of Virginia Beach. The article detailed how Warren was the only high-school student from the *Pilot's* area to accompany a regional group of Boy Scouts to the 2007 World Scout Jamboree in England, a centennial celebration that featured 40,000 scouts from 158 countries. His group was assigned to a camp with representatives from 50 other countries. Warren found himself surrounded by boys from other cultures: "We spent one day doing a service project. I painted fences and made friends with scouts from Angola . . . I played cards with Australians, shot baskets with the Angolans, went shopping with a new friend from Hong Kong" (Warren, 2007).

Warren summarized his experience by pointing to the particularly fond memory of trading his uniform for a ceremonial Japanese scout uniform. His piece, however, suggested he left with more – a desire to integrate these new, quite alien, individuals into his existing relationships. He wrote that during the airplane ride back he decided to attend the next World Scout Jamboree in Sweden in 2011. "Only next time," he said, "I am going to bring along all my friends from [my] troop to meet my new friends from the Jamboree in England" (Warren, 2007).

In October 2007, Naomi Burke, a 76-year-old "spokesmodel" from Chesapeake, VA, described how she had decided, in 1992, to enter the "Ms. Chesapeake

Senior Citizen" competition. Even though she entered her first-ever pageant at the age of 61, she thought, "What the heck. Nothing to lose – just have a good time" (Burke, 2007). She won that contest, and then unsuccessfully competed at the state level. She emphasized, however, that her involvement in the pageant led to other experiences: "Since then, I've been in Christmas parades and the Neptune Festival parade. Yes, that was me in 'The New Detectives,' 'The FBI Files' and 'The Haunting' [series] filmed at New Dominion Pictures and shown on the Discovery Channel" (Burke, 2007).

Burke closed by sharing that her husband said she should have entered pageants when she was young, but she reminded him she was working and raising five children during those years. The more important point, she told readers, is to not shy away from a new challenge at any time in your life, because you don't know what can come from it.

In these pieces, Co-Pilot highlighted the pro-social value of curiosity. These particular contributors stressed the worthiness of pursuing one's curiosity: it provides new experiences from which to learn and grow. However, moving beyond the benefits that accrue in the purely private sphere (improved personal skills, novelty, new friendships), the pieces also cast curiosity as a route toward engagement in the public sphere (whether it was in Toastmasters, the Boy Scouts or participating in civic parades). By affirming openness to novelty, contributors tried to draw a connection between the private benefits of curiosity and a sense of an enhanced and more expansive individual capacity to connect and contribute to public life.

Curiosity pieces, then, attempted to show how individuals took their impulses and, in the course of their own individual journey, used them to contribute in the public sphere. For Co-Pilot, these types of articles came close to speaking to the concerns of the larger community. They fell short, however, because contributors were focused on their individual perspectives, the Co-Pilot discouraged potentially contentious pieces and the newspaper provided no additional contextual reporting.

Citizenship Values in Co-Pilot Contributions

Citizenship stories in Co-Pilot often appeared as brief mentions of organized activities (e.g. a car wash for children of incarcerated parents sponsored by Phi Theta Kappa, or a gift shop for charities run by an organization of military spouses). These pieces did not offer a clear window into the values of the contributor; instead, these brief articles communicated how one could support an organization's efforts. Other pieces, however, offered a clearer connection to Peterson and Seligman's citizenship definition – pro-social efforts that are customarily closely aligned with a formalized initiative.

In its first month, Co-Pilot printed a story on the New Chesapeake Men for Progress from Geraldine Minter, a volunteer with the group and a 46-year-old prevention specialist from Chesapeake, VA. Minter highlighted the organization's second annual forum and its related sponsorship of a parent-education conference. She said both sessions were designed to emphasize to a group of 250 young black men and their parents the need for black youth to stay on track with their education. She cited research that indicated under-educated black men are "more disconnected from the mainstream society, and to a far greater degree than comparable white or Hispanic men" (Minter, 2007). The New Chesapeake Men for Progress was determined to convince the young men and their parents that black children must embrace two things: (1) the need to stay in school, because there is a "relationship between learning and earning" and (2) the need to take responsibility in life and relationships. She finished by observing, "sometimes [our young men] will fall, but together, we can help them to rise" (Minter, 2007).

One contributor pointed to how multiple groups were working together to help improve the community. Tara Davis, an Americorps/Vista volunteer in Norfolk, wrote that a local fraternity, Beta Zeta Upsilon, supported a project that allowed children of incarcerated parents to beautify a local nursing home. "By cleaning out flower beds, sowing grass seed and planting pansies, the 10 children had the opportunity to learn about the environment and take pride in improving their community," she wrote (Davis, 2007). Not only was Beta Zeta Upsilon due to shortly receive a national award for its effort, but the members were going forward with several other college associations to start a child-mentoring program.

Kevin Brewer, a 46-year-old York County, VA, quality-assurance manager, described how volunteers for the Tidewater Search and Rescue (TSAR) contributed to their community. That summer, TSAR members helped local authorities find a missing child. Brewer detailed how he and his fellow searchers assisted the hunt for two-year-old Matthew Hollis, who had left his yard wearing only a diaper. His fellow volunteers, all trained in search techniques, assisted local authorities; a TSAR member found Hollis at the end of a 17-hour hunt. Discussing the power of citizens working together, Brewer said that the rescue was meant to be, with each citizen working in a specific position as part of a team. Furthermore, he said:

> They had all come together for the team to make the "find." The TSAR member who found Matthew embodied the entire search effort, everyone played a part in [that search member's] being in the right location, at the right time with the right teammate.
>
> (Brewer, 2007)

These contributions to Co-Pilot revealed a conception of citizenship as a more formalized effort among individuals to help their local communities. Particularly of interest is how these portrayals of citizenship emphasized how community members banded together, not only to work in service of a common interest, but also to maximize established or newly mastered skill sets. In the New Chesapeake Men for Progress story, Minter described how volunteers set up speeches and ran workshops that attracted 250 attendees. Clearly, in her account, the citizens who orchestrated the forum had specific organizing and managing abilities. Davis' contribution on Beta Zeta Upsilon pointed out that the fraternity developed skills to work with kids of incarcerated parents through a formalized outreach program offered by a Norfolk non-profit organization. Finally, Brewer's account of TSAR's rescue demonstrated how citizens came together to apply search skills to find the missing child. Citizenship, according to these Co-Pilot contributors, called for channeling both desire and expertise into an organized effort to help others. However, while these accounts are laudable, as was common with the curiosity pieces, they were anecdotal. Neither contributors nor Co-Pilot attempted to contextualize how citizens struggle with ongoing concerns in the greater community.

Kindness Values in Co-Pilot Contributions

Kindness pieces in the Co-Pilot tended toward accounts of seemingly random benevolent acts by citizens, without the contributor providing a clear-cut message to the reader. Other contributors, however, attempted to use accounts of kind acts to convey the value of altruism. In fact, the very first edition of Co-Pilot featured a piece from Linda Shuman about her five-year-old son, Robby, and his efforts during the 2006 holiday season. While out on a shopping trip with his mother, Robby persuaded her to buy a suncatcher painting kit. When she asked why, "he replied he would sell them at our church . . . so he could buy toys for kids who don't have moms and dads" (Shuman, 2007). The church, friends and family all responded, and Robby made additional kits to meet demand. He raised more than $1,000 that was used to buy toys for a Norfolk homeless shelter.

Alison Schoew, a technical writer from Chesapeake, VA, submitted a stream-of-consciousness piece that illustrated the random opportunities for kindness. After a tough day at work, and a frustrating evening in rush-hour traffic, she decided to be "a small gift to someone else." At the grocery store, she noticed the "checkout gal looks tired." Schoew asked the woman about her "I Love Louisiana" pin and then wished her well. "She seems pleased to be seen as a proud New Orleans woman," noted Schoew, "not just as someone scanning my salad fixings." Schoew finished the piece with an account of helping an older man with his umbrella. She concluded:

> My life is demanding, but I don't have to be. I can make a fresh start by
> being open, aware and gentle. Each day . . . I try to lift myself out of my
> world by simply remembering to be a small gift for someone else.
>
> (Schoew, 2007)

In a very personal piece, Brenda Taylor, a 62-year-old office manager from
Chesapeake, VA, shared how, after she had experienced the recent loss of her
mother and a bitter divorce, she found that her aunt, Alice Wilkins, was in need.
When Wilkins' husband died, Taylor packed up her belongings and moved in
with her aunt as a temporary housemate. What was supposed to last only a couple
of days turned into a stay of more than a year, Taylor wrote. She said:

> My mom's younger sister taught me the joy in dropping everything to catch
> a glimpse of a spectacular sunset. . . . She taught me it's OK to smile and
> laugh in the face of incredible sadness and adversity. . . . What began as a
> way for me to help has become so much more. In giving, I have been given
> to, and both of us have been blessed with a new beginning.
>
> (Taylor, 2007)

Co-Pilot's pieces on kindness, as these examples show, often highlighted how
altruism served as a social good. Contributors focused on how a sense of kindness allowed one to identify the needs of others. Furthermore, these stories
displayed that true kindness was a willingness to help others with no expecta-
tion of extrinsic reward. Additionally, each piece, by keeping a focus on the
recipients of the kindness, allowed the authors to present themselves as role
models for the value of such benevolence while avoiding the appearance of a
self-aggrandizement that could compromise their messages. However, despite
the morally uplifting nature of these accounts, these pieces, by their very nature,
transmitted truncated, episodic renditions of primarily private lives. Therefore,
kindness stories also struggled with touching upon issues of compelling interest
across the newspaper's community.

Implications

Over its nine-month run, Co-Pilot attempted to demonstrate a second wave of
public journalism by encouraging readers to submit local news. In this way, the
section tried to approximate some of the approaches used by hyper-local news
websites. However, from almost the beginning, the page's editor faced a significant challenge – readers often needed a lot of priming to submit pieces, and
the ones they did submit were not news in the sense of the Enlace model
demonstrated in *El Correro*. Co-Pilot's admonition that contributors stay away

from controversy not only likely dampened submissions, but also led those who did write to cast news from within private-sphere perspectives. "When people submitted to Co-Pilot, they were looking less outward into their communities and more toward their own personal experiences and family stories," said Anderfuren (personal communication, July 30, 2008).

Accordingly, what was intended to be a community-news page driven by citizens was often filled with incidental reminiscences from readers' lives. Additionally, as this study reveals, more articulate contributors used the section to speak to personal values. Attributes such as curiosity, citizenship and kindness, which are normally situated within the more private realm of interpersonal relationships, were cast by these contributors as valuable news for others to know. However, larger questions remain about other factors that contributed to citizens using the page this way.

First, as Haas has said, participatory journalism's hyper-local news focus, as often demonstrated on community websites, leads to contributions that reinforce the notion that communities are characterized by shared values and goals (2007, p. 154). This dynamic was apparent within the pages of Co-Pilot. Readers/contributors tend to see the hyper-local format as an opportunity to reify what makes a community cohesive; a ripple effect follows as others offer similar accounts. Therefore, it is not surprising to see that Co-Pilot contributors submitted pieces about private events that conveyed their sense of essential community values. For participatory journalism, this presents a double-edged sword. Janowitz (1967) pointed out that highly personal news at a highly local level does help to develop community values through public expression of those values. At the same time, he indicated that woven into this dynamic is a type of storytelling that is concerned with "status and self-respect" (p. xviii) that is "related to family attributes and community orientations" (p. 215). Participatory journalism, therefore, encounters the difficulty that the personal framing of stories can, indeed, minimize the concerns of those community members who are not part of this paradigm of status, attributes and orientations.

Second, Haas has described such hyper-local efforts as featuring a "journalistic division of labor." Journalists still report news while local residents "are encouraged to contribute articles related to their private interests and concerns" (2007, p. 153). This two-tier approach to news, where journalists' own, but separate, work is in close proximity to that of citizen contributors sends the message to readers: "you write on your world; we'll still do the real news." This bifurcation of the journalistic world and the realm of citizens constrains participatory journalism from realizing a more citizen-engaged news. This is clearly shown in the Co-Pilot's case – contributors provided accounts from the private sphere of family and personal networks that had no apparent link to a sense of news that concerned the area's wider public sphere.

Third, there is the practical matter of citizens having the time, skills, resources and inclination to provide a news account, even about an event that occurred in their daily, private lives. Anderfuren indicated that Co-Pilot was designed to allow amateurs to drive content, but submissions were, at times, sporadic. Pieces often required much editing, with Anderfuren devoting considerable time verifying the spelling of names and the accuracy of facts. "Stories often needed a lot of editorial work on them, as contributors would leave out vital information that would help us understand their stories and photos," she said (personal communication, July 30, 2008). Obviously, if individuals have such difficulty telling cogent and complete stories about their own personal experiences, writing about wider community concerns would prove even more daunting.

By the time the Co-Pilot was discontinued in the spring of 2008, the section had not clearly established that this model of participatory journalism was a second wave of public journalism. Co-Pilot attempted to embrace the legacy of public journalism by devoting a portion of the newshole as a forum where citizens could bring news accounts into the traditional, printed newspaper. However, Co-Pilot did not realize a key theoretical impetus of public journalism – to involve citizens in the construction of news with the goal of helping civic life go well. The section's emphasis on bringing private (but commonly assumed) pro-social values into the printed paper was not sufficient to spark citizen dialogue about larger community issues. In fact, by highlighting what appeared to be uniform values in the community, Co-Pilot was further walling-off potential contributions from citizens who had concerns about ongoing conflicts or dysfunctions in their neighborhoods.

Reflecting on Co-Pilot as a possible descendant of public journalism, Anderfuren said:

> The goal of public journalism was to engage the community it covers, but the experts were still in the driver's seat. This attempt was to put amateurs in the driver seat. We did that, but they didn't take us anywhere interesting.
>
> (Personal communication, July 30, 2008)

Anderfuren's observation points to a key problem that journalism must address. If newsrooms are to become more citizen-engaged – whether through the traditional printed medium or emerging, interactive technologies – they need to make sure they sit in the front seat with citizens. Journalists need to participate in the citizen reporting, contributing their skills and knowledge to extend citizen observations into a wider frame that can engage readers.

It is one thing to know that, for example, individuals like Katrina Manikad confront and overcome the fear of public speaking. It is another when journalism expands on such citizen perspectives to show how they are relevant to the wider public sphere. Taking Manikad's account further, compelling participatory journalism could provide additional insights regarding how people use competence in public speaking to advocate for the homeless, get funding for new alternative fuels or lead a protest for their right to bear arms in public places. In this way, private-sphere experiences and values can surely inform and deepen our knowledge of what is contested in the public sphere. Such citizen-engaged journalism can tell us how individuals exert themselves to make public life go well. But, as the Co-Pilot case shows, these connections between private-sphere impetus and public-sphere contestations will not just happen because citizens have a platform. Participatory journalism calls for the active hand of journalists to make private sphere, values-based reporting relevant to diverse interests within a community.

Summary

Theoretical Implications

- Participatory journalism, as Nip has suggested, appears to be a later variation of public journalism in that it devotes part of the newshole to contributions from citizens. However, participatory journalism can result in stories that are not informed with public journalism's impetus of helping civic life go well.
- As Haas has pointed out, the stories that citizens contribute within the participatory journalism model may often focus on a narrow set of personal values and interests. The Co-Pilot stories reflected this dynamic, as contributors repeatedly relayed private experiences that emphasized positive values such as curiosity, citizenship and kindness.
- Since journalists view participatory journalism as "you write on your world, we'll still do the real news," journalism has yet to incorporate citizen contributions into stories that help news consumers visualize how citizens make public life go well.

Practical Implications

- Devoting journalistic space to citizen contributors does not necessarily mean the news outlet is completely divorced from the shaping of that particular newshole. For example, in its first appearance, the Co-Pilot section informed citizens that "this isn't a soapbox or a place to grind an ax." This guideline influenced both the nature of citizen contributions and how the *Pilot* performed gatekeeping for this section.

- The lack of consistent, quality contributions to Co-Pilot points to how difficult it is for individuals to participate. Various factors can dampen citizen contributions – time, skills, resources and inclination.
- The consistent re-occurrence of citizen stories in Co-Pilot that reflected positive values presented a certain uniformity that, in the words of the section's editor, did not "take us anywhere interesting." Participatory journalism, to be more effective, should seek a diversity of voices, perspectives and contestations.

Reflection Questions

- The Co-Pilot was seen as an experiment, rather than a fundamental change in the way that journalism would be done at the paper. How might the very label "experiment" actually serve to inhibit such a participatory journalism effort?
- The Co-Pilot editor revealed that contributors had difficulty telling cogent and complete stories that sprang from their own personal experiences. How might the editor telling contributors to avoid "ax-grinding" have influenced the contributions? What do these factors say about participatory journalism's potential.
- Should journalists take a more active role in how citizen contributions are presented in news outlets? Why or why not? If so, where should journalists start?

Note

1. All three coders agreed that "curiosity" appeared in 8 percent, "citizenship" appeared in 7 percent and "kindness" appeared in 5 percent of all the elements. Coder agreement on "love of learning" appeared in only seven instances and "humor" in two. Coders agreed that "creativity" appeared in 8 percent of all elements, but the vast majority of those instances involved identification of children's artwork and is therefore not included in this analysis.

References

Anderfuren, M. (2007, June 6). How I started Co-Pilot: Now, it's your turn. *The Virginian-Pilot*, A11.

Brewer, K. (2007, July 23). To the rescue. *The Virginian-Pilot*, A15.

Broder, D. (1990, January 3). Democracy and the press. *The Washington Post*, A15.

Burke, N. (2007, October 12). New adventures just keep coming. *The Virginian-Pilot*, A15.

Carey, J. (1995). The press, public opinion and public discourse: On the edge of the postmodern. In Glasser, T. and Salmon, C. (eds.), *Public opinion and the communication of consent* (pp. 373–402). New York: The Guilford Press.

Charity, A. (1995). *Doing public journalism*. New York: The Guilford Press.

Davis, T. (2007, December 3). Effort to help children takes root. *The Virginian-Pilot*, A19.

Haas, T. (2007). *The pursuit of public journalism*. New York: Taylor and Francis.

Janowitz, M. (1967). *The community press in an urban setting: The social elements of urbanism* (2nd edn). Chicago: University of Chicago Press.

Manikad, K. (2007, July 2). A toast to constructive feedback. *The Virginian-Pilot*, A11.

Merritt, D. (1998). *Public journalism and public life*. Mahwah: Lawrence Erlbaum Associates.

Minter, G. (2007, June 25). A timely forum lifts up young men. *The Virginian-Pilot*, A17.

Nip, J. (2006). Exploring the second phase of public journalism. *Journalism Studies*, 7(2), 212–236.

Peterson, C. and Seligman, M. (2004). *Character strengths and virtues: A handbook and classification*. New York: Oxford University Press.

Riffe, D., Lacy, S. and Fico, F. (2005). *Analyzing media messages: Using quantitative content analysis in research* (2nd edn). Mahwah: Erlbaum Associates.

Rosen, J. (1999). *What are journalists for?* New Haven: Yale University Press.

Schoew, A. (2007, June 8). Life is demanding; I don't have to be. *The Virginian-Pilot*, A13.

Shuman, L. (2007, June 6). One little boy makes a difference. *The Virginian-Pilot*, A11.

Taylor, B. (2007, September 17). Kind act gives rise to deep kinship. *The Virginian-Pilot*, A19.

Warren, R. (2007, September 12). 100 years later, founder's vision lives. *The Virginian-Pilot*, A11.

Chapter 8

Citizen Journalism in the Community and the Classroom

Kirsten A. Johnson

We-town.com is a dual-purpose citizen journalism website launched in April 2008 in the small central Pennsylvania town of Elizabethtown. One purpose of the site is to provide a place for community members to share news that is important to them, using audio, video, pictures and text. Second, it is a teaching tool for students in the Department of Communications at Elizabethtown College. This site offers students a chance to tell stories using various types of media. So far, the site has been successful at allowing students to pursue multimedia storytelling, and also at engaging community members in debate over local issues in a converged media environment.

Typically such sites have been launched at large universities with large journalism programs, but the we-town project is unique in that it is housed at a small comprehensive college. (Elizabethtown College has about 2,000 students, with about 150 Communications majors.) Developing a project such as this on a small campus, in a small town, has both opportunities and challenges. This chapter highlights lessons learned in the launching of we-town.com, advice on effective use of a citizen journalism site as a teaching tool, and ways to use such sites to facilitate community storytelling. The chapter also highlights the site's stance on gatekeeping and censorship, namely that no explicit rules about appropriateness of content are set forth for contributors.

Citizen Journalism in Higher Education

Universities have launched citizen journalism initiatives in the past several years that have taken different forms. In many cases these sites are used as teaching tools for students, while encouraging participation from community members, as is the case for we-town.com. Some university citizen journalism sites such as MyMissourian.com and Hartsville Today partner with traditional media.

Since 2005, the New Voices Grant Program has provided funding to launch and support about a dozen higher-education citizen journalism initiatives (including all of the initiatives mentioned below except MyMissourian.com). Other higher-education projects, not discussed in this chapter, that have received support from the New Voices Grant Program include: Miami University, the University of Kentucky, Kent State University, Virginia Commonwealth University, California State University-Los Angeles, City University of New York, Michigan State University and Temple University (New Voices Grantees, 2009).

MyMissourian.com was launched in 2004 by the University of Missouri-Columbia and works in partnership with the Columbia *Missourian*, a news organization directed by professional editors, but staffed by students. At MyMissourian.com, citizens, both on and off campus, serve as writers, while journalism students act as editors. According to University of Missouri professor Clyde Bentley:

> Editors work closely with authors who "share" information rather than "cover" stories. We edit for readability and civility, not A.P. style and newspaper tradition. We know how to keep our reporters out of libel court, so this responsibility doesn't change because our authors are not on the payroll. We let writers get trivial and let them talk about what interests them.
>
> (2005, p. 27)

The *Missourian* newspaper is distributed to the community and sometimes "reverse publishes" stories from the MyMissourian.com site (*About the Missourian*, n.d.).

Another example of a citizen journalism site that has partnered with traditional media is Hvtd.com, a joint venture between *The Hartsville Messenger* (a small twice-weekly newspaper) and the University of South Carolina School of Journalism and Mass Communication. A study of the first year of this partnership by Fisher and Osteen (2006) found it is important for site operators to think like users and readers, not like publishers and journalists. They also found that recruiting citizen journalists is an important part of the process, and that, "Once you've built it, they may not come" (p. 2). Overall, Fisher and Osteen (2006) concluded that the site is successful, as it has helped them engage their readers in a "community conversation." Hartsville Today's content has been used to complement coverage in the *Hartsville Messenger*. However, the newsroom and the university have experienced problems, including the integration of Hartsville Today into the day-to-day operations of the *Hartsville Messenger*, and the reluctance of sales staff to sell advertisements on the site for fear of hurting newspaper advertisement sales (Fisher and Osteen, 2006).

An example of a citizen journalism project affiliated with an institution of higher education but not with a single traditional outlet is Madison Commons, created at the University of Wisconsin-Madison School of Journalism and Mass Communication and its Center for Communication and Democracy. The goal of the site, described more thoroughly by Robinson *et al.* in Chapter 12, is to gather news and information about communities in Madison, WI. Some content is provided by citizens, and other relevant content is linked from local media outlets that partner with the Commons. Madison Commons also supports a citizen journalism boot camp, and as of May 2007 about 70 community members had been trained (Friedland, 2007).

In 2006, Columbia College in Chicago launched ChicagoTalks.org. The site, not affiliated with a traditional media outlet, has Columbia College students and community members providing hyper-local news for Chicago residents and is covered in greater detail in Suzanne McBride's account in Chapter 9 of this book. Project directors say the site has been successful in providing quality news and in drawing people to it; however, they feel the site has fallen short of its goal of engaging citizens as journalists (Iverson and McBride, 2008).

Ohio University's E.W. Scripps School of Journalism launched the Route 7 Report, a citizen journalism effort that provided journalism training to citizens in three rural villages in southeastern Ohio. This project, also not connected to traditional media, helped citizens create a monthly newsletter and post stories on local issues to a website. According to Reader (2008), about 20 community members submitted stories, but the bulk of the content came from a core group of four people. Since it has been a struggle to get community members to participate, students have had to pick up where the community members have left off and produce content.

So, although money, talent and enthusiasm have propelled the creation of these sites, their experiences illustrate the problems of getting citizens to participate. We-town.com is no exception. Since citizen participation is central to a robust citizen journalism website, this is not an area that should be overlooked when creating one of these sites. Steps must be taken to make sure the site is relevant to the community, unique from established media in its content, and easy for citizens to use. What follows is a detailed look at the creation of we-town.com and how it encountered struggles and achieved some successes.

We-town.com

We-town.com was launched in April 2008 as the result of a grant from Elizabethtown College that brought together the departments of Communications, Computer Science, and Information Technology Services. The funds were used to buy a server to host the site, provide release time for faculty involved in the project, including the author, and to pay a computer-science student to help develop the site infrastructure. It took about eight months from inception to the time the first post was made to the site. Those eight months included times of uncertainty, failure and pure elation, as we embarked on doing something none of us had ever done before.

Objectives of the Site

Before the we-town team could begin technical and design work, it needed to determine the site's objectives. One team member had done extensive research on citizen journalism and wanted to experiment with it at Elizabethtown as a contrast to the projects being done at larger universities. In addition to providing a fertile area for future research, the site would provide mass communications students with a place to utilize their multimedia skills and serve the community through posting stories about Elizabethtown. Providing a service to the community is directly aligned with the college's motto of "Educate for Service," which made this project a natural extension of the curriculum. The team also wanted students to experience producing stories for a website, which we felt would enhance their portfolios and give them more marketable job skills. We also wanted to engage community members in the production of hyper-local news content.

A mission statement was also developed, and posted on we-town under the "About" tab. It reads:

> We-town is a unique opportunity for members of the Elizabethtown and greater Lancaster County communities to share the news most important to them by submitting photographs, interviews, stories, videos and pod casts covering community events. The website is a chance for community storytelling; a place for anyone to bring attention to current issues. The site does not generate any revenue, and is indeed, purely a tool to facilitate community storytelling.

Type of Site

After determining the objectives, we had to determine what type of citizen journalism site it should be. Currently the college operates a newspaper, a cable television station and an FM radio station. The community is also served by a weekly newspaper, the *Elizabethtown Chronicle*. So where did we-town fit in this media landscape, and what model of citizen journalism should it employ? According to Outing (2006), citizen journalism can follow various models including: readers commenting on already published articles; having a professional journalist post a small story and then allowing citizens to post their experiences about the story; combining the work of citizen journalists with the work of professionals;

a stand-alone citizen journalism site made up of contributions from citizens that is edited and separate from the core news brand; and a stand-alone citizen journalism site where stories are *not* edited prior to being posted. We decided to make we-town.com a stand-alone site where stories were *not* edited before posting. We chose this model because we wanted a free flow of information, and no formal gatekeeping process. We also decided to not be affiliated with any other media outlet because we wanted to make sure that this was truly a site to facilitate community storytelling. We didn't want anyone to think it was a commercial site or that content was being formally censored in any way.

We also thought it was important to allow anyone to contribute. We required registration before users could add content. But in order to encourage citizen participation, the registration process was designed to be very simple. All a user had to do was provide a user name (which does not have to be their real name), password and an email address. We discussed whether users should be required to provide information about themselves, and decided that, since the site was not well known in the community, the lower the barrier of entry, the better.

To Censor or Not to Censor?

We wanted to keep gatekeeping to a minimum on the site, and while we realized this could lead to uneven story quality, as well as harm the perceived credibility of the stories, we felt that the need to facilitate a free flow of information outweighed these drawbacks. One of the ways traditional media try to lend credibility to their information is through a filter-then-publish model. This means that the information that comes into a newsroom is edited prior to being released to a mass audience. Conversely, participatory journalism websites tend to operate under a publish-then-filter model, where information is released to the mass audience and only then "edited" in the form of reaction and discussion about it (Bowman and Willis, 2003). In some cases, people with journalism experience are employed as editors, whereas in other cases, visitors to the site can act as editors. The missing layer of editorial oversight may cause credibility problems (Gilster, 1997; Scheuermann and Langford, 1997).

Many citizen journalism sites do have "rules" about the content that can be posted on the site. For example, MyMissourian.com won't accept anything that contains profanity, nudity, personal attacks, or attacks on race, religion, national origin, gender or sexual orientation (Bentley, 2005). CNN's citizen journalism website i-Report.com provides 17 detailed points regarding things that are not appropriate for the site. These rules include: not posting material that is "grossly" offensive to the online community, not posting material that might instruct someone in how to do something illegal, and not posting copyrighted or trademarked materials (Terms of Use, 2009).

Even though other sites have posted rules defining appropriate content, it was decided that the we-town site would not include such rules, instead relying on community members' sense of decency. We felt declaring rules might discourage people from contributing, and in essence, silence voices that should be heard.

In the first eight months after the official launch, more than 100 posts were made, with no problems of inappropriate content in story submissions or posted comments. It should be noted that only registered users can make comments on the site. This was done primarily to control spam on the site, as well as to provide a measure of control over who was commenting on stories.

Faculty members in the Department of Communications oversee content on the site, but do not look at, or edit, stories or comments prior to their posting. Each time something new is posted or a comment is made about a story, an email message is sent to a faculty member's email account. The faculty member can then look at the post. It was agreed that if something offensive (as judged by the faculty member reading the story) is posted to the site, that the faculty member has the right to take the story off the site. As the site continues to be developed, this is an area where further discussion and research is needed.

Organization/Design of We-town

After determining objectives, a mission statement and a content model for the site, it was time to find an appropriate content-management system, as well as design the site. This was the most time-consuming part of the project. The key criterion on which the selection was made was ease of use for an end-user to add content.

WordPress was chosen as the open source content-management system for the site, and Information Technology Services at the college agreed to set up an open source server. WordPress was chosen, in part, because the administrative panel is user-friendly. Furthermore, students were familiar with Word-Press.com blogs, as they were used in several Communications courses. WordPress also allowed for easy availability of essential plug-ins for easy uploading of audio and video files, features we thought were important. Students in the Publication Design and Graphics course worked on the logo and color scheme for the site (see Figure 8.1) and concentrated on the look and feel of we-town.

Many different page layouts were considered. We decided to go with a tabbed menu across the top of the page, because we felt this would provide for the cleanest design (see Figure 8.2). We also decided that stories would be posted on the homepage in the order received, with the most recent stories at the top of the page, similar to the chronological order that blogs used. Of

Figure 8.1 We-town logo (used with permission of Elizabethtown College).

particular concern were the categories that should be used to organize the site. We eventually settled on Home, News, Features, Sports, Events, Editorial, About, Archives and Get Started, which then became the names on each tab.

On the right we chose four subheadings including *We-town*, a brief description of the site. A *Users* subheading includes a place to log in and manage stories and to subscribe to the site using an RSS feeder. Another subhead called *Tags* is used to help organize content on the site. When users post content they are encouraged to include a series of descriptive keywords called "tags" with their story, which then appear under the *Tags* subhead on the homepage. The more often a tag is used to describe a story, the bigger in size the tag gets on the homepage (see, for example "Bear Creek" in Figure 8.2). This provides an easy, visual way to see what the most popular topics on the site are – the bigger the

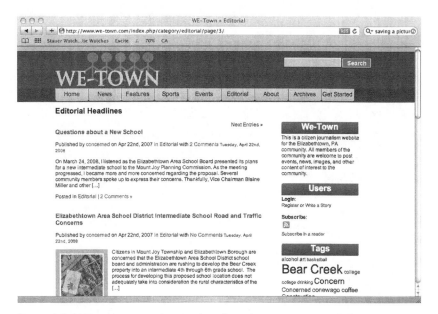

Figure 8.2 We-town site design (used with permission of Elizabethtown College).

tag, the more popular the subject. The last subhead is *Photos*. Any photo that is posted in conjunction with a story is automatically posted under this subhead on the homepage. A user can then click on the picture and go immediately to that story. This is a visual, as opposed to textual, way to find stories on the site.

Refining the Design, Populating and Publicizing

Students in several communications courses have helped design, populate and publicize the we-town.com site. In fall 2007, Communications students in the Writing for New Media course developed the content map and initial news content for the site. This included the development of protocols and proce-dures for posting and editing stories. The students also wrote directions to help users log into the site, change their passwords and post stories or upload images. The same students conducted some preliminary usability testing, evaluated the processes required to upload content to the site, and provided suggestions for improving these processes.

Content developed by Mass Communications students in the Senior Seminar Capstone course and the Digital Media Convergence and Design course included a number of stories, both hard news and features, that contained video, audio, pictures and text using techniques such as:

- Podcasts highlighting local people/events in the community;
- Video news packages about community events;
- "Natural sound" video stories, providing a "slice of life" look at the community;
- Print stories focused on controversial campus and community issues;
- Stories about sporting events not covered by local media;
- Photo ethnographies of prominent community members.

Corporate communication students in the Senior Seminar Capstone course also developed a number of initiatives aimed at attracting community interest and participation. Some of these projects included:

- A publicity campaign to bring awareness to the site and to recruit local citizens to participate;
- Creating a flyer promoting the site;
- Contacting prominent members of the community to write for the site;
- Development of public service announcements designed to run on radio and television to promote the site;
- A launch event at a local coffee house to register users and raise awareness of the site.

The launch event was held one evening in April 2008 at a coffee house in the downtown area of Elizabethtown. The location was chosen because it was off-campus and it had wireless Internet access. A student publicized the event, on and off campus, using flyers and email. People at the coffee house were given cards (about the size of a business card) with the we-town logo on it and directions for registering. The initiative was met with limited success. About 30 new users were registered during the three-hour event, but we were hoping for many more. Future community outreach will need greater publicity. Prominent community leaders should be strongly encouraged to attend, and contacts need to be made with leaders of large community organizations. Perhaps prizes and giveaways could also attract community members to such events. So far, we have experienced limited success in getting prominent members of the community to write for the site.

Results of the Experience

While formal studies have yet to be completed on the we-town experience, early evidence suggests that using the citizen journalism website to teach media convergence and to showcase students' professional skills was a success. During the end of the semester students in the Senior Seminar Capstone course were asked about their experience working with the site. Most of the nine anonymous respondents said they felt the experience prepared them for a future career:

- "This course makes you use all the skills you have learned the past four years and put them to real world use."
- "I have learned skills needed for professionalism in the field."
- "Helped with real world application."

One student commented on how the theoretical component of the course was useful: "I found the research I did for other sites helped me with the work I did with the we-town site."

Students' knowledge of converged media and citizen journalism prior to working on the we-town.com site was minimal. Most of them had only been exposed to the ideas of media convergence and citizen journalism sporadically in courses prior to participating in this project. They simply did not have enough prior exposure that was intentional enough in nature. For example, they had not learned how to figure out whether audio, video or text was the best way to tell a story, or how to combine these different elements to craft a compelling story. Also, the lack of earlier exposure to citizen and civic journalism theory and user-created content hindered students in gaining deep insights into the practice. By the end of the semester, many were just starting to really grasp the theory and how it applied to their particular project. In order for an experience such as working on we-town to be meaningful, students should be introduced to the concepts of converged media and citizen and civic journalism early in their college careers. This will allow for a clearer cognitive model to be established for work in more advanced courses. This particular introduction to citizen journalism should become easier in the coming years as the practice becomes more popular and well-known. Also, the Department of Communications has launched a New Media concentration that focuses on new delivery platforms in communications. Earlier exposure to the concepts of media convergence and citizen journalism should result in higher-quality projects from students, since they will not have to spend as much time familiarizing themselves with basic concepts.

When creating content for the site, students had trouble thinking beyond stories created for a single medium. Instead of thinking about the best way to tell the story, they often wanted to stick to one method of storytelling, be it print, video or audio. Challenging students to think about telling the story using more than one media platform made them uncomfortable. They often wanted to decide prior to heading out on a story assignment whether they were going to do a video, audio or print story for the site, and had to be instructed to let the content dictate the form the story would take.

Part of this reluctance undoubtedly came from going through a curriculum that did not teach them how to work across different media platforms. The college's current course offerings of News Reporting and Writing for the Print Media and Broadcast Writing send a message that these are separate and distinct ways of thinking about stories. We plan to rectify some of these issues with the launch of a New Media concentration that has two newly created courses: Writing for New Media and Digital Media Convergence and Design. Both of these courses aim to help students understand the intersection of good storytelling across platforms and new technologies that can be used to tell stories. The Mass Communications and Corporate Communications programs are still being offered. Thus far, the New Media concentration has not attracted as many students as we had hoped, but this may be due to lack of marketing.

Another area where we encountered problems was in setting clear expectations for students creating content for the site. Many students were hesitant to commit to exactly what they would produce. While use of an existing form that required students to explain their goals and objectives, as well as pre-production, production and post-production strategies, was helpful, many students were not specific enough about what they would produce.

Conclusion

The launch of we-town.com met our initial objectives. The site allowed students to produce high-quality multimedia projects, led students to a greater understanding of citizen journalism and new media, and engaged community members in producing content. As has been the case with other citizen journalism sites, the last objective – getting community members involved – has been the most challenging. Immediately following the launch of we-town, several community members wrote stories on the site about a controversial plan to build a new elementary school in the district. Eighteen new stories from community members were posted to the site in three months. Following this flurry of activity, community posts have been limited to about two or three a month. We must examine ways to raise awareness about the site and encourage community members to contribute. We are developing a marketing plan, producing a video greeting and tutorials, and conducting usability testing. It is our hope that these things will improve participation by making community members more cognizant of the site and making the site more user-friendly and welcoming. Very few people in the community have heard of citizen journalism and aren't sure what to expect from the site, so the videos and tutorials should help to ease their worries.

University-based citizen journalism sites can benefit the community and the students. The community benefits from the posting of stories that are hyperlocal and relevant. Students benefit from the multimedia skills gained by writing, editing and posting stories online. Citizen journalism sites are also a great way for students to showcase their work. Often students can feel like they are working in a vacuum, producing work that will be seen only by the professor and classmates. Sites such as we-town give students the chance to share their work with an audience.

Additionally, we-town's position on pre-censorship makes it an interesting case study. The team's decision not to post rules of conduct or describe appropriate content was a risky approach that proved to be successful. Team members felt it would be a mistake to pre-censor any content, as this may limit the number of voices involved in the community conversation. Thus far, this policy has not posed any problems and community members have not abused this privilege. Only time will tell as to whether or not we-town is able to maintain this position, and will certainly provide opportunities for further research.

Elizabethtown College's size also makes this project unique. Many citizen journalism projects, such as the ones cited at the beginning of this chapter, are at large universities. Elizabethtown is a small comprehensive college with about 2,000 students, situated in a small community. This comes with both positives and negatives. One positive is that because the college is so small it is easy to access administrators when the idea for a new project arises. Also, because of the small size of the department and classes (typical enrollment about 14), we can easily experiment with new ways of teaching and new projects. Some negatives of being at a small college are that it is difficult to attract outside funding for projects when competing with large universities. Also, at a department level, we are limited in the number of students we can commit to new projects because there just aren't that many students available. Elizabethtown does not have a journalism school, but rather a Communications Department comprised of Corporate and Mass Communications students. Allowing the Corporate students to work on the project has allowed them, in many cases, to gain multimedia experience they would not have otherwise had. Also, these Corporate students have been vital in promoting the site both internally and externally.

Higher education, in fact, has attributes that make it a highly effective testing and learning ground for citizen journalism projects. The availability of a free student workforce to populate the project site and supplement content posted by community members, college resources (such as computer labs and audio and video equipment) to support the project, and the ability to sustain a site without the worry of making a profit, are all strong arguments for using higher education as a place to experiment with different models of citizen journalism.

Summary

Theoretical Implications

- The role of established media outlets as gatekeepers of information is challenged in the citizen journalism model. Decisions need to be made about who can post and to what degree the content will be edited. The concept of what is and is not news and the idea of who is and is not a reporter are changing.
- While there are several models of citizen journalism, none has been established as the best way to blend student and citizen involvement.
- University-sponsored citizen journalism sites need to carefully develop models for encouraging community participation and test them.

Practical Implications

- Citizen journalism sites are a unique way to engage students in multimedia reporting, and are a vehicle for creating connections between the campus and community.

- It is difficult for students to think across different platforms (audio, video, print) when covering stories, particularly when a "silo" approach to teaching reporting and news writing has been their experience.
- Involvement in a citizen journalism site does not have to be limited to students studying mass communications or journalism. Students studying corporate communications can help promote the site and encourage community participation.
- Encouraging participation from community members is difficult. Just because a citizen journalism site is launched does not mean community members will automatically participate.

Reflection Questions

- What are some ways colleges and universities can partner with local media to create citizen journalism websites?
- What is the best model for engaging students in a citizen journalism project?
- What does the future look like for citizen journalism sites in higher education?
- Should content posted by citizen journalists be edited prior to being posted on the site? What are the consequences of *not* editing the stories prior to being posted? What are the consequences of editing the stories prior to being posted?
- What are some ways to more fully engage the public in citizen journalism websites?
- What are some good strategies for marketing and promoting citizen journalism websites?

References

About the Missourian. (n.d.). Retrieved February 25, 2009, from www.columbia-missourian.com/p/about/.

Bentley, C.H. (2005). Reconnecting with the audience. *Nieman Reports* 59(4), 26–28.

Bowman S. and Willis, C. (2003). *We media: How audiences are shaping the future of news and information*. Retrieved October 20, 2005, from www.hypergene.net/wemedia/weblog.php.

Fisher, D.J. and Osteen, G. (2006). *Hartsville today: The first year of a small-town citizen journalism site*. Retrieved November 13, 2006, from www.j-newvoices.org/index.php/site/story_spotlight/hartsville_todays_cook_book/.

Friedland, L. (2007). *The Madison Commons project*. Retrieved February 20, 2009, from www.j-newvoices.org/site/story_print/59/#finalprogress.

Gilster, P. (1997). *Digital literacy*. New York: John Wiley & Sons.

Iverson, B.K. and McBride, S. (2008). *Creating community connections.org*. Retrieved February 20, 2009, from www.j-newvoices.org/site/story_grantees06/creating_ community_conversations/.

New Voice Grantees. (2009). J-lab: The Institute for Interactive Journalism. Retrieved February 20, 2009, from www.j-newvoices.org/.

Outing, S. (2006). The 11 layers of citizen journalism. Retrieved May 16, 2006, from www.poynter.org/content/content_view.asp?id=83126.

Reader, B. (2008). Route 7 report: Regular, dependable, popular, and in print. Retrieved February 20, 2009, from www.j-newvoices.org/site/story_print/98/.

Scheuermann, L.E. and Langford, H.P. (1997). Perceptions of internet abuse, liability, and fair use. *Perceptual and Motor Skills*, 85, 847–850.

Terms of Use on i-Report.com. (2009). Retrieved February 4, 2009, from www. ireport.com/terms.jspa.

Chapter 9

The Changing Face of News in a Major U.S. City

Hyper-Local Websites Try to Fill the Void in Chicago

Suzanne McBride

Readers of Chicago's hyper-local news websites had a smorgasbord of choices on January 30, 2009. They could read that prostitution continues to be a problem in one South Side neighborhood. They were reminded about an upcoming forum for candidates to replace former U.S. Rep. Rahm Emanuel, recently named as White House chief-of-staff. They could find out about a local environmental lawyer who wants Chicagoans to use more wind and solar power, a recent march for immigrant rights and a Westside group helping renters who were losing their homes to foreclosure. And there was commentary – lots of commentary – on former Illinois Governor Rod Blagojevich, who had been removed from office a day earlier, and the latest development with Drew Peterson, who had been questioned about the death of his third wife and the disappearance of his fourth.

That same day the city's two daily newspapers – the *Chicago Tribune* and *Sun-Times* – covered Blagojevich and Peterson, too. Both papers devoted their front pages to the governor's ouster, with the *Tribune* filling four pages inside and the *Sun-Times* three. But neither paper had much coverage about the city's 77 neighborhoods, beyond some breaking crime news and a few features. On that day – like many others before and since – Chicago's growing number of Web-only news sites offered readers the local coverage the city's two major dailies failed to provide. The major daily newspapers' diminished devotion to local coverage has created a news vacuum that the hyper-local news sites work to fill in the nation's third-largest city.

Seasoned news professionals run these mostly non-profit sites, which rely on grants and other private support rather than advertising. While professional journalists and college-level journalism students produce most of the content, there has been some citizen involvement. Some sites focus on local neighborhood news, while others offer commentary and criticism about the city's mainstream media outlets as well as everyday life in Chicago. All of these sites provide Chicagoans with news and information the major dailies do not offer and attempt to increase civic engagement in specific neighborhoods and across the city.

As these hyper-local sites seek to build citizen engagement, they struggle with resolving what interactivity and citizen involvement can offer toward redefining the content and purpose of news versus desires to preserve traditional journalism values and standards. The question is two-fold: (1) how should established definitions of news be re-constructed? And (2) who should be responsible for balancing these new definitions against traditional notions of journalistic standards? These questions are especially vital when applied to hyper-local news sites operated by individuals who came from traditional journalistic backgrounds.

Community News in Chicago

Chicago has a history of vigorous news coverage at the local level. For more than 100 years, the city was home to the legendary City News Bureau, where raw recruits learned the basics of news coverage in Chicago's police precincts (Howlett, 1999). The bureau ended its run as an independent organization in 1999 when it was taken over by the *Chicago Tribune*, which ran the bureau for a few years before it closed for good in 2006. The local news websites today are inheritors of the tradition of neighborhood coverage by papers described nearly 60 years ago by Janowitz (1952, 1967) and of an even earlier tradition of immigrant press coverage (Park, 1929).

Park and Janowitz were University of Chicago sociologists who operated from that institution's tradition of using the city as a "natural laboratory for sociological investigation" (Rogers, 1994). They were interested in the impact of the local press on community integration and expression of community values. In his study, Janowitz counted 82 neighborhood papers with a combined circulation of nearly 1,000,000 in 1950 (1967, p. 26). The fundamental hypothesis of his work was "that the community newspaper participates in the process of integrating the individual into the urban social structure" (p. 61). This was accomplished through providing local news with a focus on helping build and maintain local traditions and identities. These local newspapers also "democratized prestige" by celebrating individual and group accomplishments at a neighborhood level. At their core, these papers emphasized news that was tied to each neighborhood community's common interests. Janowitz saw these community papers as operating somewhere between the "mass media" function of citywide papers and the interpersonal word-of-mouth communication that spreads information throughout a neighborhood. The local, community-focused newspaper fulfilled functions not suited to either of those levels of communication. A key distinction between the metro press and community papers was that, at the citywide dailies, news items from local communities "would get into the daily press only . . . because of human or dramatic interest" while the community papers would cover them as matters of "routine interest to readers" (p. 72).

Today, topics lacking the high profile that would merit coverage in Chicago's daily papers are the province of several websites serving the city or parts of it. Chicago is not unique in this regard; Web-based hyper-local journalism is a growing phenomenon. A study by J-Lab: The Institute for Interactive Journalism (2007) identified nearly 500 citizen news media sites nationwide. But Chicago may be unique – or at least unusual – in having a half dozen such news sites not affiliated with each other or with any common organization in one metropolitan area. This case study elaborates on some recurring approaches offered by this assortment of sites, as well as unique elements of some of them, to help explore how they "provide Chicago residents with the information they need to make smart decisions about public affairs" (Dougherty, 2009).

Filling the Gaps in Local News

Former *Chicago Tribune* investigative reporter Geoff Dougherty launched Chi-Town Daily News (www.chitowndailynews.org/) in late 2005 after becoming frustrated with his employer. "My time there convinced me that our city's newspapers were doing a terrible job of covering Chicago," he wrote a short time later in *Nieman Reports*, adding:

> The *Tribune* didn't regularly cover the Chicago Housing Authority, an agency that spends millions in public funds every year. Chicago has the nation's largest civil justice system, but no reporter was assigned to cover it full time. Each Chicago public school has a local school council, independently elected to set the annual budget and evaluate the principal, and they meet each month. Nobody at the paper covered these meetings. The *Tribune* had more reporters stationed in Europe than on the South Side of Chicago.
>
> (Dougherty, 2007, p. 62)

Chi-Town's daily offering of news stories is mostly produced by professionally trained journalists, with occasional contributions from citizen journalists who've attended special training workshops. An approach similar to Chi-Town Daily News has been taken by Chicago Talks, founded by this chapter's author and Columbia College Chicago colleague Barbara K. Iverson, both of whom wanted to improve neighborhood news coverage in Chicago by training citizen journalists and then publishing their work. Originally, the plan called for Columbia College to train the citizen journalists and Dougherty's site to edit and publish their work. But the parties could not agree on how money from a grant would be spent and how exactly citizen journalists would be involved, resulting in two independently operated sites.

In an average week, ChicagoTalks publishes five to six news stories, including occasional investigative pieces, while Chi-Town Daily News produces five or six times that number of daily stories. Both sites emphasize news over commentary, though Chi-Town has some blogs. And both edit the copy before posting it, adopting the gatekeeper role of the traditional news organizations where the founders of both sites spent much of their careers. While both sites allow for readers to comment on the content, this feature is only sporadically used. A difference between the two is that ChicagoTalks also operates in partnership with other local news operations, including *Streetwise* (a weekly newspaper sold by homeless street vendors), the Community Media Workshop and the New Communities Program operated under the auspices of the Local Initiatives Support Corporation/Chicago (LISC).[1]

The New Communities site (www.newcommunities.org/index.asp), which LISC launched in 2004, features the work of journalists called scribes – some with decades of experience – who report on efforts to rejuvenate the West, Southwest and South Side neighborhoods. Each of the 16 neighborhoods also operates its own website, and all can be accessed through New Communities. Some of the local grassroots sites post articles at least a few times a month, including the Logan Square site (www.newcommunities.org/communities/logan/), which publishes in both Spanish and English. Andrew Mooney, senior program director for the LISC/Chicago office, describes what his staff is doing as service journalism that fosters the flow of information between and among neighborhoods and groups (personal communication, February 11, 2009). The non-profit group realized years ago the importance of being able to disseminate news from its 16 neighborhoods, especially with little reporting being done on these struggling areas by the traditional news outlets.

Another source for Chicago neighborhood news is the "News Tips" site offered by the Community Media Workshop (www.newstips.org/). Since its founding in 1989, Community Media Workshop has at least twice a month published short stories – known as "news tips" – about "the other Chicago, the oft-neglected neighborhoods and back streets of Chicago, where the problems are felt most deeply and where solutions are likely to be born" (Who We Are, 2009). The non-profit organization has one employee producing the now-weekly "news tip," while the rest of the staff offers training to other non-profits on how to effectively tell their stories to the media. Thom Clark, president and co-founder of the Community Media Workshop, has plans to launch a "Community News Project," which would provide readers with "thoughtful, civic-minded and original multimedia enterprise reporting done by experienced journalists, including perhaps some who've been laid off by the city's alternative weekly, the *Chicago Reader*" (personal communication, January 13, 2009).

Beachwood Reporter founder Steve Rhodes described his site (www.beach-woodreporter.com/) as a "news and culture review" that aims to offer readers a virtual public square. "We don't let just anyone put anything they want on the site," said Rhodes, a former reporter for the *Chicago Tribune* and *Chicago* magazine (personal communication, February 2, 2009). That, Rhodes said, is in contrast to Windy Citizen (www.windycitizen.com), whose founder, Brad Flora, said he strives for the site to be "the go-to place for the best of the local Web in Chicago" (personal communication, February 25, 2009). Flora, who earned a graduate degree from Northwestern University's Medill School of Journalism in 2007, described his site as a tool that lets Chicagoans rate, discuss, discover and share local community news on the Web. After a redesign in January 2009, the site featured some original reporting along with more than 40 citizen blogs covering local news, people and places on such subjects as disability rights, feminism and homelessness. Before the redesign, the site featured news articles on local and national issues produced largely by students and recent graduates from Medill. Now Windy Citizen's content "is really just links and posts" helping people find material they wouldn't otherwise find on their own, Flora said. He considers Twitter to be his site's main competitor. He noted, however:

> We're offering a different way of cracking that nut, and the two aren't mutually exclusive at all. . . . The great thing about what we're doing is that all these new sites that launch in Chicago, they're no longer competitors but just more stuff for us to link to. The more competition in this space, the more we benefit, because we're doing so much less than any of them. The link is the unit of commerce on the Web. All you need to do is get your links to matter more than the other guy's and you can do something special.
>
> (Personal communication, February 25, 2009)

Public data compiled from a variety of places is at the center of Adrian Holovaty's EveryBlock.com (www.everyblock.com/). The former *Washington Post* staffer describes the site, launched in January 2008, as "a new way to keep track of what's happening on your block, in your neighborhood and all over your city" (About EveryBlock, 2009). Starting with Chicago, New York and San Francisco, and available in 15 other cities across the country by October 2009, EveryBlock provides nearly 20 types of information. Users can find crime data, business license information, lost-and-found postings and bike rack installations, searchable down to a street address. EveryBlock's information, culled from various public sources, is designed to answer the basic question: What's happening in my neighborhood? This includes:

- Civic information such as building permits, crime stats and restaurant inspections that in many cases is already on the Web but buried in hard-to-find government databases.
- News articles and blog entries, classified by geography, so site users can find mainstream media coverage near particular locations.
- Other information that readers might not be aware of, such as local photos posted to the Flickr photo-sharing site and user reviews of local businesses on Yelp (About EveryBlock, 2009).

The EveryBlock team says it is seeking to expand the traditional definition of news:

> We like to toss around the word "news" to describe all of this, and that might surprise you at first. Isn't news what appears on the front page of *The New York Times*? Isn't news something produced by professional journalists? Well, it *can* be – and we include as much of that on EveryBlock as possible. But, in our minds, "news" at the neighborhood or block level means a lot more. On EveryBlock, "Somebody reviewed the new Italian restaurant down the street on Yelp" is news. "Somebody took a photo of that cool house on your block and posted it to Flickr" is news. "The NYPD posted its weekly crime report for your neighborhood" is news. If it's in your neighborhood and it happened recently, it's news on EveryBlock.
>
> (EveryBlock FAQ, 2009)

In a magazine profile, Holovaty explained that EveryBlock "is one piece of the puzzle. It's never going to replace narrative or investigative journalism" (Johnson, 2008, p. 10). He was non-committal about whether he planned on making the site more participatory by featuring user-generated content – articles, images and video submitted by average readers not trained as journalists. Is EveryBlock journalism? Its operators write on the website that they "don't want to argue over semantics" but instead "prefer to spend our time building a web site that people find useful – whether the academics call it 'journalism' or not" (EveryBlock FAQ, 2009).

Citizen Involvement in Content Generation

Financing these Web-only sites is a challenge. Most are organized on a non-profit basis, relying largely on grants to pay their operating costs. The John S. and James L. Knight Foundation has provided nearly all of the funding for Chi-Town Daily News and EveryBlock, through separate grants that are part of a five-year, $25 million campaign by the foundation to promote online experiments in innovative journalism. The level of funding that sites manage to attract has a significant implication for their ability to use paid professional journalists and how much content comes from them.

By early 2009, Chi-Town – the best-funded of the local sites, with a budget of about $500,000 annually – employed eight full-time staffers. Most were professionally trained journalists, some with years of experience. One of Chi-Town's first hires, however, was a social worker with experience organizing for media justice and civil rights. His job: recruit everyday Chicagoans to report for the site, alongside its group of paid professional journalists. The Chi-Town Daily News report is the largest of any of the city's Web-only news outlets; most days, it features four to five stories primarily produced by the professionally trained journalists. During a February 2009 town hall meeting of Chicago journalists – which he later recounted on his blog – Dougherty said that with a $2 million annual budget, a local-news website could provide more complete local coverage than the city's dailies (Dougherty, 2009).

That demand for new content never lets up. To increase story count, many Chicago sites turn to volunteers. Chi-Town is trying to build a network of citizen reporters to supplement its paid staff. ChicagoTalks relies on journalism students at Columbia College wanting to get their work edited and published. And Beachwood Reporter and Windy Citizen use unpaid contributors who have a passion for a particular topic.

Unlike a traditional newsroom in which reporters get paid and follow a regular schedule, the volunteers and the work they do for Chicago's hyper-local news sites is far less predictable. Early on, ChicagoTalks worked with several residents interested in covering stories in their neighborhood, and in most cases, the site was fortunate if citizens provided just one article before they ran into impediments that limited further involvement. Chi-Town has had a similar experience; one case study reported: "As a publication that relies on a community of contributors who make a substantial personal commitment, the largest problem for the Daily News is retaining volunteers" (Hampel, 2008).

Relying on non-professional journalists also raises questions of quality of the contributions that come to a site. As the Beachwood Reporter's Rhodes said, there needs to be a standard for what will be published because readers expect filtering. "We don't let just anyone put anything they want on [our] site," he said. Roughly one dozen "hard-core contributors" to the Beachwood Reporter, along with another dozen "floating on the edges," operate at a quality above citizen journalists, he said (personal communication, February 2, 2009). In similar fashion, Mooney has pushed for a code of standards for the work published by LISC, in recognition that his non-profit is a part of the growing number and types of people and groups creating journalism (personal communication, February 11, 2009).

Another major challenge: getting participation and engagement from neighborhood residents across the city, the audience for whom much of the content is geared. Reader comments – one way to measure engagement – rarely can be found on either ChicagoTalks or Chi-Town Daily News. And other sites, including Community Media Workshop and LISC's New Communities, don't even offer a comment option. One study noted that discussion on Chi-Town

> is minimal and there are no other features on the site that aim to build community among readers . . . the Daily News site has not developed the kind of online community that enlivens many participatory media sites – comments on articles and personal details about authors are practically nonexistent.
>
> (Hampel, 2008)

Lou Rutigliano, an assistant professor in communications at DePaul University who studied websites in Chicago as part of his doctoral research, said sites such as Chi-Town and ChicagoTalks – with their multi-source news stories – may seem too traditional for local residents to get involved. "Being too journalistic inhibits community residents from participating," Rutigliano said. He noted that although both sites have published a number of stories about the Uptown neighborhood, "there was no community participation" on either site. "But look at [the blog] Uptown Update.[2] There's a ridiculous amount of participation. . . . If you try to turn it into journalism, does that go away?" (personal communication, February 11, 2009).

This imperative to engage residents has been a central theme of the Knight Commission on the Information Needs of Communities in a Democracy. At its fall 2008 meeting in Chicago, the commission said it was clear from community forums held in California, Montana and Pennsylvania that people yearn for access to meaningful information and to be engaged in civic life (Knight Commission, 2008). Mooney, the head of Chicago's LISC office and a commission member, said it is essential that the public gets news and information that will benefit communities and engage citizens. "Over the next 10 years, not only here but nationally, we're going to see a lot of efforts . . . that will be aided or blocked by technology we don't even know of yet," he said. "It's not just a question of providing information . . . but that the information can be acted on" (personal communication, February 11, 2009).

In the meantime, digital media has not filled the void created by cutbacks at newspapers, Mooney said, nor does he expect that it will. He predicted a number of models will continue while others emerge. "Journalism in the future is going to be much more varied," ranging from watchdog/investigative journalism like what ProPublica produces and "service journalism" done by groups like LISC, to spot news and disaster coverage done by amateur and citizen journalists, he said. Mooney, who was once a stringer for City News Bureau, said for residents to remain or become engaged in their neighborhoods, it is critical that streams of information from a variety of sources be developed. No one news outlet can or should perform this important function, he said (personal communication, February 11, 2009).

Conclusion

In their short existence, Chicago's Web-only local news sites have continued on the well-traveled path of public journalism and begun, in small ways, to build on the work of established media outlets such as *The Wichita Eagle* and *The Charlotte Observer* that helped define the practice. Like their print predecessors, these hyper-local sites are trying, as Merritt states in Chapter 3 of this book, to make "public life go better." But they share something else with their public journalism forerunners: the tension between traditional news values and innovative approaches.

Some of the sites – most notably LISC and also Community Media Workshop – have helped build civic life in some of Chicago's most economically challenged neighborhoods by creating virtual places for residents to get information about their community and for local groups to get the word out about what they are doing. In so doing, they are approaching construction of improved civic life from a traditional journalistic mindset as described by Ryfe and Mensing in Chapter 4. Historically, there has been little coverage by the city's newspapers of many of these neighborhoods, and that is not likely to change in light of the financial turmoil roiling the newspaper industry. This will give these websites an important role in informing residents, an initial step toward engagement.

Other sites – Chi-Town Daily News and ChicagoTalks – similarly use a traditional news-values approach to target coverage at the local level, reporting on stories that the city's newspapers generally don't cover anymore (if they ever did at all). For example, the dailies do not cover meetings of local school councils, of which there are more than 600. Whether hyper-local online coverage of these topics has led to more civic engagement is unclear. The sites' operators report anecdotally that more people have attended community meetings after learning about an issue on their sites but as Rutigliano noted, this approach is not the most effective one for ascertaining whether the news site helped foster citizen involvement.

But other sites go beyond traditional conceptions of journalism, using interactive means to connect citizens with community information in novel ways. EveryBlock.com, for example, has created new tools for Chicagoans to easily access government information about crime, new businesses and other information the site compiles. Local publications, including The *Chicago Tribune* and *Sun-Times*, have added a widget from EveryBlock to their websites. This gives their readers easy access to data that, until now, was available only to those few persistent, patient citizens who took the trouble to visit government offices and submit Freedom of Information Act requests. Traffic on EveryBlock is high, suggesting Chicagoans are looking at the site, but as with other sites the information-engagement connection is so far undetermined.

But some question whether EveryBlock or sites that rely on citizen journalists are the answer. EveryBlock "is a journalistic tool that can be part of a journalistic mix. I don't think raw data alone is it," Rhodes said (personal communication, February 2, 2009). He wishes the Knight Foundation's $25 million were directed to already existing media outlets to do better reporting and higher-quality journalism. Rhodes said:

> People are always trying to come up with these [new] ideas because we know our media is failing us. Now people are turning to citizen journalism and technology. But what really bums me out is that we should be doing better journalism, not coming up with some alternative way of doing it.
> (Personal communication, February 2, 2009)

Chi-Town Daily News has recruited everyday Chicagoans, most with no journalism background, to report on issues that until now had been mainly covered by professionally trained journalists, thus giving citizens the opportunity to be participants in public affairs rather than victims or spectators (Rosen, 1999). However, Chi-Town and other sites that publish citizen journalists' work are careful to teach these contributors the basic rules of objective reporting and either prohibit or discourage citizen journalists reporting on issues or events they are involved with.

Perhaps one important evolution in public journalism will occur when the publishers of these new media outlets reconsider and even throw aside the trustee model of journalism as outlined by Schudson (1999). Under this model, long-employed by the traditional media:

> journalists are to provide news according to what they themselves as a professional group believe citizens should know. The professional journalist's quest for truth and fairness, exercising sound and critical judgment as measured by a jury of peers, should dictate the shape of the news.
> (p. 120)

But would a greater number of citizens become involved in these sites and could richer content be produced if there were general acceptance that "journalists are unavoidably players" and should take a step "away from traditional journalistic detachment?" (Merritt, 1998, pp. 141–142). It could be difficult for these Chicago website publishers – many of whom worked years for major news organizations before launching their sites – to make the "mental leap" described by Merritt:

> If we're not talking about detachment, they say, then we must be talking about attachment, then we must be talking about abandoning such indisputably important and useful roles as watchdog, outsider from government, independent observer, uninvolved-and-thus-credible source of information.
>
> (1998, p. 142)

The first step away from this privileging of professional journalists as the sole source of news would be to allow readers some unfettered access to the Chicago sites. None of the Chicago sites allow readers to post unedited content, though some do allow unfiltered comments. It appears that this time-honored practice should be reconsidered, especially if it leads to more civic engagement among readers.

Summary

Theoretical Implications

* The increase in citizens involved in online journalistic enterprises raises questions about how news is defined and what it means to be a journalist, which could lead to new definitions.
* Many mainstream journalists, including some who operate Chicago's new online ventures, adhere to the more traditional definition of who is a journalist and what counts as legitimate news content, creating a barrier for greater involvement by citizen journalists in reporting on issues they are involved with.

Practical Implications

* The shrinking local news coverage produced by traditional media outlets will lead to more Web-only sites that aim to increase civic engagement among their readers.
* The hunger for local news and information is leading to a rise in the number and type of people who do the work formerly done only by traditional journalists.

- While some citizens want to be involved in an online news operation, it is still a struggle to keep them interested and engaged in a site over time.

Reflection Questions

- How can the burgeoning online-only news outlets get everyday residents interested in using the sites as well as contributing to them? Should the volunteer model of getting citizens involved in a site continue, or should sites explore options such as paying citizens for content?
- In neighborhoods where hyper-local sites are flourishing, have residents become more involved in their local schools, crime-watch groups and other civic activities? In what ways can civic engagement be measured?
- What should online-only news operations be doing to attract new readers and increase site traffic, which under the traditional advertising model could lead to increased revenue? Should there be more collaboration between sites, with cross-branding and links?

Notes

1. The aim of LISC is to support comprehensive community development in 16 of the city's most challenged neighborhoods. Its New Communities program website is: www.newcommunities.org/index.asp.
2. Uptown Update is a local blog operated by an anonymous Chicago resident: www. uptownupdate.com/.

References

About EveryBlock (2009). Retrieved March 19, 2009, from http://www.everyblock. com/about.

Dougherty, G. (2007, winter). Picking up where newspapers leave off: A former investigative journalist launched an online local news web site in Chicago. Nieman Reports. Retrieved March 19, 2009, from www.nieman.harvard.edu/reportsitem. aspx?id=100128.

Dougherty, G. (2009, February 23). Ravings from the editor: The $2 million newsroom. Retrieved March 19, 2009, from www.chitowndailynews.org/Ravings_ from_the_editor/The_2_million_newsroom,22987.

EveryBlock FAQ. (1999). Retrieved March 19, 2009, from www.everyblock.com/ about/faq/.

Hampel, M. (2008). The Chi-Town Daily News: Creating a New Supply of Local News. The Berkman Center for Internet & Society. Retrieved January 26, 2009, from http:// cyber.law.harvard.edu/sites/cyber.law.harvard.edu/files/Chi-Town%20Daily%20 News_MR.pdf.

Howlett, D. (1999, February 26). Legendary news bureau to close; City News in Chicago was training ground for renowned writers. USA Today, A4.

Janowitz, M. (1967). *The community press in an urban setting: The social elements of urbanism* (2nd edn). Chicago: University of Chicago Press.

J-Lab: The Institute for Interactive Journalism (2007, February). *Citizen media: Fad or the future of news?* Retrieved March 19, 2009, from http://www.kcnn.org/research/citizen_media_report/.

Johnson, S. (2008, August 17). Cyberstar: Adrian Holovaty is as red-hot as a techie can get. His EveryBlock.com tells you all about your neighborhood – including who's taking bribes. *Chicago Tribune Magazine*, 8–11, 15, 28.

Knight Commission on the Information Needs of Communities in a Democracy. (2008). Informational meeting, Chicago Public Library, Chicago, IL, November 17.

Merritt, D. (1998). *Public journalism and public life: Why telling the news is not enough* (2nd edn). Mahwah: Lawrence Erlbaum Associates.

Park, R. (1929). *The immigrant press and its control*. New York: Harper.

Rogers, E.M. (1994). *A history of communication study: a biographical approach*. New York: The Free Press.

Rosen, J. (1999). The action of the idea: Public journalism in built form. In Glasser, T. (ed.). *The idea of public journalism* (pp. 21–48). New York: The Guilford Press.

Schudson, M. (1999). What public journalism knows about journalism but doesn't know about "public." In Glasser, T. (ed.). *The idea of public journalism* (pp. 118–133). New York: The Guilford Press.

Who We Are. (1999). Retrieved March 19, 2009, from www.newstips.org/interior.php?section=About+CMW.

Open Source Interview

Online Dialogue, Public Life and Citizen Journalism

Tanni Haas

You, and other scholars such as Jay Rosen, Tom Warhover and Mark Deuze, have mentioned that traditional journalists will need to come to terms with the inevitability of news construction through the online world. One consistent thread in these observations is that the online world encourages dialogue as a vital component of relaying and understanding news. This dialogic aspect is, of course, antithetical to traditional journalistic principles and practices of detached, fact-oriented reporting. How do you see both public journalism and citizen journalism building a bridge that will allow traditional journalists to successfully adjust and contribute to a more dialogic news product?

For public journalism, I think the challenge is to show traditional journalists that it is indeed possible to create a dialogic news product which relies on the participation of a wide spectrum of citizen voices, and that such citizen participation enriches the news product in a variety of ways. I am thinking here in particular of the many race-relations initiatives that public journalism has been involved with over the years. These initiatives have sought the input of people of different racial backgrounds, and the resulting news coverage has clearly shown that there is no "detached" way of reporting on race-relations and no single, authoritative "fact" of race that people can agree upon across racial divides. Indeed, these initiatives clearly show that journalists' reporting is inherently influenced by their own racial affinities, and that citizens' views on given race-related issues are refracted through their particular racial identities. For citizen journalism, I think the challenge is to show traditional journalists that the distinction between "news" and "views" (or "facts" and "values") is fundamentally flawed. Indeed, virtually all citizen journalism initiatives show that citizens' choice of issues and internal discussion of those issues are grounded in their particular views on given issues.

In the same vein, what opportunities do you think technology, especially online interaction, can offer for developing the "conver-

sational commons" that you propose as a means for public journalism to be more effective?

I think that online interaction can offer an incredible means of furthering the idea of a "conversational commons." Through online interaction, public journalists would be able to solicit a wide spectrum of citizen voices, offer citizens opportunities to elaborate on issues of particular concern to them and encourage citizens to deliberate about those issues with others. The challenge, however, is to moderate those online interactions in such a way that they do not disintegrate into brute shouting matches – to ensure that citizens genuinely listen to one another rather than merely "shout" their own views as loud as possible. We know from the vast literature on computer-mediated interaction more generally that the anonymous nature of online encounters does not always bring out the best in people. Put differently, the challenge for public journalists would be to ensure that citizens' online interactions resemble as much as possible the best of offline encounters. Here public journalists could find much inspiration in the many offline encounters that have been organized over the years in the form of focus groups, roundtable discussions and town hall meetings.

Reader Comment

Online interactions do offer exciting possibilities for conversation about community but they require a different skill set (and tool set) than most traditional journalists possess. The qualities that make for a successful journalist, for example, don't necessarily prepare the same person to be a successful moderator of a vibrant online community.

(Donica Mensing)

Also as part of this redefinition of news, the mainstream news media are giving some opportunities for users to publish their stories. Do you think this involvement of users helps achieve the goal of enhancing public life? If so, in what ways?

In theory, I don't think there is any limit to how much user-generated content could contribute to the enhancement of public life. In practice, however, I am very disappointed with how mainstream news media are soliciting such content. Instead of encouraging citizens to comment on a wide spectrum of public issues of concern to them, most mainstream news media operate in terms of a journalistic division of labor whereby journalists assign themselves the responsibility of covering properly public, political issues while encouraging citizens to cover private, personal issues.

> **Reader Comment**
>
> News organizations that are serious about public journalism could do much to make user-generated content more collaborative throughout the reporting process, rather than simply being a place to publish.
>
> (Donica Mensing)

The Internet seems to be a medium that privileges the formation of communities of interest. How are these similar to and different from geographic communities? Will this difference shape the kinds of public problems on which these communities (with the assistance of journalists) might work?

While I realize that the distinction between "communities of interest" and "geographic communities" is a common one, I find this distinction misleading, even suspect. Indeed, I would argue that, even in the smallest of localities, you will find social groups with unequal degrees of political power. In this sense, I would prefer to dispense with the notion of "community" altogether, under the assumption that there are no substantive values which unite given localities, but rather that various social groups within those localities have different, and often conflicting, political interests. A much more accurate and productive way of describing given localities would be to distinguish between different "publics" whose interests might conflict but could be mediated through adherence to the procedural, but not substantive, value of rational–critical deliberation. To return to my answer to a previous question, the challenge for journalists would be to acknowledge those divisions among citizens, and then to try to facilitate the kinds of online interactions that would allow all citizens, whether politically powerful or not, to voice their particular concerns – and to hear each other out. Indeed, one of the great sins of mainstream journalism continues to be the glossing over of political conflicts of interest under the assumption that we live in a classless society characterized by common values.

> **Reader Comment**
>
> Perhaps local journalists could most fruitfully focus their work on those issues where communities of interest and geographic communities intersect and overlap.
>
> (Donica Mensing)

Can an online conversation produce a discussion that looks anything like a Habermasian deliberation? If not, what would journalists have to do to prompt such an online conversation in their local communities?

I certainly think it would be possible for journalists to facilitate online discussions that resemble the ideals of Habermasian deliberation. However, it would require journalists to be much more mindful than they currently appear to be of what they are trying to accomplish and to take a much more active role in moderating those discussions. Most importantly, journalists would need to ensure that as wide a spectrum of citizens as possible is included in given discussions. This might require journalists to offer citizens various incentives to participate, especially to those who rarely participate in such discussions, whether in the form of financial remuneration or a promise to make use of their input in subsequent coverage. Second, journalists would need to ensure that all citizens have an equal opportunity to participate in those discussions, including by curtailing the contributions of those who tend to dominate the discussions and encouraging those who are silent to speak up as much as possible. Finally, journalists would need to encourage citizens to not only state their views clearly and comprehensively – and genuinely listen to those of others – but also to state their reasons for espousing certain views. Indeed, without extensive and reciprocal reason-giving, citizens could not be said to engage in rational–critical deliberation in the Habermasian sense of the term.

Following up on that, how would this activity be similar to and different from what public journalists did in the past (convening meetings, moderating discussions, etc.) to provoke such conversations?
This activity would be very similar to what public journalists have done in the best of offline encounters, whether in the form of focus groups, roundtable discussions or town hall meetings. In many of these offline encounters, public journalists have done precisely what I mention above: worked to include as wide a spectrum of citizens as possible, ensured that all citizens were offered an equal opportunity to participate, and encouraged citizens to state their views and reasons for espousing those views. The added challenge online is, of course, the strong measure of anonymity as well as the asynchronous nature of the discussions. As previously mentioned, we know from the vast literature on computer-mediated interaction more generally that it can be difficult to moderate online discussions in a democratic manner. A few participants often try to monopolize the discussion, couch their views in the strongest possible terms while paying little attention to those of others, and offer little, if any, evidence in support of their views. Moreover, the asynchronous nature of online discussion could make it difficult, although by no means impossible, for journalists to maintain a strong sense of continuity. Simply put, in contrast to offline encounters, where participants are spatially and temporally co-present, online discussions occur among participants who may be widely dispersed in space and whose contributions are offered over a long time span. This is likely to make for a somewhat disjointed discussion whose conversational "red thread" can be difficult to locate at times.

> **Reader Comment**
>
> Experience indicates that online discussions are often more successful if combined with face-to-face meetings. The public journalist of the future would have to be skilled at gathering participants, networking, training, encouraging, listening, responding and participating both online and offline. Successful online moderation requires an intense amount of offline work.
>
> (Donica Mensing)

In *The Pursuit of Public Journalism* you argue that citizen media as currently configured are not contributing much to creating that "conversational commons." But *could* they? What would have to happen for venues such as blogs and hyper-local sites to meet traditional public journalism goals such as fostering effective deliberation and problem-solving of public issues?

It is true that citizen media, notably hyper-local sites, do not at present contribute much to a "conversational commons." The most serious impediment, as I note above, is the prevailing journalistic division of labor whereby journalists take on responsibility for reporting on properly public, political issues while encouraging citizens to report on private, personal concerns. This is a relatively easy problem to rectify, however. Instead of operating their sites in terms of this journalistic division of labor, journalists could simply dispense with this distinction and encourage citizens to contribute reporting and commentary on all public issues of concern to them. As to the question of what would need to happen to blogs to meet traditional public journalism goals of fostering effective public deliberation and problem-solving, I believe the main challenges are to gain much more independence of mainstream news media and engage in genuine deliberation across ideological divides. As I detail in my book, the empirical research literature clearly shows that blogs tend to mimic the news reporting and commentary of mainstream news media sites and primarily inspire deliberation among people of similar political persuasions.

Following up on that, could facilitation and guidance of citizen journalism efforts by representatives of traditional news organizations in a new sort of "pro–am" approach help bring about this elevation of the citizen media?

I am not convinced that a so-called "pro–am" approach to news coverage is the best remedy for the problems that I mention above. To the extent that weblog writers tend to mimic the news reporting and commentary of mainstream news media, rather than engage in their own, independent news coverage, I believe the best approach would be to try to keep mainstream news media and blogs as separate as possible. If we are to broaden the domain of news coverage beyond that provided by mainstream news media, it would be much better to encourage weblog writers to build up their own, independent news-gathering and reporting entities. In the best of worlds, mainstream news media and weblog writers would not collaborate on news coverage. Rather, weblog writers would become so independent and powerful that their news coverage would force mainstream news media to truly take note of them and to enlarge their own news coverage in light of their contributions. In Habermasian terms, the multitude of weblogs in the "periphery" of the political public sphere would become so powerful that they would influence the functioning of the mainstream news media occupying the "center" of the political public sphere.

Reader Comment

I think it's important to acknowledge the development of a complex news ecology, where some mainstream news organizations incorporate more and more citizen voices in their work – iCNN, BBC, *Guardian*, the *New York Times* – and others do not. Some citizen sites mimic traditional news practices and others do not. Some organizations form around communities of interest and others turn hyper-local. Will there be a "center" to the political public sphere of the future?

(Donica Mensing)

In this same book, you discuss how many forms of online journalism, instead of encouraging or facilitating public deliberation, tend to privilege news content and discussion around an assumption of shared values and goals. You point out this leaves many community members out of the stories. This is a striking observation, as public journalism also criticized journalists as working from shared values and goals that resulted in news content that was disengaged from what citizens cared about. So, while the technology of news gathering and distribution changes, and, over time, the professionalism of the "reporter" may be different, we are still left with the inevitable place of values. What lessons does public journalism have to offer citizen journalism on this issue?

The most important lesson public journalism has to offer citizen journalism with respect to values is that it should not assume there are any overarching, substantive values to which all citizens subscribe. Indeed, any reference to shared values and, by implication, shared political interests is bound to privilege certain dominant values and political interests over other more marginalized ones. That said, to encourage and facilitate genuine public deliberation, citizen journalism ought to operate in terms of the procedural, but not substantive, value of rational–critical deliberation: the idea that all citizens ought to be offered the opportunity to participate in public deliberation, and that all views and the evidence offered in support of those views ought to made available to criticism, evaluation and continuous refinement in the light of other views and supporting evidence.

Reader Comment

Just an observation about this comment: many citizens would likely struggle with a separation between procedural and substantive deliberation. Values and emotions tend to drive participation and engagement. Rational–critical deliberation may not be valued, familiar or desired by many participants.

(Donica Mensing)

Part III

Looking Ahead
Public Journalism 2.0

One of the editors had the pleasure during summer 2008 of moderating a panel at an academic convention ambitiously titled "The Future of Print Journalism." He quipped at the start of the session that if the panel members really did manage to describe that with any certainty, they would all be quitting their jobs and forming a new consulting firm. Needless to say, despite some interesting observations during the following 90 minutes, no clear or absolute future was defined. Prognosticating about journalism's inscrutable future is a difficult task.

So in a similarly ambitious way that, it is hoped, does not cross the line to hubris, Part III offers some ideas about a future in which journalism may be enhanced through citizen journalism practices informed by public journalism principles. The issues and themes explored through the volume so far – defining what constitutes news, gatekeeping, the roles of citizen contributors versus professionally trained journalists, managing the logistics of citizen journalism operations and getting consistent, quality contributions – all relate to the question of what lies ahead.

This final section of the book begins with two models for participatory journalism that start from an assumption that professional journalists and citizen contributors both have a role, and the relationship between the pros and the contributors will be a major factor in defining whether news presentations can meet the aspirations of public journalism. Joyce Nip presents a seven-part model demarcated by different levels of professional involvement in the news mix – from completely controlled professional production at one end of the spectrum to pure citizen journalism at the other. She then describes how, at each point along the continuum, the pro–am relationship affords opportunities for different types of coverage that extend on the impetus of public journalism. Book co-editor Jack Rosenberry offers a model of his own, a set of best-practices for professional journalists called an "online coverage framework." This paradigm redefines news presentations and the role of professional journalists by articulating how online interactivity can bring trained journalists and citizen contributors together to create the kind of coverage envisioned by proponents of public journalism.

These two theoretical pieces are followed by another case study, by Sue Robinson and colleagues at the University of Wisconsin-Madison, which explores the evolution of that university's Madison Commons civic engagement project from a basic news-posting model toward a truly interactive one. This piece provides a comprehensive look at the group's efforts to maximize the promise and overcome the challenges of a news space reliant on citizen-contributed news. Their piece offers insights into both the pragmatic concerns that will face such initiatives in the future, but also theoretical perspectives on how such an effort needs to adequately define community space and the publics that will use such a forum. Part III concludes with an Open Source interview with Jan Schaffer, whose career has followed the arc of the civic and citizen journalism movement's evolution over most of the past two decades, first as director of the Pew Center for Civic Journalism and then as executive director of J-Lab: The Institute for Interactive Journalism. As such she is uniquely qualified to discuss some of the connections and separations between citizen and civic journalism.

Chapter 10

Routinization of Charisma[1]

The Institutionalization of Public Journalism Online

Joyce Y.M. Nip

When public journalism emerged in the late 1980s, local news outlets were, by and large, the channels through which people learned about the recent happenings of the world. By 2009, audiences in communication-rich countries had access to a global network of news information supplied not only by local news outlets, but also regional and global news suppliers, citizen journalism sites and first-hand news sources such as government and corporate websites. Competition in the new environment has affected how news is reported – normalized, personalized, dramatized and fragmented (Bennett, 2008) – in ways that are far from what public journalism suggests. Technologies in the new environment, however, provide opportunities for audience engagement, which could be used to achieve the goals of public journalism.

In earlier works I explored a "second phase" of public journalism with a typology of audience participation that consisted of five models: (1) traditional journalism, (2) public journalism, (3) interactive journalism, (4) participatory journalism and (5) citizen journalism (Nip, 2005, 2006). The five models of audience participation varied in the extent and form of participation by ordinary people in news production, with citizen journalism involving the people to the greatest extent, and traditional journalism the least. Citizen journalism was used to refer to the practice in which the people were entirely responsible for gathering content, along with envisioning, producing and publishing the news product. Unlike in some other uses (Bowman and Willis, 2003; Gillmor, 2005; Lasica, 2003), the term was distinguished from participatory journalism, where the audience played a role in the news-making process framed by journalists. Another model, interactive journalism, allowed audience initiatives after the news was published, such as adding story comments or clicking on links to find additional information. Public journalism, as a movement that experimented with a wide range of practices in engaging citizens, encompassed elements of interactive and participatory journalism.

Since then, many have expressed dissatisfaction with the terms "participatory journalism" and "citizen journalism." "User-generated content" has become a widely accepted way of describing what is produced. Many other terms – notably "network journalism" (Bardoel and Deuze, 2001), "professional participatory storytelling" (Deuze, 2005), and "pro–am journalism" (Rosen, 2006) – have also been coined to describe the new form of participation of ordinary people in journalism. The people involved are sometimes called "produsers" (Bruns, 2005), reminiscent of the "prosumers" forecast by Alvin Toffler (1980). There is no shortage of categorizations of these new forms of audience participation either (e.g. Outing, 2005; Cohn, 2007).

Unlike those attempts that seemingly seek to exhaust the various combinations of relationships between journalists and audience in different work procedures and technology conditions (Outing, 2005; Rosen, 2006; Cohn, 2007), the continuum I shall present explores a different framework. It does not aim to account for the technologies used, although I recognize their importance as enabling and constraining conditions for audience participation. It does not aim to differentiate the various work models that could exist among the amateurs, although such information is valuable for understanding the limitations and possibilities of audience contribution. Nor does it aim to incorporate the work procedure between journalists and audience, except when it is illustrative of the relationship between them. Instead this chapter shows that key criterion used in demarcating the various modes of audience involvement is the degree of control by the news organization. In my view, this is the most fundamental factor that influences the role of the non-professionals in the journalism process, and hence the possibility of achieving the goals of public journalism.

Seven Modes of Citizen Connection in News Making

Depending on the relative control by the journalists and the citizens, the involvement of the people in news-making could take seven modes, as shown in Figure 10.1.

Professional Incorporation

This is a practice used in traditional journalism, where journalists seek out and incorporate the views or experiences of ordinary people in reporting their

1	2	3	4	5	6	7
Professional incorporation	Professional co-option	Citizen response	Guided professional reporting	Guided citizen reporting	Citizen submission	Citizen journalism

Figure 10.1 Seven modes of citizen connection in news-making.

stories. The views and experiences of the common people would not be accessible publicly, and sometimes not even expressed, without journalists taking the initiative. In news stories, these incorporations usually appear as short direct quotes used to show the impact of government or commercial policies and measures on ordinary people.

Professional Co-option

In this mode of connection, journalists follow up and re-purpose stories or comments published by citizens. The journalist takes the initiative to follow citizen-published content, and makes the decision of what to develop and the direction of the development. In other words, citizen content is used as one of the sources for story discovery. The re-purposed content then forms part of the news product.

Professional co-option has become common in Hong Kong and China. The second-largest-circulation newspaper in Hong Kong, for example, *The Apple Daily*, has a team of reporters who monitor the popular online forums, blogs and video-sharing sites. Reporters use these online outlets as sources for stories that range from vandalism and bullying in schools to complaints about companies and government departments (Yip, 2008). Some newspapers in China, such as *Wuxi Daily* and *Ram City Evening Post*, contain special sections that publish stories sourced from citizen posts online.

Citizen Response

Here, members of the audience take the initiative of reacting to stories published by journalists, through responses to the pieces, to the journalists who produced them or to other news users who produce content. This mode of participation is enabled by interactive journalism. A common form for it is comment boxes that follow news stories published online. Less customary are message boards and online chat sessions on current issues. Usually, the contributed content is published with only retrospective moderation; comments are edited or removed only when they violate standards such as use of vulgarity or threatening language. In this setting, citizens are allowed to raise topics and have a higher degree of control of input, but their contributions remain as responses rather than original news content.

Guided Professional Reporting

At this level, citizens may be involved in more than one stage of the news process, including shaping the news agenda, forming the story perspective and providing information during reporting. In this mode, the news outlet offers a

more open-ended opportunity for citizen participation. Thus, guided professional reporting seeks out considerably more citizen engagement than professional incorporation, although the journalists remain responsible for producing
the work. For this to happen, news organizations need to have mechanisms in
place that reach out to people for input. A common form is the call for readers
to send suggestions on stories and topics, which would be pursued by
journalists.

Guided Citizen Reporting

In this mode, journalists and citizens reverse their roles from the ones in guided
professional reporting. Here, citizens produce the work (news or commentaries), with the journalists doing the guiding. A common type of guidance is topic
suggestion. The assignment desk on MSNBC's Citizen Journalists Report
(www.msnbc.msn.com/id/6639760/), for example, suggests that readers
whose homes were damaged by Hurricane Katrina send in their stories, videos
and photographs of the rebuilding of their homes. The guidance goes a little
deeper when an angle is suggested for the pursuit of a story. On the twentieth
anniversary of the June 4, 1989 Tiananmen Square massacre in China, BBC's
"Have Your Say" (http://news.bbc.co.uk/2/hi/talking_point/default.stm)
sought reader comments on whether the demonstrations that eventually led to
the massacre had any impact: "China has boosted security ahead of the anniversary of the killings. Did the protests change the country?"

Citizen Submission

Citizens sometimes contribute entirely out of their own initiative without any
journalistic prompting. Many photographs and videos of the 2004 Asian tsunami
and 2005 London Underground bombing were voluntary citizen submissions. As
a regular mode of audience participation, citizen submission is normally solicited
by news organizations for publication in spaces designated for such a purpose.
Examples are CNN's iReport (www.ireport.com/), MSNBC's "FirstPerson"
(www.msnbc.msn.com/id/16713129/), and Yahoo! News' "You witness
news" (http://news.yahoo.com/you-witness-news). The feature on BBC's
"Have Your Say" that asks: "Have you got a good story?" (http://news.bbc.co.
uk/2/hi/talking_point/your_news/7593687.stm) is another example.

   Different degrees of input from professional journalists may apply: In some
cases, citizen-submitted content is published without filtering or editing as far
as possible; in other cases, selection and editing is made by journalists before
publishing. The news organization provides the frame of presentation by giving
it a headline, and letting it appear on a page under a classification of categories.

Usually the citizen publishing space is distinctly separate from the journalists' publishing space. Some citizen submissions become part of the news product through professional co-option.

Citizen Journalism

This is the only mode in the typology that does not involve professional journalists. While the phrase "user-generated content" may be a more comprehensive term, I prefer "citizen journalism" because of its association with public life. Citizen journalism could take the form of citizen media, such as proprietary websites and blogs, or it could be content published on open media spaces such as blogs hosted by blog service sites, or messages posted on forums hosted by portal sites or online community platforms. Citizen journalism differs from citizen submissions to news sites in that it is published without frames provided by either an individual professional journalist or a news organization.

The recent species of news operations run by entrepreneurs outside of mainstream media is often called "citizen journalism." Many of them are hyper-local ones, but some are large national or transnational sites (e.g. Merinews and OhmyNews). Most of them rely mainly on citizens who are paid little or nothing for their contributions, but also have professional editors who oversee the operations. Where these editors are not the entrepreneurs themselves, they tend to be paid full-time staff. OhmyNews, for example, had a staff of about 50 overseeing more than 26,000 citizen reporters (Gillmor, 2003). That is why they are more appropriately classified as citizen submission, not citizen journalism. (Chapter 9 of this book, by Suzanne McBride, describes several such U.S. hyper-local operations in Chicago.)

Aiming at Public Journalism in Different Modes of Citizen Connection

Public journalism has three main goals: (1) to connect to the community; (2) to engage individuals as citizens; and (3) to help public deliberation in search for solutions (Nip, 2006). These goals are generally accepted by journalists, although the techniques used for achieving them have aroused controversy (Poynter Online, 2003). The act of giving opportunities to the audience to participate in news-making is itself a democratic gesture, one which affirms and facilitates the exercise of the individual's freedom of speech. In this sense, it is consistent with public journalism's ultimate goal of enhancing democracy. Whether the gesture serves the specific goals of public journalism stated above, however, depends on the frame of participation provided (Nip, 2006). The history of public journalism has seen experimentation with multiple techniques in six main areas of practice (Nip, 2008), which can be fruitfully applied to the seven modes of citizen connection.

In Professional Incorporation

Most of the modes of connection discussed in this chapter are provided only online. Despite the increasing popularity of the Internet, however, many people do not have the resources to access news online, or prefer to receive it through traditional print and broadcast media. The digital divide will therefore allow the mode of professional incorporation to remain valuable. Advocating a journalism that moves beyond many traditional journalistic practices, public journalism has specific suggestions for incorporating citizen perspectives into news, including:

- Reaching beyond officials and quasi-officials to ordinary people using techniques such as civic mapping – an attempt to map the informal leaders of a community (Schaffer, 2001);
- Interviewing in a way that opens up conversation, and following the interviewee's pace; and
- More frequently and more prominently citing "real people."

These practices are as applicable today as before, except that new communication technologies and electronic databases can make some of them, such as civic mapping, much easier.

In the other modes of citizen connection that are facilitated by online exchanges (except citizen journalism), the extent to which the goals of public journalism are served depends mainly on three conditions: (1) that ordinary people, not just the elite, have the opportunity to participate; (2) that the content and topic selected is relevant to public life; and (3) that the frame of participation provided encourages a public perspective.

In Professional Co-option

A study conducted in 2004 found that political reporters and editors tended to follow elite blogs but not citizen blogs generally (Farrell and Drezner, 2008). Indeed, a study in 2004 reported that some editors described blogs as "extremely dull," "mediocre" or of "very marginal interest" (Thurman, 2008). But a more recent study in 2006 found that journalists have become more appreciative of the value of citizen journalism (Hermida and Thurman, 2008), as editors acknowledged that a newspaper's audience could be "very knowledgeable about certain areas." Some editors, however, still described blogs as "massively overrated" and as "a bit of fun" (Hermida and Thurman, 2008). Realization of public journalism principles would require that professional co-option reaches beyond elite citizen content.

Public journalism started with coverage focused on elections and community-wide action projects. Then it turned to specific community issues such as race, immigration, families and youth (Friedland and Nichols, 2002). In co-opting citizen-published content (column 2 in Figure 10.1), journalists can select from among views and experiences related to elections, government and community issues that are clearly relevant to public life. Disseminating this type of content on the platform of the news organization would serve to connect to the public concerns of the community, which is one of the main goals of public journalism.

Consistent with public journalism principles, these professional news reports should aim to facilitate public understanding and stimulate citizen deliberation addressing the problems behind the stories. As citizen content tends to highlight individual experiences, journalists probably need to change the angle of the story to focus on the issue, and provide historical background or information related to larger civic concerns. Journalists can include possible solutions to the problem, and, in that way, reveal the values behind different courses of action and help spark constructive civic dialogue. (Burton St. John, in Chapter 7 of this book, further identifies how journalists need to make the link between private values and compelling public concerns.)

In Audience Response

Similarly, journalists should select stories and topics about public issues when they solicit responses from the audience. Public journalism advises addressing the people as citizens, which means contextualizing them as learners, participants and decision-makers of public affairs, with the capacity to contribute to public life as a deliberative body (Rosen, 1997). One of the main goals of public journalism is to create spaces where news users can interact with each other, deliberate and solve problems. Creating a civilized environment and equal opportunity for participation is fundamental (Nip, 2006). Online moderation (like the mediation provided in the town hall meetings sponsored by public journalism projects) could enhance opportunities for deliberation. User registration helps to ensure responsible behavior.

In Guided Professional Reporting

For tapping into the concerns of citizens – the basis of guided professional reporting – public journalism newsrooms have already devised various listening techniques. They include conducting polls, surveys, town hall meetings, focus groups, readers' panels, organizing intimate living room or kitchen conversations, opening up news meetings and sending reporters to "third places" (Harwood and McCrehan, 2000). Another technique is building citizen databases, as done by the Spokane (WA) *Spokesman Review* (Ken Sands, personal communication, March 2005) and Minnesota Public Radio's Public Insight Network (Andrew Haeg, personal communication, January 9, 2005). In some of these approaches, news workers who were involved in long-form reporting projects engaged citizens for their input in a back-and-forth cycle. The same as when co-opting citizen content, journalists should avoid polarizing the issue, but report on areas of agreement in addition to differences. For long-term community issues, journalists should frame the story to include the progress (or lack of it) made in solving the problem.

In Guided Citizen Reporting

Beyond journalists giving story ideas to amateurs to pursue, guided citizen reporting requires substantial resources from the news organization. Deeper-level journalistic guidance is justified if the education provided to the contributors is valued. The "Your Turn" column introduced in *The Spokesman Review* in 1994, for example, required that the column editor sit together with contributors to work on conceptualizing, writing and editing the pieces (Rebecca Nappi, personal communication, March 23, 2005). The *Savannah* (GA) *Morning News* used the Neighborhood Newsroom program for this kind of education from 2001 to 2004 (Nip, 2008).

In Citizen Submission

When space is provided for news users to submit stories or commentaries, the frame provided is critical. A call for submission of photographs of the 2008 Wenchuan earthquake in China surely engages the audience as citizens; a similar call for pet photographs (as often happens) does not. MSNBC's "First Person," the network's first citizen journalism project, called for politically relevant citizen contributions during the Democratic and Republican conventions in 1996. You Witness News and iReport ask for news-oriented items, prompting potential contributors to think with a larger, public perspective.

In Citizen Journalism

Apart from co-opting content from citizen media, news organizations could connect to them in systematic ways. Domingo *et al.* (2008) found that 37.5

percent of the newspapers studied provided space for citizen blogs. Short of that, news organizations could relate to selected citizen journalists as informal leaders, and invite them to make suggestions for news coverage or to take part in discussion forums on public issues. To amplify the impact of major stories, citizen journalism sites could be invited to highlight and comment on the issues being covered, just as public journalism newsrooms allied with other news outlets to highlight major coverage. Hyperlinks to the news organization could be built on selected citizen journalism sites. In return, news organizations could use their websites to recommend (through links) some of the citizen sites.

Promises and Limitations on the Future of Public Journalism

Two decades of experience in public journalism has produced many successful examples of citizen engagement, along with controversies about some of its practices. Where public journalism has been less successful is resolving a certain applied and theoretical vagueness regarding some of its fundamental concepts. Many have pointed out that public journalism, also known as civic journalism, lacks a clear definition. Advocates have said that they aimed to help democracy by building the public, but they have also said they aimed to strengthen the community. Schudson (1999) said that the public and the community might not be complementary as was implied. Here, I shall try to clarify the relationship between the two, for the purpose of defining the scope of relevance for audience connection.

Some scholars of democratic theory doubt that there is one collective called "the public." This discussion accepts the notion of multiple publics, each formed around different interests, professions or locales (Fraser, 1990; Gitlin, 1998; Negt and Kluge, 1993; Warner, 2002). A public differs from a community in one key way: A public is formed on the basis of a shared common good; this is not necessarily an attribute of a community. A community is bound by a sense of belonging among members who share something in common – such as a language, a certain value orientation, style of dress or type of activity – and have social interactions and social ties with each other (Anderson, 1983; Castells, 1997; Cohen, 1985; Effrat, 1974; Elias, 1974; Janowitz, 1952; Wellman, 1999). With this distinction, it becomes clear that stories that strengthen the sense of belonging to a geographic community, such as reports about a carnival in town or a prominent figure in the community, have little direct relevance to building the public, enhancing a common good or supporting democracy. With this understanding, we can see that the topics covered by public journalism projects – first community-wide problems, then specific issues such as race, immigration, families and youth – were selected to help publics who were struggling with these issues at different levels.

The advent of new online technologies increases the convenience in practicing public journalism. Early attempts at "public listening" to ordinary citizens placed journalists in the position of wandering around the streets and talking to people haphazardly or knocking on people's doors one after another. The Internet and mobile broadcasting help to overcome logistical and resource limitations such as these that often constrained public journalism practices.

Similarly, news organization websites provide increasing opportunities for readers to contribute (Domingo *et al.*, 2008; Hermida and Thurman, 2008). These opportunities span the various modes of participation described above. Professional co-option (column 2 in Figure 10.1) has been going on for a number of years. Blogs shot to fame when traditional journalism outlets discovered and reported on blogs critical of U.S. Senate majority leader Trent Lott and CNN news executive Eason Jordan. These accounts seeped from non-traditional sources into the mainstream press, and they had impact. Lott eventually left his leadership position and Jordan resigned from CNN.

A 2007 study of 16 online newspapers in nine countries found significant opportunities for citizen response (column 3 in Figure 10.1), with 68.8 percent providing commentary spaces to journalist stories or blogs, and 56.3 percent providing journalist-driven forum spaces. However, guided professional reporting (column 4 in Figure 10.1) and guided citizen reporting (column 5 in Figure 10.1) were relatively rare: even the most superficial level of seeking story suggestions from readers (37.5 percent) or suggesting topics for readers to cover (6.3 percent) was uncommon. Opportunities for citizen submission (column 6 in Figure 10.1) were often provided, with 62.5 percent allowing contributions of photos, video and audio, and 31.3 percent allowing citizen stories (Domingo *et al.*, 2008).

Public journalism started with a focus on special projects then struggled to be integrated into day-to-day news work. Providing features of audience connection on professional news websites institutionalizes user engagement as part of routine news-making. Some of these features, as the above discussion shows, seek to engage users as citizens in public issues. They signal the integration of public journalism in day-to-day news routines. In this respect, it is a small step of success for public journalism. Looking to the future of public journalism, the question is how to get news organizations to build in more of the features of audience engagement, and to use them toward strengthening the community/ public and democracy.

Whether, and how, this might happen is questionable because a combination of factors has created an unfavorable environment for the future of public journalism. Public journalism emerged in the United States in the late 1980s partly in response to declining newspaper circulation, and partly as a reaction to the undesirable state of public affairs reporting, especially of the 1988 presidential election. It was a movement that involved the industry and the profession, as well as academia and philanthropic foundations. As of this writing, however, foundations that once provided financial support for many public journalism projects have identified other initiatives for engaging citizens. Academic interest in the subject has also receded.

Back then, newspaper owners were convinced that people who felt connected to their geographical communities were more likely to read newspapers (Batten, 1989). Technological and social changes have revealed that multiple communities exist both in geographical localities and online spaces, and that other factors also affect news consumption. Theoretical developments have clarified that community-building and democracy-enhancement have no necessary connection. The continued decline of citizen consumption of news through traditional news outlets has resulted in closures of news operations, as well as huge cutbacks in staffing and resources for those that remain. In this environment, it is easy for the profession to turn its focus away from the democratic ideals of journalism and value audience engagement for community-building with a goal of commercial success. In this consideration, the features of audience engagement would be used for engaging people as private individuals, not citizens.

Research has found that even with audience participation, journalists tend to retain control on the published content (Domingo *et al.*, 2008; Hermida and Thurman, 2008; Örnebring, 2008). The seven modes of citizen connection presented earlier help to classify the various participatory and interactive features provided on news websites. With the exception of citizen journalism, professional journalists retain control in all the other modes, to varying degrees, on the issues as well as the frames in which news users are engaged. In some of the modes, they also decide which particular "news users" can participate. It is this control that gives professional journalists the possibility to use the features for the goals of public journalism. Twenty years of experimentation in public journalism has provided rich experience which journalists can draw upon, even though the present conditions of the news industry will make efforts for a more citizen-engaged press a struggle.

Summary

Theoretical Implications

- Features of online news can be analyzed with a typology of five models of audience participation (traditional journalism, interactive journalism, public journalism, participatory journalism, citizen journalism) and a continuum of seven modes of citizen connection (professional incorporation,

professional co-option, citizen response, guided professional reporting, guided citizen reporting, citizen submission and citizen journalism).
- Professional incorporation is the mode used in traditional journalism.
- Citizen response is the mode provided in interactive journalism.
- Guided citizen reporting and citizen submission are modes provided in participatory journalism.

Practical Implications

- Public journalism practices that give a voice to the people are particularly applicable to the modes of professional incorporation and citizen journalism.
- Public journalism practices in presentation are particularly applicable to the professional co-option mode.
- Public journalism practices in addressing the news user as citizen are particularly applicable in the modes of citizen response, guided citizen reporting and citizen submission.
- Public journalism practices in listening are particularly applicable to guided professional reporting.

Reflection Questions

- Do news reports that increase a sense of belonging to the community help democracy indirectly?
- Apart from news reports about problems and issues, what other topics for news reports are relevant to public well-being?

Note

1. The title is built upon a term coined by sociologist Max Weber to describe the institutionalization of new practices, often driven by economic forces. Considering the flux that journalistic business models are currently struggling with, Weber's term is appropriate here. Additionally the term captures well how public journalism practices inform part of the routines of online journalism – that is, the routinization achieves to a certain extent the goals of public journalism without the term "public journalism" obscuring the process.

References

Anderson, B. (1983). *Imagined communities: Reflections on the origin and spread of nationalism.* New York: Verso.

Bardoel, J. and Deuze, M. (2001). Network journalism: Converging competences of media professionals and professionalism. *Australian Journalism Review* 23(2), 91–103.

Batten, J.K. (1989, April 3). America's newspapers: What are our prospects? Lecture delivered at University of California, Riverside. No. 24 in the *Press-Enterprise* lecture series.

Bennett, L.W. (2008). *News: The politics of illusion* (8th edn). New York: Longman.

Bowman, S. and Willis, C. (2003). *We media: How audiences are shaping the future of news and information*. The Media Center at The American Press Institute. Retrieved May 18, 2009 from www.hypergene.net/wemedia/download/we_media.pdf.

Bruns, A. (2005). Some Exploratory Notes on Produsers and Produsage. Retrieved May 10, 2009 from http://snurb.info/index.php?q=node/329.

Castells, M. (1997). *The power of identity*. Malden: Blackwell.

Cohen, A.P. (1985). *The symbolic construction of community*. Chichester: Ellis Horwood Ltd.

Cohn, D. (2007, September 6). Network journalism versus citizen journalism versus the myriad of other names for social media in the news world. Retrieved March 30, 2009 from http://newassignment.net/blog/david_cohn/sep2007/06/network_journali.

Deuze, M. (2005). Towards professional participatory storytelling in journalism and advertising. *First Monday* 10(7). Retrieved May 15, 2009 from http://outreach.lib.uic.edu/www/issues/issue10_7/deuze/index.html.

Domingo, D., Quandt, T., Heinonen, A., Paulussen, S., Singer, J.B. and Vujnovic, M. (2008). Participatory journalism practices in the media and beyond. *Journalism Practice* 2(3), 326–342.

Effrat, M.P. (1974). Approaches to community: Conflicts and complementarities. In Effrat, M.P. (ed.). *The community: Approaches and applications* (pp. 1–32). New York: Free Press.

Farrell, H. and Drezner, D.W. (2008). The power and politics of blogs. *Public Choice* 134, 15–30.

Elias, N. (1974). Towards a theory of communities. In Bell, C. and Newby, H. (eds.). *The sociology of community: A selection of readings* (pp. ix–xli). London: William Clowes & Sons Ltd.

Fraser, N. (1990). Rethinking the public sphere: A contribution to the critique of actually existing democracy. *Social Text* 25/26, 56–80.

Friedland, L.A. and Nichols, S. (2002). Measuring civic journalism's progress: A report across a decade of activity. Retrieved April 18, 2009 from www.pewcenter.org/doingcj/research/measuringcj.pdf.

Gillmor, D. (2003, May 18). A new brand of journalism is taking root in South Korea. *San Jose Mercury News*, as republished by Ohmy News. Retrieved May 18, 2009 from: http://english.ohmynews.com/articleview/article_view.asp?menu=c10400&no=153109&rel_no=2#A%20new%20brand%20of%20journalism%20is%20taking%20root%20in%20South%20Korea-San%20Jose%20Mercury%20News.

Gillmor, D. (2005). A citizen journalism breakthrough. Retrieved May 18, 2009 from http://dangillmor.typepad.com/dan_gillmor_on_grassroots/2005/04/a_citizen_journ.html.

Gitlin, T. (1998). Public sphere or public sphericules? In Liebes, T. and Curran, J. (eds.). *Media, ritual and identity* (pp. 175–202). London: Routledge.

Harwood, R.C. and McCrehan, J. (2000). Tapping civic life: How to report first, and best, what's happening in your community. Pew Center for Civic Journalism/Tides Center and The Harwood Institute for Public Innovation. Retrieved August 18, 2009 from http://www.pewcenter.org/doingcj/pubs/tcl/index.html

Hermida, A. and Thurman, N. (2008). A clash of cultures. *Journalism Practice* 2(3), 343–356.

Janowitz, M. (1952). *The community press in an urban setting.* Glencoe: Free Press.

Lasica, J.D. (2003). What is participatory journalism? *Online Journalism Review* 7 (August). Retrieved May 18, 2009 from www.ojr.org/ojr/workplace/1060217106.php.

Negt, O. and Kluge, A. (1993). *Public sphere and experience: Toward an analysis of the bourgeois and proletarian public sphere.* Minneapolis: University of Minnesota Press.

Nip, J.Y.M. (2005). Exploring a second phase of public journalism. Paper presented at AEJMC Mid-Winter Regional Conference, February 11–12, 2005. Kennesaw State University, GA.

Nip, J.Y.M. (2006). Exploring the second phase of public journalism. *Journalism Studies* 7(2), 212–236.

Nip, J.Y.M. (2008). The last days of civic journalism: The case of *Savannah Morning News. Journalism Practice* 20(2), 179–197.

Örnebring, H. (2008). User-generated tabloid content in *The Sun (UK) and Aftonbladet (Sweden). Journalism Studies* 9(5), 771–785.

Outing, S. (2005, June 15). The 11 layers of citizen journalism. Retrieved March 30, 2009 from www.poynter.org/content/content_view.asp?id=83126.

Poynter Online. (2003, April 10). Civic journalism embraced, but cautiously. *The American Journalist Survey.* Bloomington: Indiana University. Retrieved May 18, 2009 from www.poynter.org/content/content_view.asp?id=28835.

Rosen, J. (2006, August 15). The Era of Networked Journalism Begins. Retrieved March 30, 2009 from http://journalism.nyu.edu/pubzone/weblogs/pressthink/2006/08/15/ear_ntw.html.

Rosen, J. (1997). Public journalism as a democratic art. In Rosen, J. Merritt, D. and Austin, L. (eds.). *Public journalism: Theory and practice – lessons from experience* (pp. 3–24). Dayton: Kettering Foundation.

Schaffer, J. (2001, May 22). Civic mapping. Morris Communications Workshop, Augusta, GA. Retrieved May 18, 2009 from www.pewcenter.org/doingcj/speeches/s_augustacivicmapping.html.

Schudson, M. (1999). What public journalism knows about journalism but doesn't know about "public." In Glasser, T.L. (ed.). *The idea of public journalism* (pp. 118–133). New York: Guilford Press.

Thurman, N. (2008). Forums for citizen journalists? Adoption of user generated content initiatives by online news media. *New Media & Society* 10(1), 139–157.

Toffler, A. (1980). *The third wave.* New York: Bantam Books.

Yip, W. (2008). The impact of user-generated content on mainstream newspapers in Hong Kong. Unpublished M.A. thesis. Hong Kong Baptist University.

Warner, M. (2002). *Publics and counterpublics.* New York: Zone Books.

Wellman, B. (1999). The network community: An introduction. In *Networks in the global village: Life in contemporary communities* (pp. 1–47). Boulder: Westview Press.

Chapter 11

Common Knowledge, Civic Engagement and Online News Organizations

Jack Rosenberry

The original impetus for civic journalism was a desire by some journalists and academics to address what they saw as the inability of mainstream journalism to help the public come to common judgment concerning many political issues, a situation that still persists. Despite unprecedented access to information from newspapers and magazines – along with broadcast, cable, satellite television and the Internet – the general public has, in the view of many observers, become disempowered and unable to affect the decisions and operations of government (Gans, 2003). Critics point out that news operations too often are either passive transmitters of political "spin" or arrogant know-it-alls, making them part of the problem rather than part of the solution (Fallows, 1996).

The goal of this chapter is to outline a set of normative "best practices" for online news coverage. Specifically, this examination explores how traditional news organizations can more effectively perform their Fourth Estate role of assisting in the formation of public opinion so that citizens can have a greater impact on public policy. These normative suggestions are grounded in theory, but at the same time have pragmatic applicability. The premise is that if more media organizations used these tools, or something like them, to improve citizen engagement, then the political communication system that underlies our self-governing society could begin to function more effectively in small but significant ways.

The online coverage framework described here provides an opportunity to rejuvenate public affairs coverage by traditional media in ways that emulate the public journalism ideal of creating a civic commons. This study explores how news organizations can use interactive tools as a different means to achieve that end.

Public journalism was always about more than purely information delivery, and so is online news. The interactivity that distinguishes the Internet from other mass media can be used to facilitate shared constructions of meaning that are crucial to public deliberation. Traditional mass media approaches such as print or broadcast news reports are good at creating awareness (agenda setting) but not so good at helping to create public judgment (Yankelovich, 1991). This distinction creates room for novel approaches. As Singer (2003) succinctly put it, "The Web offers both citizens and journalists new options related to information, discourse and decision-making. . . . Journalists who see their role as crucial to democracy have an opportunity to expand that role in a meaningful way" (p. 52).

A New Role for Journalists

Modern journalism needs new strategies because the traditional model of political communication – the "if-you-publish-it-they-will-engage" theory of journalism and democracy rooted in Progressivism – leaves much to be desired. As Gurevitch and Blumler describe the classical view:

> The existence of a free press enshrines the democratic concept of the political accountability of power holders to ordinary citizens. . . . [A free press] implicitly stands for the assumption that readers, viewers, and listeners are offered material on the basis of which they can make up their own minds about who the "good guys" and the "bad guys" in politics are.
>
> (1990, p. 273)

But, as journalist and press critic James Fallows notes, this classical view has lost credibility because: "far from making it easier to cope with public challenges, the media often make it harder" (1996, p. 7). Neuman, Just and Crigler are even more blunt, saying: "The system of political communication in the United States seems to be falling short of its potential" (1992, p. xv). It is worth noting that these observations date to the time frame – the early to mid-1990s – when public journalism was developing as a route toward addressing some of the shortcomings that vexed these observers.

These critics describe a journalistic ineffectiveness rooted in the incorrect assumption that information access or supply leads automatically to engagement. Putting it another way, the system allows but does not encourage public participation. Some early observers saw the Internet as offering potential for a paradigm shift in civic engagement through either network-facilitated plebiscitary democracy (Grossman, 1995) or development of online-based deliberative discourse (Buchstein, 1997). But a vibrant public sphere that can guide enlightened development of public policy as they envisioned has not developed on its own. While online interaction can support democratic discourse, it needs facilitation to do so effectively (Dahlberg, 2001; Barber, 1997; Wilhelm, 2000).

But who should the facilitators be? This is where a new role and function for journalists from traditional news operations could emerge, using the interactive power of online journalism to leverage traditional roles. The traditional media are far from perfect, but they still occupy a pivotal place within the political communication system largely because they perform a "core function" with regard to public life:

> These media put illumination of policy, power, ideology and self-interest at the center of their productions and do so in every issue or edition. This is not to say the traditional news outlets always or even usually augment democracy; an enormous literature documents the gap between journalistic ideals and traditional journalism's actual contributions to democratic life. It is merely to say that the media in this category are generally regarded as having the highest probability of contributing to democratic citizenship.
>
> (Entmann, 2005, p. 50)

Interactive online journalism has an audience that is already engaged as participants *in* the communication as cyber-democratic theory envisions rather than being passive recipients of messages *through* it as traditional news models are constructed. This makes them participants in a process with the kind of structure (supplied by news organizations) that Entmann says is valuable for credibility, based on common knowledge provided by surveillance of the environment through exposure to the news site. It follows that if facilitation is a key to effective cyber-democratic discourse – as Dahlberg, Barber and others maintain – then journalists are naturally well-placed to facilitate such conversation among their interactively engaged audience. In doing so, they can essentially "marry" the best parts of cyber-democratic theory to traditional views of the Fourth Estate to reclaim their eroded role in ways that are not possible under traditional source–message–channel–receiver models of mass communication.

In research done following the 2000 presidential election, Singer extensively quoted one of her survey respondents, who stated the case for online facilitation eloquently:

> This medium is about the empowerment of our community, to facilitate interaction with interesting or meaningful people, to house "forums" in which users can exchange ideas and information, to focus on the local angles, to give people a voice.... Newspapers have always been the bridge between newsmakers and readers. With interactive Internet applications, we have a way to enhance that role and make that bridge a two-way thoroughfare. This is good for the newspaper, good for the online service and good for the users. We're muddling through the continuing chaos of an election [in 2000] in which roughly half the voting public is going to feel

disenfranchised, no matter what the outcome. This is a good time to be in the "enfranchisement" business.

(Singer, 2003, pp. 49–50)

As this quote shows, journalists can use online technology to reformulate their approach toward public affairs journalism. "Too often the alternative to the conventional journalistic role of 'gatekeeper' has been posited as one of 'advocate' . . . Other possibilities exist and should be explored, including the role of 'democratic midwife'" (Gurevitch and Blumler, 1990, p. 286). In a practical sense, this means taking the journalistic role of providing information for surveillance and social cohesion needs and combining it with facilitated discourse using interactive tools. A crucial feature that separates this approach from notions of basic cyber-democracy is that the involvement of the newspaper, a community institution with a traditional role in political discourse, gives the information exchanged and expressed there a certain prominence and institutional support. This in turn makes the interaction more meaningful because traditional media outlets, especially newspapers, are where the public historically has turned for accurate, credible information and analysis about those who hold power (Entmann, 2005).

Emphasizing the importance of legacy news organizations in this process is not meant to disparage those who work outside such institutional settings, many of whom do extensive and high-quality work (as, for example, documented in several case studies in this book). But rather, by bringing facilitated civic discourse under the tent of the online newspaper's institutional authority, journalists can begin to encourage a renewed sense of enfranchisement among the citizenry. As a democratic midwife, the Fourth Estate can reassume the role that has been eroded away by public cynicism about politicians and the political process, and the media's links to both.

A New Strategy – The Online Public Affairs Coverage Framework

But how should this "midwifery" be conducted? What specific prescriptions should online news organizations use for this endeavor? A logical starting point is to recognize the role of the news organization as an institutional actor within the political communication system – as described by Entmann and others – and build upon it.

While merely providing information is not a sufficient condition for creating the conditions under which discourse can flourish, it still is a necessary one because "journalists have a responsibility to recognize and augment the capacity of the audience to learn politically relevant information" (Neuman et al., 1992, p. 120).

Indeed, developing a common base of knowledge is seen as a key component of effective deliberation (Fishkin, 2000). So journalists must continue to provide surveillance of public affairs issues, but also add the established and emergent capabilities of the online environment to build upon merely supplying facts (Graber *et al.*, 1998). The blueprint for online journalists should include using that potential to provide information in interactive ways (e.g. hyper-local stories and related links) that augment traditional, linear story-telling approaches.

Recognizing that simple information dissemination is not enough leads to another role for online journalists, based on Kovach and Rosenstiel's idea that:

> As citizens encounter an ever-greater flow of data they have more need – not less – for identifiable sources dedicated to verifying that information, high-lighting what is important to know and filtering out what is not. . . . The role of the press in this new age becomes working to answer the question "where is the good stuff?" Verification and synthesis become the backbone of the new gatekeeper role of the journalist, that of the "sensemaker."
>
> (2001, p. 48)

In a similar vein, Campbell (2004) suggests "a public knowledge model, in which citizens, experts and journalists collaboratively pool their intelligence." These ideas reinforce the notion that a new role for online journalists also ought to include helping citizens interact with officials in politics and government as well as with each other.

To summarize, a new role for online journalists that can help reclaim the mantle of the Fourth Estate can be built around the following online practices:

- Using interactive tools to present public affairs surveillance information more effectively;
- Providing venues for citizen voices linked with the authority and credibility of the news organization;
- Providing places for citizen-to-citizen interaction on public affairs issues;
- Providing spaces for citizen-to-official interaction on public affairs issues; and
- Combining institutional and citizen voices.

This framework is drawn from theories of cyber-democracy. These theories affirm the potential for online interaction to promote engagement by providing participants with greater access to information and breaking down barriers of time and space for information exchange. Online journalists are well situated to advance this process, with that facilitation put into practice through devices or techniques such as:

- Rich sets of links to government, political, citizen activist and other sites that can help citizen-readers "find the good stuff";
- Citizen viewpoints (such as blogging and news commentary) hosted within the site such that institutional authority accompanies the citizen voices;
- Moderated and facilitated online conversation that connects citizens with each other (replacing the unmoderated screeds now found online in many so-called "discussion" forums and story comment add-ons), and perhaps building connections between citizens and news-makers as well;
- "Pro–am" coverage and commentary models that combine institutional and citizen voices.

Certainly, many of these devices are already used by some news sites. The suggestion here is to employ them in combination in a strategic, purposeful way to shape and direct engaged deliberation by citizen-readers. Such an effort offers an untapped opportunity for news operations to compensate for shortcomings in contemporary news presentation supporting public life.

Online News Sites as a Venue for Cyber-Democratic Engagement

Assessing the capacity of these practices to revitalize the Fourth Estate requires consideration of not only whether online legacy news organizations *can* contribute to improving political communication and deliberation but also requires exploring what they *uniquely* bring to the process. In other words:

- Why should this be the journalists' responsibility?
- What is gained when they are the ones doing it?
- What might stand in the way of them doing it effectively?

Shared Understanding

The answers to the first and second of these questions are rooted in the ability of the online news site to provide not only two-way (interactive, conversational) tools for information exchange, but to supplement it with a base of credible common knowledge and an impartial venue where citizens can make connections. Dumping information on the public doorstep is not sufficient to promote discourse or develop engagement (Gans, 2003; Yankelovich, 1991). But lack of gatekeeping in the interactive environment can allow for presentations of unverified and unreliable information from questionable sources, or allow audience members to customize news reception in disadvantageous ways. As Sunstein notes: "There are serious dangers in a system in which individuals bypass general interest intermediaries and restrict themselves to opinions and topics of their own choosing" (2001, p. 16).

Sunstein, in fact, argues forcefully on behalf of a public forum in which citizens are not only free to *express* a wide variety of ideas and arguments but also are obliged to be *exposed* to the same variety. Traditional mass media are a key source of such exposure in ways that most blogs and citizen-activist sites are not. "A heterogeneous society benefits from shared experiences, many of them produced by the media," Sunstein notes. "These shared experiences provide a kind of social glue, facilitating efforts to solve shared problems, encouraging people to view one another as fellow citizens, and sometimes helping to ensure responsiveness to genuine problems and needs" (2001, p. 103).

Thus, the value of the online newspaper's involvement is that it can provide both a customized experience and a shared one that helps build credible, common understandings. Creating such understandings has always been the province of journalism. So, while the online coverage framework emphasizes the two-way flow of information – with users doing some gatekeeping for themselves and contributing ideas to the collective presentation – it also is understood that this happens within the context of a general news site and that material presented therein reflects the values of general-interest journalism. A base of reliable, common information, much of it from local media outlets, is one characteristic that contributed to the effectiveness of the Minnesota E-democracy project investigated by Dalhberg (2001).

The Importance of Opportunity

Sunstein's ideas draw on one of the inspirations for the public journalism move-ment, John Dewey, who said: "The important consideration is that *opportunity* be given ideas to speak and to become the possession of the multitude. The essential need is the improvement of the *methods and constitution* of debate, dis-cussion and persuasion" (Dewey, 1927, as quoted in Sunstein, 2001, p. 45, emphasis added).

The emphasized passages are meant to highlight another key aspect of the online public-affairs coverage framework, which is that implementing its devices cannot guarantee that an online news site's activities actually will affect public discourse, knowledge or engagement. Rather, what the implementation of these devices really does is *create the conditions* under which engagement can take root. (In some ways, this is akin to describing the conditions required for a Habermasian "ideal speech situation" to occur.) As Dewey notes, the key vari-ables are opportunities for deliberation to occur and the methods by which it may develop. Fishkin addresses the same issue, noting that

The fact that our present, quiescent, disengaged public has not bothered to think enough about politics to have public opinions (rather than political preferences) worthy of the name does not mean that it might not arrive at more informed and more deliberative opinions under conditions designed to truly engage it.

(1991, p. 58)

Sirianni and Friedland (2001) offer a similar approach, saying that deliberative democracy hinges on "expanding the opportunities of citizens themselves to deliberate."

These views about the importance of opportunity are reinforced by findings from an investigation of political discussions in an online setting, which found that "extending opportunities for participation can attract new voters, thereby changing the decision-making environment" (Stanley and Weare, 2004). Seen from this perspective, providing opportunities for developing communication and engagement may be not only a necessary condition for effective discourse, but in some ways could be a sufficient condition as well.

Information Plus Conversation

The online coverage framework can create common knowledge and offer opportunities for interaction in neutral, managed forums. Moreover, this approach can enhance exposure to political information and interpersonal discussion about the political realm, which research shows can be a powerful combination if the goal is citizen engagement. According to one study, "media use and social networks work together to produce civic engagement" (Shah *et al.*, 2001, p. 471). Similarly, the combination of political discussion and exposure to political information via the Internet has a significant impact on political knowledge and efficacy:

The impact of mass mediated information on a person's understanding of politics and participatory behavior should be highest if this person is exposed to relevant information on the Web and *at the same time* talks about it to other people, thereby learning other ways of thinking about the issue and developing a better understanding of it.

(Nisbet and Scheufele, 2004, p. 881, emphasis added)

"At the same time" has been emphasized here because, while Nisbet and Scheufele probably did not mean for the expression to be taken literally, the online environment *does* allow this to happen in literal fashion: online news sites can offer both exposure to public affairs information and real-time discussion of it involving journalists, audience members and perhaps even news-makers themselves. Significantly, public conversation could extend from the news site's base of credible, vetted and verifiable information.

Online papers can, and should, create the conditions for effective discourse. And the conditions *do* matter; that is Habermas' "ideal speech" argument in a nutshell, as well as Dewey's. Creating conditions and opportunities is also the underpinning of the framework as presented here – that involving the online news organization adds the institutional support missing from "raw" cyber-democracy. But the unanswerable question is: if online journalists build better communication systems, what will the audiences do with them? As already noted, Gans (2003) and Yankelovich (1991) both say a fundamentally flawed assumption of the traditional model is that greater information will encourage greater engagement.

One answer to limitations on the traditional model of information dissemination lies with emphasizing the active engagement of the online audience through an interactive, hyper-enabled environment. Such active engagement is missing from the traditional arrangement that Gans and others call inadequate. The studies by Shah *et al.* and by Nisbet and Scheufele show that the Internet's ability to combine the characteristics of mass-mediated and interpersonal information flow could spur audience attraction to online papers that leads to greater civic engagement.

Barriers to Success

But how the audience and the journalists use the coverage devices employed by online papers will have an impact on the ultimate effectiveness of such processes. Meaningful discourse requires that individuals seek common ground, a key theme of work by Sunstein (2001) and Cohen (1997). The idea of journalists as facilitators can address this need. But one of the implications of online access is that users can sort and select the information they receive so that it is narrowly tailored to their own interests – a phenomenon sometimes referred to as creating "The Daily Me" (Negroponte, 1995, p. 145). Facilitating civic engagement through online news sites operated by professional journalists trained in creating a news report that reflects the interests and needs of the whole community provides some protection against such provincialism, but offers no guarantees.

The most significant barrier is that implementing the online public-affairs coverage framework will require journalists to adopt new roles, which some may be reluctant to accept. The traditional description of an editor's job involves fact-checking and re-writing reporters' stories, not recruiting citizen bloggers and moderating online discussions. Singer's work (2003) illustrated that adopting and adapting to these new roles will take some time. Editors in her survey mentioned tools such as interactivity and use of multimedia, but did not endorse them with much enthusiasm. The recent hollowing out of many news-rooms, leaving the remaining journalists strapped to merely produce daily reports, is another impediment.

The inertia of tradition could mean mainstream journalism will be slow to change. The steps taken so far by many organizations to incorporate citizen con-tributions without direction or facilitation, such as hosting message forums that end up filled with anonymous personal attacks and unverifiable observations, con-tribute nothing meaningful to the discourse. Taking such a laissez-faire approach to incorporating interactive technology on the news site – "We post reader-submitted stories; we've got blogs; we Twitter; isn't that enough?" – has the same shortcomings as the cyber-utopian view that the network will automatically and inevitably lead to a dynamic, engaged public. The lesson of public journalism is that building a public and fostering effective deliberation requires thoughtful, guided informational exchanges. That's still true even in the interactive age.

Conclusion: A Step Toward Civic Engagement

As proponents and practitioners of public journalism can attest, reforming a dysfunctional political communication system is no easy task. One answer, although it may seem too facile, is for all of the actors involved – politicians and officials, members of the public, and members of news organizations – to seek out practical, specific reforms that contribute to reducing the systemic prob-lems. This is hardly a radical suggestion, and certainly not a panacea. Rather, it is an idea drawn from the philosophy behind the proverb that the longest journey begins with a single step.

From the perspective of journalism and the public, the "single step" pro-posed here is an online public-affairs coverage framework rooted in the five practices described earlier. It is a practical and realistic, yet theoretically grounded, approach. It stresses using the power of interactive communication available to Internet-based news organizations to create conditions that can facilitate both greater understanding of public affairs by the public and expanded civic engagement through online discourse. By itself, this would not fix the system. But it is a step in the right direction. The ideas suggested here follow and build upon past suggestions for press reform, including ones underlying the public journalism movement. But what is significantly different here is incorpo-ration of technology to facilitate the reforms, without resorting to the kind of technological determinism that says productive discourse and effective engage-ment will emerge easily or automatically simply because the Internet allows efficient interactive communication.

Journalists, news-makers and audiences all have a role to play in public affairs discourse, and share culpability when the political communication system does not work effectively. But one thing is certain: whatever the prerogatives of audiences and officials, the first step must be taken by journalists, the traditional sources for information about public life. Implementing the online public affairs coverage framework may or may not be a sufficient condition for fixing a broken political communication system, but doing something like it is a necessary one. In doing so, journalists might meet a goal expressed by James Carey (quoted in Kovach and Rosenstiel, 2001, p. 18), who said: "Perhaps in the end, journalism simply means amplifying the conversations of the people themselves."

Summary

Theoretical Implications

- The traditional "if-you-publish-it-they-will-engage" theory of journalism and democracy is no longer operative. But while traditional media are far from perfect in their support of democracy, they still occupy a pivotal place in the political communication system.
- The online environment promotes engagement by (1) providing participants with greater access to information and (2) breaking down barriers of time and space for information exchange. This has applications for development of public opinion and mobilization, sometimes called "cyber-democracy." But online interaction supports democratic discourse best when it is facilitated rather than left to develop on its own.
- The interactivity of online news (in comparison with traditional reporting forms) can be used to create shared constructions of meaning, which are crucial to public deliberation.
- Theories of cyber-democracy (online political engagement) and traditional journalism can compensate for each other's shortcomings. Journalistic presentations do not automatically promote civic engagement, but the news organizations can provide the structure and facilitation that it requires to make it practical and effective.

Practical Implications

- Theories of cyber-democracy can be used to develop a set of normative "best practices" for enhanced online coverage by traditional news organizations. In a practical sense, this means taking the journalistic role of providing information that fills surveillance and social cohesion needs and combining it with facilitated discourse using interactive tools.

- These devices primarily create the conditions under which engagement could take root, but offer no guarantees that it will.
- If more media organizations used such tools to improve citizen engagement, then the political communication system could function more effectively.

Reflection Questions

- Can merely providing opportunities for interactive civic engagement online be not only a necessary condition for coming to common judgment, but a sufficient one as well?
- What specific types of "moderation" and "facilitation" can journalists provide that will offer the greatest likelihood of helping citizen-readers come to common judgment?
- What is the likely impact of further fragmentation in the news delivery system as news consumers build their own customized presentations rather than attending to the broad scale of surveillance offered by traditional news sites?

References

Barber, B. (1997). The new telecommunications technology: endless frontier or the end of democracy? *Constellations* 4 (2), 208–226.

Buchstein, H. (1997). Bytes that bite: the Internet and deliberative democracy. *Constellations* 4 (2), 248–263.

Campbell, C. (2004). Journalism and public knowledge. *National Civic Review* 93 (3), 3–11.

Cohen, J. (1997). Deliberation and democratic legitimacy. In Bohman, J. and Rehg, W. (eds.). *Deliberative democracy: essays on reason and politics* (pp. 67–91). Cambridge: MIT Press.

Dahlberg, L. (2001). Extending the public sphere through cyberspace: the case of Minnesota e-democracy. *First Monday* 6 (3). Retrieved May 17, 2003 from http://firstmonday.org/issues/issue6_3/dahlberg/index.html.

Entmann, R. (2005). The nature and sources of news. In Overholser, G. and Hall Jamieson, K. (eds.). *The Press* (pp. 48–65). New York: Oxford University Press.

Fallows, J. (1996). *Breaking the news: how the media undermine democracy*. New York: Pantheon Books.

Fishkin, J. (1991). *Democracy and deliberation: new directions for democratic reform*. New Haven: Yale University Press.

Fishkin, J. (2000). Virtual democratic possibilities: prospects for Internet democracy. Presented at Internet, Democracy and Public Goods conference, Belo Horizonte, Brazil, November 2000. Retrieved January 15, 2005 from: http://cdd.Stanford.edu/research/papers/2000/brazil_paper.pdf.

Gans, H. (2003). *Democracy and the news*. New York: Oxford University Press.

Graber, D., McQuail, D. and Norris, P. (1998). Introduction: political communication in a democracy. In Graber, D., McQuail, D. and Norris, P. (eds.). *The politics of news, the news of politics* (pp. 1–16). Washington, DC: CQ Press.

Grossman, L. (1995). *The electronic republic: democracy in the information age.* New York: Viking.

Gurevitch, M. and Blumler, J. (1990). Political communication systems and democratic values. In Lichtenberg, J. (ed.). *Democracy and the mass media: a collection of essays* (pp. 269–289). New York: Cambridge University Press.

Kovach, B. and Rosenstiel, T. (2001). *The elements of journalism: what newspeople should know and the public should expect.* New York: Crown Publishers.

Negroponte, N. (1995). *Being digital.* New York: Alfred A. Knopf.

Neuman, W.R., Just, M.R. and Crigler, A.N. (1992). *Common knowledge: news and the construction of political meaning.* Chicago: University of Chicago Press.

Nisbet, M. and Scheufele, D. (2004). Political talk as a catalyst for online citizenship. *Journalism & Mass Communication Quarterly* 81 (4), 877–896.

Shah, D.V., McLeod, J. and Yoon, S.-H. (2001). Communication, context and community: an exploration of print, broadcast and Internet influences. *Communication Research* 28 (4), 464–506.

Singer, J.B. (2003). Campaign contributions: online newspaper coverage of election 2000. *Journalism & Mass Communications Quarterly* 80 (1), 39–56.

Sirianni, C. and Friedland, L. (2001). Deliberative democracy (entry in *Civic Dictionary*). Civic Practices Network. Retrieved January 15, 2005 from http://www.cpn.org/tools/dictionary/deliberate.html.

Stanley, J.W. and Weare, C. (2004). The effects of Internet use on political participation: evidence from an agency online discussion group. *Administration and Society* 36 (5), 503–528.

Sunstein, C. (2001). *Republic.com.* Princeton: Princeton University Press.

Wilhelm, A.G. (2000). *Democracy in the digital age.* London: Routledge.

Yankelovich, D. (1991). *Coming to public judgment: making democracy work in a complex world.* Syracuse: Syracuse University Press.

Chapter 12

Madison Commons 2.0
A Platform for Tomorrow's Civic and Citizen Journalism

Sue Robinson, Cathy DeShano, Nakho Kim and Lewis A. Friedland

The hope inherent in democratic self-rule lies in citizens' identity construction via communal relationships and an attachment to place. In other words, "for democracy to work, community is necessary" (Friedland, 2001, p. 358). As Internet usage has grown, citizen media projects have tried to recreate, resurrect and renegotiate community spaces online. Some form of a deliberative public sphere is often the aim of these websites, which experiment with different economic, philosophical and structural models. While most citizen media seem to succeed on some level in regards to virtual communal gatherings, questions of information credibility, significance and authority have also nagged the projects.

The citizen journalism model examined in this case study tried to resolve those issues by combining participatory initiatives with traditional journalistic concepts and standards. This project developed with the aim of creating a place for communication where people's communities could intersect with their political and economic institutions through journalism. Informed by the theory of John Dewey (1927) and Jurgen Habermas (1962/1989, 1981/1987), Lewis A. Friedland (2001) of the University of Wisconsin-Madison had developed a theory of integrated community via communicative action: by building a new online platform where all communicative networks could merge, community – and thus democracy – might thrive. In March 2006, he and a doctoral student, former CSPAN editor Chris Long, established Madison Commons.org. The idea was that the citizen media website would become a link between the associative public–private realms of the individual and the institutional aspects of political, economic and cultural life of the state.

This chapter scrutinizes the mission of Madison Commons, its initial implementation, the challenges and successes, and, finally, its plan for progression. Specifically, this chapter catalogues how the site evolved from a clearinghouse of mostly textual information produced by citizens trained in the journalistic tradition to a Web 2.0 platform that explores community integration through interactive features. It concludes with an evaluation of how well this citizen journalism effort operates as a realistic application of the "communicatively integrated community" theory (Friedland, 2001).

As of 2009, the project had succeeded minimally on all three levels of relational engagement; it enhanced, to some degree, associative, organizational and institutional relationships. For example, the site aggregated community-oriented news, parceling it by neighborhood. This ordered collection served to knit together a textual representation of contemporary Madison, WI. However, the site's mission to empower citizens through journalistic training and self-generated content did not develop as hoped, and this reduced the level of individual communicative action. Realities of habit, time constraints, structural issues (such as a lack of deadlines) and technological impediments all interfered with the model's ability to become a hub for civic engagement. Proposed initiatives for the project's second phase, however, included an experiment in resolving many of the current challenges, and should showcase Madison Commons 2.0 as a site to build community through journalistic-grade content.

Foundational Concepts: Civic and Citizen Journalism

The University of Wisconsin-Madison's citizen-media experiment began around the same time that dozens of other participatory journalistic websites blossomed in cyberspace. A few of these sites thrived while many others failed. All have had the potential to transform the very idea of journalism. Some of the better-known ones included OhmyNews (thrived), Backfence (failed), Slashdot.com (thrived), wikinews (in progress) and Bayosphere (failed). On a more hyper-local level, MyMissourian, iBrattleboro, WestportNow and the Northwest Voice were providing virtual platforms for communities across the nation in late 2008 and early 2009. Challenges for citizen journalism sites have been both institutional and communal in nature, ranging from economic considerations such as software expenses to a lack of substantive civic participation.

Each project has employed a different economic, structural, cultural and civic model for citizen media. OhmyNews, for example, was conceived as editorially moderated but citizen-fueled, relying on journalists transforming from gatekeepers (White, 1950) into gatewatchers and information filterers (Bruns, 2005). The MyMissourian site targeted specific community niches using an open-source approach that its administrators say succeeds because of a hyper-local focus and forums that "self-correct" when discussion disintegrates (Bentley et al., 2006). Citizen media news sites have at their core a sense of social responsibility and libertarianism that suggests citizens will civically engage in a responsible way when they are given the tools to do so (Bentley et al., 2006; Deuze, 2001; Glasser, 2004).

This premise has long existed at the heart of civic and public journalism, a trend emerging from the social movements of the 1970s and 1980s (Friedland, 2003; Glasser, 1999; Rosen, 1999). The assumption of civic/public journalism suggests that by incorporating readers into the process of journalistic production, the quality and relevance of public information and public life will improve. Originally this idea manifested in reader–journalist forums and reader-driven agendas for both political and community-centered news coverage. Its inherent philosophy depends on the reporters, editors and publishers embracing a civic mindset for all content production by insisting that a concern for community-specific needs governs all newsgathering, reader collaboration and publishing (Friedland, 2003; Glasser, 1999; Rosen, 1999). Public journalism initiatives, however, tended to emphasize that this process of citizen-engagement began with the professional journalists in corporate newsrooms.

Online, citizen media projects start with individuals who exist outside the institution of the press. Citizen journalism relies on amateurs to report and broadly disseminate information external to the journalistic gatekeeping process. It is the self-referential, monitorial individual and his/her relationships with others and their commercial media who matter for a vibrant, deliberative online public sphere (Papacharissi, 2010, in press). Online sharing sites and discussion forums shift focus from orienting and instrumental functions of news production to dialogic and monitorial information exchanges (Deuze, 2003). Ideally, through this increased dialogue, citizens flesh out and address community needs (Gillmor, 2004).

Foundational Concepts: Community

These trends in the transformation of news production matter because such shifts in information control are inevitably linked to civic engagement, political participation and the health of the republic. The Internet has the potential to rebuild or at least enhance communal relationships that have become increasingly fragmented in a multimodal society. As Schuler noted:

> Communities can be thought of as living systems. And just as a human body has a skeletal system, circulatory system, and other systems that sustain its life, a community has several "systems" or "core values" that help sustain its life.
>
> (1995)

Schuler identified six core values: culture and conviviality, education, strong democracy, health and social welfare, economic equity and opportunity, and information and communication. He stressed that "community information is critical to community networks, and information that supports the core values is especially valuable" (Schuler, 1995). Scholars have long theorized that community cannot exist without vibrant communication (Hawley, 1986; Hawley and Wirt, 1974; Matei *et al.*, 2001; Park, 1938; Wirth, 1946). Furthermore, theorists suggest that for self-rule to work, there must be significant public deliberation (Friedland, 2001; Merritt, 1998). A vibrant, healthy community depends on trust, reciprocity and solidarity – achieved in part through communicative action that exercises interpersonal, organizational, associative and institutional ties (Friedland, 2001; Habermas, 1981/1987).

Much scholarship has begun to examine what new media forms might mean for concepts of community. For example, a 1998 edited volume about mobile communication, *Displacing Place*, theorized that our geographic sense of place is being reconceptualized into virtual worlds, where a "mediapolis" offers interconnectedness within a hybrid space of physical–virtual realms (Kleinman, 2007). Some scholars maintain that the Internet might destroy community on some level. Bimber (1998) suggested the Internet leads to a deinstitutionalization of society that dissolves social–political–economic associations and creates a general sense of disconnection. Others have found that greater use of the Internet translated to less interpersonal communication, resulting in poor group cohesion (Kraut *et al.*, 1998).

At the very least, citizen use of the Internet is changing conceptions of community, shifting community structures, and recontextualizing communicative action for both public and private spheres of society. For an alternative mode of civic engagement to thrive, however, any citizen media project must be characterized by access to information and a certain level of productive reciprocity (Papacharissi, 2010, in press). It must also feature a combination of interactive involvement, personalization and contiguity of content (Yaros, 2010, in press). Additionally, it should take into account the changing nature of the expectations, purposes and authority of knowledge today. Boundaries of information are becoming "liquid" and difused; successful communicative action is being evaluated more for measures of group cohesion, personalization and self-definition than for political action (Atton, 2002; Deuze, 2007; Rodriguez, 2001; Matheson, 2010, in press). Indeed, it is the quality and level of *connectedness* that seem to matter (Jung *et al.*, 2001).

The University of Wisconsin-Madison citizen media project, Madison Commons, sought to explore how community might be re-invigorated through facilitating the integration of people's worlds – their private, social and political spheres. At the same time, the project's administrators wanted such an integrated engagement to maintain a standard of learned knowledge to facilitate informed deliberation. As the blogosphere proliferated, two broad approaches to the questions of information accuracy and fairness have developed. The "crowds" approach operates under the "self-correcting" theory that enough eyes on any story should ensure the ultimate validity of the information in it. Madison Commons chose the more traditional paradigm: that the press's formal industry standards of fairness and accuracy should be applied to citizen journalism as well – an approach consistent with one of citizen media's pioneers, Dan Gillmor. Even while arguing that people collectively know more than the individual journalist, Gillmor (2004) was fundamentally concerned with the credibility of information in this new age.

Unfortunately, the original model of Madison Commons has stumbled over people's changing communication expectations as well as their communal gratifications. Thus, both its mission and implementation must be revised and reapplied. This chapter takes stock of these efforts since 2006. The next section describes the model as an applied framework, followed by a detailed accounting of the project's implementation and its next phase for a Web 2.0 environment. A conclusion offers the theoretical and practical lessons we might take away from this effort.

Madison Commons: A Model, an Experiment

The concept of Madison Commons as a workable model stemmed from the idea that at the community level, the societal system – the self-regulating economic and political structure – meets the lifeworld, described by Habermas (1981/1987) as a multi-dimensional set of interactions that compose people's culture and social relations. The philosophy of Madison Commons holds that communities persist even within a fractured society. This view holds that boundaries between interpersonal, associative, organizational, institutional and mediated networks might no longer be distinct (if they ever were) and, therefore, reifying a sense of place is essential for vibrancy and relevancy for individuals within a community. Ideally, Madison Commons would create a virtual community overlaying a geographic place that would expand people's interpersonal networks and make associational networks more visible. In the process, such a platform should produce communication and, more importantly, *deliberation*, creating new relational ties across neighborhoods and city sub-regions.

The Commons draws (not surprisingly) from commons theory, most prominently developed by Elinor Ostrom (1990) and colleagues. A commons is best understood literally – as a pool of natural and other resources used by many but owned by none (Hardin, 1968). Levine (2001) and Bollier (2002) show how the commons model can be applied to the Internet. The Madison Commons attempts to re-localize the commons model of management for the Internet, taking quite literally the idea that local communication resources can be collectively managed.

The Madison Commons, then, is a practical experiment with theoretical intent. The model depends on multiple contributors and users; this collective management, production and usage increases the resource yield for all. It attempts to increase the links between local social capital and community integration by drawing on networks across the community, including some social associations that may remain largely disconnected from each other or, often, unknown.

These links build on the structure of "weak ties," one of the most influential concepts in contemporary sociology of community, first developed by sociologist Mark Granovetter (1973, 1982). Weak ties are those links from one person to another that are not primary (close friends, family) but secondary (acquaintances, friends of friends and, increasingly, connections to others on the Internet). Granovetter and others have posited that much of social life is made up of weak ties, and this is increasingly so as community weakens and more of life is lived online. While our traditional images of community draw on images of closely knit strong ties, the structure of weak ties dominates in late modern societies. This increases the challenge of any community-building project like the Madison Commons: the task is not only to connect strong networks, but also to link networks of weak ties that are, by definition, looser and more ephemeral.

Connecting these networks makes them visible and builds that imagined community (Anderson, 1991) so that – in this case – a broader vision of Madison can be sustained. But because it draws together both mass and networked media, the imagined community is both extensive (ranging broadly across the entire community through newspapers and broadcast) and intensive (reaching deeply into both micro-local neighborhoods and personal networks). This particular model convenes a networked public sphere of local discussion that can warn of social problems early and transmit them to the attention of broader groups of social actors, both formal (government) and informal (associations and residents). Finally, this virtual place is governed as a commons, owned by no one institution (governmental or private), open to all and freely used by all.

Madison Commons: The (Web 1.0) Initiative

Wisconsin's capital city with some 225,000 people, Madison boasts a vibrant physical community, including more than 120 registered neighborhood associations. Madison Commons endeavored to bring people from these neighborhoods together and raise awareness of their shared and unique experiences as Madison residents. Using a town commons approach, the project was based on three layers of physical collaboration: community and neighborhood partnerships that drive local newsgathering; local media collaboration; and the University of Wisconsin-Madison School of Journalism & Mass Communication as a host, administrator and caretaker.

During the early planning, staff members of neighborhood planning councils, which are quasi-official community organizations spanning city regions, helped identify significant issues at the neighborhood level and provided individuals to participate in citizen journalism workshops. Partnerships were developed with local media, which agreed to allow their stories to be republished on Madison Commons, as long as they could publish content originating on the site in exchange. In addition, journalism students from the university were encouraged to report on neighborhood issues. Graduate students functioned as editors. Foundation grants supported the online platform, new technology and graduate student responsibilities.

Training

A fundamental Commons principle held that all volunteer citizen journalists needed to complete journalistic training before publishing articles on the site. In workshops, volunteers became familiar with basic journalism principles such as fairness, accuracy, transparency and thoroughness. The project trained adults to report on hyper-local issues and people rather than on state or national matters. In 2007 and 2008, Madison Commons trained more than 70 individuals, with an average of eight people attending a series of six workshops. The project gave citizen journalists broad latitude to select topics for each assignment, although they were encouraged to write about their neighborhoods.

By 2008, the training had been greatly modified. Although there were fewer difficulties recruiting workshop participants than originally anticipated, the Commons heard from individuals who wanted to get trained but had scheduling conflicts. The project offered many of these people a one-time introductory workshop; the Commons provided nine of these seminars in 2008. These one-day workshops emphasized journalistic responsibilities that citizens must employ to create fair and accurate stories, but did not walk these participants through actual reporting and writing stories. The new format appealed to people: registration increased 100 percent in 2008, from fall 2006.

Challenges

While finding citizens to undergo training was easier than initially anticipated, keeping them as contributors was a more formidable challenge. Of the 70 initially trained individuals, only ten contributed to the Commons following completion of their training and their efforts were inconsistent, ranging from just six to two stories over a year. Between October 1, 2006 and September 30, 2007, 10 percent of the stories published on the Commons were original articles written by citizen journalists.

Four individuals who took part in a focus group of contributors cited busy personal schedules and lack of story ideas as the main obstacles in writing for the Commons. All suggested that if they were asked to write about a specific issue and given a deadline, they would be more inclined to contribute.

This lack of citizen journalist participation resulted in greater dependence on stories published first in other outlets and republished on Madison Commons. Between October 1, 2006 and September 30, 2007, 78 percent of stories that were published on the Commons originally appeared in one of its local media partners. Another 12 percent of the stories were first published in neighborhood newsletters.

Technology also posed a significant challenge. With a limited staff and budget, the project could not quickly implement features that would make involvement more accessible for citizen journalists. For example, one writer developed a Commons blog that dealt with diversity issues within the city, but the process for updating the blog was cumbersome and hindered real-time dialogue with readers.

Successes

Despite the limited participation, there were successes, including the formation of crucial relationships between citizens and community organizations. In late 2006, the project partnered with the city's Department of Planning to provide a writing workshop for newsletter editors at the Neighborhood Roundtable Conference. Citizens also developed relationships with newsletter editors in the city's neighborhoods. Commons' citizen journalists reported for neighborhood newspapers or became neighborhood newsletter editors. In addition, each of the participants during the fall 2006 workshop series had an article published in a media-partner outlet. Therefore, even if trainees were not writing original stories for the Commons, they became communicatively engaged with their communities, and carried with them the skills and journalistic principles developed during training, such as commitment to accuracy and transparency. Furthermore, these actions introduced citizen-generated content to organizations that had previously been closed to outside contributors. Finally, the Commons also served as an outlet for university students to publish work that focused on neighborhood people or issues.

The Shift to Madison Commons 2.0

Nevertheless, by 2009 it had become apparent that the Madison Commons project needed to be reconceptualized. In particular, the application of the model needed to evolve into a more participatory platform without compromising the credibility, relevance and significance of the information published on the site. To achieve this goal, three main challenges had to be addressed: participation in editorial content creation, interactive information-service features and site administration.

Editorial Content

First, direct participation by citizen journalists had to be made easier. "Easier participation" should not imply that anyone can post anything into the site, which would contradict the initial premise that citizen journalists need to be trained. Rather it means that site administrators should implement diverse ways of participating. As of the end of 2008, the only way to contribute content was to undergo the workshop training and write full-fledged news articles or post short comments to articles. This approach was helpful in maintaining the quality and credibility of the site, but it discouraged potential contributors. Those who were trained still did not feel confident enough to select stories and manage their time so that they could compose journalistic-grade articles.

To cope with this challenge, administrators want to offer three ways to produce significant content. The news articles written by trained citizen journalists would continue to be the main feature. A second contributive method would be blogs hosted on the site. Finally, site administrators planned on adding discussion forums with both editorially determined and free topics open to anyone, regardless of training. The three venues would come together in a concept called the "editorial stub." In a "stub," the editor posts some basic information, and the users can contribute to the topic as news articles, blog posts or forum posts. Relevant entries would be selected, categorized and integrated into the stub as hyperlinks.

Information Services

The second challenge for Madison Commons involves boosting the site's number of visitors and their return rates. To draw attention to the site, the Commons is investigating the use of various local information service features such as event calendars and themed maps. Users must be the ones to maintain these services to maximize the interactive functions of the Internet, a concept often emphasized by the proponents of the buzz phrase "Web 2.0" (O'Reilly, 2005). Three specific ideas to achieve this are: an RSS news aggregator to catch the latest entries of the local blogosphere; an event calendar function with more links to relevant news articles, search options and location maps; and community maps available as a directory-type service (for example, a map showing gasoline prices in various neighborhoods).

Site Administration

The third challenge for the next phase of Madison Commons 2.0 is administrative. The structure of the site at the end of 2008 relied heavily on the contribution of the editors who initiated the project as a social experiment with the hope the site would become a communally-run public sphere. Madison Commons must move from "project" designation to a self-sustaining structure that is citizen generated. This will involve transitioning from the academic-team management to a community-led initiative. To this end, administrators hoped that active neighborhood associations would play a key role. Going forward, organizers plan to tap local community networks to find ways to organize a sustainable managing team for the content on the site. Finally, advertising revenue may also be a way to pay both server hosts and administration services.

Conclusion

By 2009, the Madison Commons project had entered a crucial phase. To realize the envisioned community platform, it must bring together Madison residents in a meaningful way on three interconnected levels – associative and interpersonal, organizational and institutional – while maintaining a standard of information credibility. This website, cognizant of the private–public tensions in any town commons, attempted to structure informal talk into a mixture of professional-grade journalism and civic dialogue. The project trained more than 70 people in journalistic techniques and provided dozens of citizen-generated, neighborhood-focused news stories. Citizens applied the training they received through Madison Commons' workshops to their writings for neighborhood association newsletters, thus enhancing the cross-community organizational relationships. The aggregating function of the site – collecting news articles from local media and sorting them by neighborhood and issues – reformulated the daily happenings in a manner relevant to residents. Finally, the site encouraged mainstream media outlets to enhance their neighborhood focus, giving content to institutional press outlets that would not have it otherwise – a key goal laid out in Merritt's (1998) guide to an idealized public life. These last elements developed the citizen–institutional relationship from the standpoint of the citizen (as opposed to the power elites). All of these successes of the project suggest that, on some level, the site touched upon the three identified tiers of communicative action – associative and interpersonal, organizational and institutional.

That said, much remains to be done to show that such a site can help achieve a communicatively integrated community. Through this experiment, it became apparent that citizen journalists are often constrained by a specific set of needs and interests to a point that they do not automatically produce the information needed by the community as a whole. Any revised site must take this into account, along with the realities of habit, time constraints, structural issues (such as a lack of deadlines) and technological impediments that could interfere with any model being fully functional. Thus, any citizen journalism site must seriously consider how it can help facilitate new conceptions of community and notions of acceptable civic engagement.

Furthermore, this research suggests that the boundaries between interpersonal, associative, organizational, institutional and mediated networks persist. In other words, the networks of weak ties discussed in this chapter require a series of stronger links to result in sustainable activity on the citizen journalism site. (It may also be the case that a greater quantity of weaker links can do the job as well; the answer is not clear at this juncture.) For example, one possible explanation for this site's struggles might have to do with the attempts to erase or blend previously well-established societal delineations, such as between the professional journalist and the "regular" person. This research indicated that rather than empowering citizens, formal journalistic training had the potential to disenchant people, depending on the individual motivations for online engagement and confidence level regarding information production. All this must be taken into account as the Madison Commons' administrators move forward. This chapter offered some possible pathways that the direction of this project – and similarly ambitious citizen journalism sites – could take.

Summary

Theoretical Implications

- The information needs of a community and the motivations of individual citizens do not necessarily match. Citizen journalists have specific sets of interests that do not automatically produce the information needed by the community as a whole.
- While the form of community information may change, the community still needs basic information about local government bodies, non-profit organizations, schools and businesses. This has traditionally been produced by newspaper journalism. There is no evidence to date that individual or blog-based reporting, with its emphasis on self-description and promotion, can provide this kind of comprehensive information.
- Boundaries between interpersonal, associative, organizational, institutional and mediated networks persist, and citizen journalism sites must find ways to overcome these barriers in order to succeed.

Practical Implications

- Realities of habit, time constraints, structural issues (such as a lack of dead-lines) and technological impediments interfered with the model's operation. Thus, any citizen journalism site should strategically employ the interactive functionality of these online sites to foster deeper connections to less geographic notions (and broader understandings) of community and, particularly, civic engagement.
- Viable citizen journalism cannot discount any of the ingredients of viable community, such as trust, reciprocity, a sense of place (even if merely virtual) and shared experiences.
- Formal journalistic training has the potential to disenchant people instead of empowering them, depending on the individual and his or her confidence level and motivations for online engagement.

Reflection Questions

- How are people's very concepts of community ("imagined" or otherwise) changing because of interactive technologies?
- If citizen journalists embrace fragmented interests, how can they harness these special niche energies to enhance a sense of the collective within a local community?
- Do these findings suggest that journalistic-grade content produced by citizens might not be a viable, or even desired, standard by either citizen journalists or readers?
- In a world where network integration promotes weak relational ties and connections based on self-interest, is a true commons – virtual or not – still possible?
- What is the critical mass of users and producers required for a citizen journalism site to become self-sustaining? How does the critical mass of citizen journalism compare to critical mass for sustained community, and must one necessarily replicate the dynamics of the other?
- Finally, from a more macro perspective, what would be the adequate scope of the community (topically, geographically or otherwise) that any citizen journalism site must cover to be considered successful and, more importantly, beneficial for democracy?

References

Anderson, B. (1991). *Imagined communities: Reflections on the origin and spread of nationalism*. London, New York: Verso.
Atton, C. (2002). *Alternative media*. London: Thousand Oaks, Sage.

Bentley, C., Hamman, B., Littau, J., Meyer, H., Watson, B. and Welsh, B. (2006). The citizen journalist movement: MyMissourian as a case study. In Tremayne, M. (ed.). *Blogging, citizenship and the future of media* (pp. 239–259). New York: Routledge.

Bimber, B. (1998). The Internet and political transformation: Populism, community, and accelerated pluralism. *Polity*, XXXI(1), 133–160.

Bollier, D. (2002). *Silent theft: The private plunder of our common wealth.* New York: Routledge.

Bruns, A. (2005). *Gatewatching: Collaborative online news production.* New York: Peter Lang.

Deuze, M. (2001). Online journalism: Modeling the first generation of news media on the World Wide. *First Monday*, 6(10). Retrieved October 2, 2004 from http://firstmonday.org/issues/issue6_10/deuze/index.html.

Deuze, M. (2003). The web and its journalisms: Considering the consequences of different types of newsmedia online. *New Media & Society*, 5(2), 203–230.

Deuze, M. (2007). *Media work.* Cambridge: Polity.

Dewey, J. (1927). *The public and its problems.* New York: Holt-Rinehart & Winston.

Friedland, L.A. (2001). Communication, community, and democracy: Toward a theory of the communicatively integrated community. *Communication Research*, 28, 358–391.

Friedland, L. (2003). *Public journalism: Past and present.* Dayton: Kettering Foundation.

Gillmor, D. (2004). *We the media: Grassroots journalism by the people, for the people.* Sebastopol: O'Reilly Media, Inc.

Glasser, M. (1999). *The idea of public journalism.* New York: Guilford Press.

Glasser, M. (2004). The new voices: Hyperlocal citizen media sites want you (to write)! *Online Journalism Review.* University of Southern California. Retrieved June 12, 2009 from http://ojr.org/ojr/glaser/1098833871.php.

Granovetter, M.S. (1973). The strength of weak ties. *American Journal of Sociology*, 78, 1360–1380.

Granovetter, M.S. (1982). The strength of weak ties: A network theory revisited. In Marsden, P.V. and Lin, N. (eds.). *Social structure and network analysis* (pp. 105–130). Beverly Hills: Sage.

Habermas, J. (1962/1989). *The structural transformation of the public sphere* (T. Burger, trans.). Cambridge: MIT Press.

Habermas, J. (1981/1987). *The theory of communicative action: Lifeworld and system: A critique of functionalist reason, Vol. 2* (T. McCarthy, trans.). Boston: Beacon.

Hardin, G. (1968). The tragedy of the commons. *Science*, 162 (December), 1243–1248.

Hawley, A.H. (1986). *Human ecology: A theoretical essay.* Chicago: University of Chicago Press.

Hawley, A.H. and Wirt, F.M. (1974). *The search for community power.* Englewood Cliffs: Prentice Hall.

Jung, J.-Y., Qiu, J.-L. and Kim, Y.-C. (2001). Interconnectedness and inequality: Beyond the divide. *Communication Research*, 28(4), 509–537.

Kleinman, S. (ed.). (2007). *Displacing Place: Mobile communication in the 21st Century.* New York: Peter Lang.

Kraut, R., Patterson, M., Lundmark, V., Kiesler, S., Mukopadhyay, T. and Scherlis, W. (1998). Internet Paradox: A social technology that reduces social involvement and psychological well-being? *American Psychologist*, 52(9), 1017–1031.

Levine, P. (2001). Civic renewal and the commons of cyberspace. *National Civic Review*, 90(3), 205–212.

Matei, S., Ball-Rokeach, S.J. and Qui, J.-L. (2001). Fear and misperception of Los Angeles urban space: A spatial–statistical study of communication-shaped mental maps. *Communication Research*, 28(4), 429–463.

Matheson, D. (2010, in press). What the blogger knows. In Papacharissi, Z. (ed.). *Journalism & Citizenship: New Agendas.* Mahwah: Lawrence Erlbaum/Taylor & Francis.

Merritt, D. (1998). *Public journalism and public life: Why telling the news is not enough.* Mahwah: Lawrence Erlbaum Associates.

O'Reilly, T. (2005). What is Web 2.0? Design patterns and business models for the next generation of software. O'Reilly Media. Retrieved October 21, 2007 from www.oreillynet.com/pub/a/oreilly/tim/news/2005/09/30/what-is-web-20.html.

Ostrom, E. (1990). *Governing the commons: The evolution of institutions for collective action.* Cambridge and New York: Cambridge University Press.

Papacharissi, Z. (2010, in press). The citizen is the message: Online media and civic journalism. In Papacharissi, Z. (ed.). *Journalism & Citizenship: New Agendas.* Mahwah: Lawrence Erlbaum/Taylor & Francis.

Park, R.E. (1938). Reflections on communication and culture. *American Journal of Sociology*, 441, 87–205.

Rodriguez, C. (2001). *Fissures in the mediascape: an international study of citizens' media.* Cresskill: Hampton Press.

Rosen, J. (1999). *What are journalists for?* New Haven: Yale University Press.

Schuler, D. (1995). Creating public space in cyberspace: The rise of new community networks. *Internet World.* Retrieved October 14, 2007 from www.scn.org/commnet/iwdec.html.

White, D.M. (1950). The gate keeper: A case study in the selection of news. *Journalism Quarterly*, 2, 383–390.

Wirth, L. (1946). Consensus and mass communication. *American Sociological Review*, 13, 1–15.

Yaros, R. (2010, in press). The PICK model for news online: An integrated model for citizen engagement and situational understanding of complex news. In Papacharissi, Z. (ed.). *Journalism & Citizenship: New Agendas.* Mahwah: Lawrence Erlbaum/Taylor & Francis.

Open Source Interview
Civic and Citizen Journalism's Distinctions

Jan Schaffer

Let's start with a couple of questions about some of the work you have done with two of the organizations that helped shape the contours of civic journalism, and now citizen journalism. The Pew Center for Civic Journalism helped in defining civic journalism by funding certain projects. When proposals from news organizations reached the Pew Center, what operational components did you look for in deciding that it was a project worthy of funding as a citizen journalism effort? What sorts of suggestions did you give to organizations to help make their work more "civic" in nature?

The possibilities for doing journalism that could engage the public in new and different ways expanded between 1993 and 2002, and so the kinds of things we funded at the Pew Center for Civic Journalism also changed and expanded over the decade and they moved away from just funding enterprise projects. We looked for a diversity of projects, a diversity of news outlets, geographic diversity, fresh topics, fresh approaches to covering the topics and new ideas for involving citizens.

We started with "convening projects" such as Tallahassee's Public Agenda project that gathered citizens in the statehouse to wrestle with a future agenda for the city. We funded bottom-up projects like Charlotte's "Taking Back our Neighborhoods" that involved citizens in framing the root causes of crime in the city as the starting point for the journalism.

With the publication of the first edition of our "Tapping Civic Life" guide later in the 1990s, a joint project with Richard Harwood, we began to look for civic mapping projects that made civic journalism a daily (not a project) enterprise that called for going out into neighborhoods, visiting so-called "third places" and talking to so-called community "catalysts" and "connectors." It's gratifying how frequently I come across people today still using those terms.

By the end of the decade we were funding and rewarding with the Batten Awards for Excellence in Civic Journalism projects that sought public engagement through digital entry points, such as New Hampshire Public Radio's Tax Calculator or the *Everett Herald*'s Waterfront Renaissance clickable map.

We sought to have the projects operate independently with no intervention from a funder, which in my view is not appropriate.

Moving from directing the Pew Center for Civic Journalism to executive director of the J-Lab, you have gone from working with mainstream news organizations in trying to improve public life to helping citizens as well as journalists to use digital technologies to report about and engage in public life. Do you think this change in your own role is indicative of any diminishing role of mainstream news organizations in enhancing public life?

No. As with the expansion of the kinds of projects we funded through the Pew Center, my work in the digital news sphere is reflective of the expanding possibilities for enhancing citizen engagement through new media venues. I also continue to work with legacy news organizations and will soon launch a major project with mainstream outlets, so I don't really see a "change" in my role. I also think that while there are promising possibilities for news and information that is gathered and produced by non-professional journalists, most citizens are dismayed at the cutbacks curtailing journalism at so many mainstream news organizations.

Moving on to some more general discussion of the field, "citizen" journalism is also known by a number of other names. Which one do you prefer, and why?

I prefer the term "new media makers" and J-Lab will soon be launching a Community Media Toolkit by that name. These new media makers are involved in both random and organized "acts of journalism." Random as in the posting of eyewitness videos or photos of some catastrophic event. Organized as in launching a community news site that has an architecture of topics or beats. Not all citizen media makers aspire to do "journalism." Some, such as individual bloggers, often don't do journalism at all. Others produce content that has a lot of journalistic DNA. We do a disservice to emerging players in the new media ecosystem and to our own understanding of what's evolving by lumping them all under one rubric. A broader name allows us to start to distinguish and codify emerging media players.

Reader Comments

I've always had misgivings about the term citizen journalism, but have continued to use it. As for the term "new media makers" this feels a bit too broad to me. It seems that anyone who posts anything online could be considered a "new media maker." What I think makes citizen journalism special is that there is some element of storytelling involved (whether or not it adheres to journalistic standards doesn't matter) and there is some connection and relevance to the community. This community connection is becoming even more important as newspapers go out of business, leaving small communities uncovered. I've always liked the term community storytelling, because it gets to the heart of what is really being done – storytelling about the community. Also, to non-journalists, this term is less threatening than citizen journalism.

(Kirsten Johnson)

In my work with the Hispanic community it has become clear that "citizen journalism" has a different connotation to those who aren't legal citizens. I like "community journalism" as it puts the focus on the subject of the journalism and not who is doing it.

I agree with Kirsten that "new media makers" is very broad and could refer to any content posted online. When Jan says that not all media makers aspire to do journalism, that's true. But if we are addressing content that focuses on public issues for the sake of building community, there has to be some definition beyond using particular tools for whatever purpose.

If "journalism" is too intimidating to people, "storytelling" could be an alternative. As we open up journalism to more voices and tools and outlets, however, perhaps it will lose some of its power to intimidate. As "journalism" expands and encompasses the everyday acts that regular people engage in to share and report and aggregate and comment on in their communities, it may be a perfectly fine word to use for what we're talking about.

(Donica Mensing)

Is citizen journalism necessarily civic journalism, or is there a distinction between the two?

Civic journalism involves journalists using the media to engage citizens in public issues – by deliberating on public agendas, framing issues, civic mapping. And often the journalists aspired to engage the citizens in the *journalism*, more than the community.

So-called citizen journalism involves citizens engaging in the community by using media as a form of civic participation. In other words, their acts of making media *are* the participation. They don't seek to cover community; they seek to build it. They are entirely different in my view in terms of motivations and conventions. They sometimes can have similar outcomes. But they cover communities from the inside-out, not from the outside-in. And I'd suggest that we are already seeing that they do their journalism much differently than traditional journalists.

Reader Comments

When citizens use media as a form of civic participation, when do their efforts really indicate news or tilt more toward private interests? To be more precise, can citizen journalists build community and, at the same time, provide news? The two terms aren't necessarily the same, but they aren't mutually exclusive either. So, are there some examples you can point to where citizen journalism is both building community and providing legitimate, credible news?

(Burton St. John III)

Jan's response suggests that "journalists" are by definition outside of their communities and "citizens" by definition are from the inside. She seems to indicate that citizens wouldn't engage in civic journalism because civic journalism is more about journalism than community.

What if we mix up those categories? What if journalists were to act more like citizens in terms of their attachment, connection and investment in community life? What if journalists and citizens act together on work that has community building at its core? This seems like one possible evolution of public journalism in an age of citizen journalism.

(Donica Mensing)

If there is a distinction, what would have to happen for citizen journalism to become public journalism?

I see the content produced by many new media makers and the very act of producing that content as an act of civic participation, not an act of journalism. So if the goal of public journalism *was* civic participation, why would you want so-called citizen journalism to have to be intermediated, which seems to me would be the end result if it "became public journalism?"

Reader Comment

Was the goal of public journalism "civic participation" in general? Or is it the solving of public problems using journalistic tools?

(Donica Mensing)

Beyond discussing distinctions, it appears citizen journalism and public journalism share an approach: they both intend to place the citizen closer to defining and relaying news. In light of this commonality, but understanding that public journalism dates back about 20 years, how do you see the principles and practices of public journalism informing citizen journalism?

I don't think "citizen journalists" have much, if any, knowledge of civic journalism or its principles and practices. It is not of their world. Again, they care about community, not journalism per se. They care about information that can build capacity for members of a community to elect wise leaders or solve community problems or become knowledgeable about community issues. If it's in the form of a news story, that's fine. If it's just information, that's fine, too. They care about journalism only in the sense that it is largely absent in their communities or their available media is unsatisfactory. And they now have some digital tools so they can do something about that.

Far more apparent is how the principles, practices and language of civic journalism are met with such an intuitive understanding and a comfort level among new-media practitioners in mainstream newsrooms, those who are charged with constructing participatory and interactive forms of journalism. Just on a lark I searched in mid-March 2009 for mentions of civic and public journalism in the blogosphere. There were 28 for civic and 26 for public journalism tracked by Technorati just in the previous five months. And they included things like an *Online Journalism Review* article that mentioned the thinking behind London School of Economics professor and former broadcast journalist Charlie Beckett's idea of "networked journalism." "The idea is to take the best parts of the civic journalism and public journalism movements and sync these up with the possibilities of the Web," wrote the author, Nikki Usher. "Through networked journalism, Beckett urges legacy journalists to think of themselves as participating in somewhat of a pro–am kind of relationship, where mainstream journalists share the process of production with everyday citizens."

Also of note, and largely unheralded, is how the innovators from the heyday of civic journalism have continued as leading innovators and thinkers of today's journalism. Take Kate Marymont, managing editor and one of the key drivers behind the *Springfield News-Leader*'s "The Good Community" initiative in 1995. She went on to make major strides in dispatching mojos or mobile journalists in Fort Myers, FL, then broke a major municipal story there using crowdsourcing. Now she's replacing retiring Phil Currie as vice president for Gannett's U.S. Community Publishing Division. Or take Wendy Warren and Ellen Foley, both drivers behind the "Rethinking Philadelphia" initiative in the late 1990s at the *Philadelphia Daily News*. Foley went on to become editor of the *Wisconsin State Journal* and open up her front pages to reader suggestions for stories. Warren is now vice president and editor of Philly.com and the leader of one of the most recent quintessentially civic journalism projects: TheNextMayor.com, which involved citizens in the 2007 mayoral elections. The project used a textbook civic journalism template and it's unfortunate that it was not archived online. Or Steve Smith, one of Buzz Merritt's protégés at the *Wichita Eagle*, who went on to webcast the *Spokane Spokesman-Review*'s daily news meetings and engage citizens in the paper's journalism with a raft of transparency initiatives and editor blogs. Or Mark Briggs, a Batten Award winner for the *Everett Herald*'s Waterfront Renaissance clickable map that engaged 2,500 residents in redevelopment. He went on to write the best-selling *Journalism 2.0* (which J-Lab commissioned and published). Or Chris Satullo, renowned in Philadelphia for bringing "Citizen Voices" and other initiatives to the editorial page, who just moved to WHYY-TV to launch a new initiative. Or Lew Friedland, who has not only authored books about civic journalism but launched one of the first citizen-driving community news initiatives in 2006, MadisonCommons.org. Just to name a few.

Yesterday's civic journalists are today's new media innovators.

Do you see public journalism principles being articulated in participatory journalism in the current environment, i.e. are there any good examples?
Yes, I think founders of community news sites have been more willing to listen, akin to public listening. They have embraced games and interactive exercises as ways to elicit public input. They are more comfortable reporting not just what people say, but allowing them to clarify what they mean. I think they don't use conflict to define news, which was always a caveat in the civic journalism world. And I think my previous answer addressed some of this.

So far, what role do you see citizen media has played, in relation to mainstream news media, in enhancing public life in the U.S.? How about outside the U.S.?
I only focus on the U.S., although I think globalvoicesonline.org has been a great example overseas.

How do you measure the success of a citizen journalism website?
Do site operators feel they are making a difference in their community? Are the right eyeballs more than the number of eyeballs looking at the site because they need to hear the public's concerns? Are community problems being addressed? Are more people challenging incumbents for public office? Do Republican candidates show up for site-sponsored candidate forums, even when they feel the site skews Democratic, yet they can't point to any bias? Does voter turnout go up? Are more citizens willing to participate in generating content? Those are the kinds of civic impact measures that are important to citizen site operators. And we need to measure their success using metrics that are meaningful to them.

Which citizen journalism sites do you consider to be the most influential? The most innovative?
You'd have to break down the sites into those produced by citizens with no journalism backgrounds and those produced by journalists who are no longer in professional newsrooms. And you'd need to differentiate individuals' blogging platforms from community news sites. Again, I point to the dangers of an

umbrella rubric that does not fit the developments. I have some favorites, but that doesn't mean that they are the most influential or most innovative.

Voice of SanDiego.org is incredibly influential. So is NewHavenIndependent.org. NewCastleNOW.org is spritely and comprehensive. WestSeattleblog.com is very popular in Seattle. NewWest.net is an intriguing model.

What will citizen journalism look like in 10, 20 or 50 years?

I just don't know and haven't really thought about it. I'm more interested in mapping various developments in the new media ecosystem.

Chapter 13

Conclusion

A Place for the Professionals

Jack Rosenberry and Burton St. John III

One of this project's contributors, Lew Friedland, a few years ago expressed pessimism for public journalism's future (Friedland, 2004). In a follow-up for this book he says his pessimism has only worsened (Part I Open Source interview). Another contributor, Joyce Nip, in a recent article described civic journalism as being in its "last days" (Nip, 2008). In fact, one of the editors of this volume has observed that professional journalism's own sociology of work and its self-definitions undermined any true deliberation about adopting public journalism (St. John, 2007). Those sound like pretty dire assessments. Has public journalism met its demise? Is a book discussing "public journalism 2.0" the equivalent of an argument for upgrading eight-track tape machines?

Clearly, the authors hope not. The premise for this book is two-fold, presuming (1) that civic or public journalism is not dead yet, but is in need of some revitalization; and (2) that citizen journalism, while not necessarily an automatic replacement for public journalism, nevertheless could pick up the mantle under certain conditions. This assumes a kind of symbiosis in which the two practices address each other's shortcomings. The myriad perspectives offered in this volume speak to both the separation and connection points that go into defining the symbiotic relationship: defining news values, gatekeeping prerogatives, collaborative work practices, emerging models for news presentation and private versus public concerns.

As a starting point, citizen journalism has become popular and fairly ubiquitous; J-Lab's Knight Citizen News Network project identified about 800 citizen news media sites as of mid-2009 (Knight Citizen News Network, 2009). And non-news citizen media creations are even more widespread, with an uncountable number of stand-alone blogs, uploaded YouTube videos, independent and sponsored (e.g. within an online newspaper's site) message forums, and other venues in which people can put their ideas online in words and images. How much of that content seeks to "connect" producers and/or recipients in any manner related to civic engagement or search for community building and common ground is unclear. However, the current body of research regarding citizen-created news content reveals few identifiable efforts that attempt to connect audiences to news that can be considered, in public journalism parlance, as helping public life go well.

In the best-intentioned citizen journalism, site organizers and dedicated volunteers (who often are the same people) set out to cover topics that major media organizations in their communities either no longer address or perhaps never did. But even these well-constructed efforts can fall short of creating the sort of "conversational commons" that public journalism suggests is necessary to build a public that can engage with civic issues or community problem-solving. As the research and case studies in this book show, citizen journalists wrestle with defining what their coverage should entail and how it should be presented. Site organizers struggle with keeping more than a handful of contributors active at any given time. There is no denying that having many independent voices contributing to the coverage of a community has certain benefits when compared to the limited perspectives available in a mass-media gatekeeping model. However, just putting all of those voices out there offers no guarantee of a common view coalescing or of a public forming, mobilized for action. This is particularly true when many contributions from the public are of a decidedly private nature or from a narrow, personalized viewpoint. So while it has some intrinsic value, citizen journalism is no automatic replacement for the aspirations of improved community engagement that were the impetus for the public journalism movement

As for public journalism, after a period of growth in the late 1980s and 1990s, peaking from around 1994 to 2002 (corresponding roughly to the lifespan of the Pew Center for Civic Journalism), it has largely melted into the media landscape. During its heyday, public journalism tended to take the shape of special reporting projects, usually by mid-sized metro daily newspapers. These took significant time, energy and resources to organize. Many of these projects cost money that went beyond their organizations' routine budgets, for expenses such as providing reporter release-time or overtime, hiring facilitators for roundtables and public meetings, and conducting community polls. And many of these extraordinary expenses were covered with additional funding, such as Pew Center grants or money from corporate headquarters interested in supporting the innovations. But as Lew Friedland points out in his Open Source interview, the economic plight of many journalism organizations, particularly daily newspapers, undermines their ability to conduct such projects today. Such initiatives are not likely to return.

So, neither public journalism as earlier conceived nor citizen journalism in its present form is up to the task of meeting public journalism's goal of "making public life go well." Arguably, however, journalism's need – and society's need – for practices that *can* attain this have not abated. If, as Buzz Merritt notes in his chapter in this volume, citizen journalism is "a practice in search of a theory," then using the theories and aspirations of public journalism to guide an improved set of citizen journalism practices seem like a natural fit. Such an approach could help answer the questions surrounding how stand-alone citizen journalism operators might refine their definitions of "news" and gatekeeping. Applying the lessons of public journalism can help to define how professional and citizen contributors can relate to, and work with, each other in constructing today's news.

In her "final days" article, Joyce Nip succinctly summarizes practices that are the hallmarks of public journalism as: listening to the public to help shape the news agenda, giving ordinary people a voice, covering stories in ways that facilitate public understanding and stimulate citizen deliberation of the problems behind the stories, presenting news in ways that make it more accessible (making it easier for people to engage in the issues), engaging the community in problem-solving, and maximizing the impact of coverage in the community (2008, p. 180). Even when public journalism was in its prime in the mid-1990s, engaging in these practices was challenging for two primary reasons: (1) it required that traditional journalists operate outside their comfort zones in defining story topics and relating to their readers, and many were loath to do so; and (2) the logistics of implementing these practices – such as finding places for roundtable forums, getting citizens to attend and figuring out how to include them in the news coverage – were time-consuming and expensive.

Fast-forward 15 years, and the environment has changed dramatically. The audience already is a part of the news mix, driving some of the agenda and often adding its voice to a news report that is more a chorus than an aria. As a result, working collaboratively with audience members in shaping news coverage is not as far outside the comfort zone for reporters now as it was in public journalism's early days. Finished reporting projects can be more accessible and have greater impact because they need not appear in the printed newspaper, but can be left online indefinitely. This creates an ability to update them at any time and offers the prospect of links from individuals or community organizations with a stake in the topic. The projects thus become a standing community resource rather than a one-and-done effort that appears on a random Sunday morning. Deliberative techniques geared toward engagement and problem-solving – such as roundtable discussions or community forums with civic leaders – can be facilitated online, reducing if not eliminating the time-consuming and expensive logistical problems that once went into such efforts.

What this adds up to is that the modern form and practice of journalism appears ripe for re-application of some of the principles and practices of public

journalism. While it is possible for a citizen journalism operation run by operators with no formal training to engage in these practices, it is perhaps more
likely for a professional operation to adopt them, working with citizens who
are often already engaged in participatory content production through that
news organization's online site.

This does not mean that simply building this participatory structure will
make for more relevant coverage that supports greater engagement. This
volume has pointed to the various promises and challenges of achieving that.
Instead, the road to realizing a more citizen-engaged press first calls for both
professional and citizen journalists to examine how they can integrate the credibility of traditional journalistic practices into new interactive mediums. Of
course, journalists have the benefits of experience and training that have allowed
them to develop conceptual frameworks for defining news. Admittedly, as
public journalism originally observed, many of these journalistic paradigms
served to distance journalism from the public. But such dysfunctions do not
mean journalists cannot take a leading role in forming a truly citizen-engaged
press. Rather, since professional news workers have the benefits that come
from both practice and education, they also should have the responsibility of
provoking a resurgence in meaningful, community-focused news by collaborat-
ing with citizen-contributors.

As Carl Sessions Stepp notes in a review of a book about the impact of the
blogosphere on the 2008 presidential race:

> To see bloggers as supplanting traditional coverage seems misguided.
> Instead, pro–am journalism probably will become increasingly synergistic.
> Although many bloggers [described in the book] express contempt for the
> mainstream press, it is striking how often they depended on cracking tradi-
> tional media to gain credibility. The richest irony here may be that tradi-
> tional media and citizen journalists aren't so much competitors as
> codependents.
>
> (Stepp, 2009)

If it sounds like we are privileging the role of the journalist at this crucial
moment, so be it. Toward the end of his book *Public Journalism and Public Life*,
Buzz Merritt poses the question: "If not journalists, who?" (1998, p. 143)
meaning: who will take responsibility for improving public life if journalists are
unable or unwilling to step up and do so? Journalists and their news operations
are the sources to which citizens turn for information about politics and public
affairs. This leaves them uniquely positioned to take on the task as Merritt suggests they should, but this time in conjunction with citizen contributors whose
work has become an inevitable part of the coverage mix.

References

Friedland, L. (2004). Public journalism and communities (excerpt). *National Civic Review* 93 (3), 36–43.

Knight Citizen News Network (2009). Directory of Citizen Media Sites. Retrieved May 27, 2009 from www.kcnn.org/citmedia_sites/.

Merritt, D. (1998). *Public Journalism and Public Life: Why Telling the News is Not Enough.* Mahwah, NJ: Lawrence Erlbaum Associates.

Nip, J.Y.M. (2008). The last days of civic journalism: The case of the *Savannah Morning News. Journalism Practice* 2, 179–186.

St. John, B. III. (2007). Newspapers' struggles with civic engagement: The U.S. press and the rejection of public journalism as propagandistic. *The Communication Review* 10, 249–270.

Stepp, C.S. (2009, June/July). Off the Bus. *American Journalism Review* 31 (3), 47.

Appendix
Further Readings

The following list of suggested readings was compiled by Davis "Buzz" Merritt, former *Wichita Eagle* editor and author of Chapter 3 of this volume.

Readings About the Origins of Public Journalism Theory

Amusing Ourselves to Death, Neal Postman, Penguin Books (1985). The problem of information glut and its implications for journalism, especially chapter 5.

Coming to Public Judgment, Daniel Yankelovich, Syracuse University Press (1991). How the public decides and what it needs to make those decisions, especially Part 2, and chapters 5, 6, 7 and 13.

The Conversation of Journalism, Anderson *et al.*, Praeger (1994). Deals with the relationship between community and public conversation and journalism's role in it.

Meaningful Chaos, Richard Harwood, Kettering Foundation (1993). A report on interviews with average people about their view of the media and public life.

Politics For People, David Mathews, University of Illinois Press (1994). An explanation of the need for public deliberation and its role in public life.

Common Knowledge, W. Russell Neuman, University of Chicago (1992). A study of how journalism affects perceptions and the public agenda, especially chapter 7.

Is Anyone Responsible? How Television Frames Political Issues, Shanto Iyengar, University of Chicago Press (1994). An analysis of how the framing choices made by journalists affect public life.

Bowling Alone: America's Declining Social Capital, Robert Putnam, *The Journal of Democracy* 6 (1), January 1995, National Endowment for Democracy. Thoughts on the decline and potential renewal of public life.

John Dewey and American Democracy, Robert Westbrook, Cornell University Press (1993). Especially chapter 9, which addresses the crucial debate between Dewey and Walter Lippmann about the nature of democracy.

James Carey: A Critical Reader, James Carey, University of Minnesota Press (1997). Thoughts about public life, politics and the press from a leading observer and theorist, especially Part IV, pp. 191–257.

Suggested Readings about the Practice of Public Journalism

Assessing Public Journalism, Edmund Lambeth, Phil Meyer and Esther Thorson (eds.), University of Missouri Press (1998). An analysis of the history and operations of public journalism.

Doing Public Journalism, Arthur Charity, Guilford Press (1995). A look at dozens of public journalism projects, 1991–5.

Public Journalism and Public Life, Davis "Buzz" Merritt, 2nd Edition, Lawrence Erlbaum Associates (1998). One journalist's journey.

Mixed News, Jay Black (ed.), Lawrence Erlbaum Associates (1997). A collection of critiques and arguments for and against public journalism with contributed chapters by many involved in the debate.

What Are Journalists For? Jay Rosen, Yale University Press (1999). An overview and analysis by a public journalism founder.

CQ Researcher 6 (35), September 20, Congressional Quarterly (1996). A balanced analysis of the debate over public journalism.

Tapping Civic Life, Richard Harwood, Pew Center for Civic Journalism (1996). A step-by-step guidebook to help journalists delve into the parts of civic life where the real action is.

The Politics of News, Doris Graber, Denis McQuail and Pippa Norris (eds.), CQ Press (1998). Especially chapter 7 by Michael Schudson, analyzing public journalism.

The Idea of Public Journalism, Theodore Glasser (ed.), Guilford Press (1996). Glasser assembles a group of academics to explore the pros and cons of public journalism.

Public Journalism: Past and Future, Lewis A. Friedland, Kettering Foundation Press (2003). Case studies and analysis of key public journalism efforts.

Getting the Whole Story: Reporting and Writing the News, Cheryl Gibbs and Thomas Warhover, Guilford Press (2002). A comprehensive public journalism textbook.

Contributors

Jack Rosenberry is an associate professor and chair of the Communication/Journalism Department at St. John Fisher College in Rochester, NY, which he joined in 2002. Before that, he worked for newspapers for more than 20 years, including 17 years as a copy editor at the *Democrat and Chronicle*, a Gannett newspaper in Rochester. He earned his bachelor's and master's degrees at Syracuse University in the early 1980s and his Ph.D. from State University of New York at Buffalo in 2005. He is a former chair of the Civic & Citizen Journalism Interest Group of AEJMC. His research interests center on public and participatory journalism, especially as it is articulated on the online sites of traditional media organizations. His work on this subject has appeared in *Newspaper Research Journal* and *Journalism & Mass Communication Quarterly*. He also is the author, with Fisher colleague Lauren Vicker, of *Applied Mass Communication Theory: A Guide for Media Practitioners* (Pearson/Allyn & Bacon, 2009).

Burton St. John III (Ph.D., Saint Louis University, 2005) is an assistant professor of communication at Old Dominion University in Norfolk, VA, which he joined in 2005. He has more than 18 years' combined experience in public relations and broadcasting. He has served as a research chair for the Civic & Citizen Journalism Interest Group of AEJMC. He was a 2006 Page Legacy Scholar, receiving funding through the Arthur W. Page Center at Penn State University to study the press and propaganda. His works on the press, the public sphere and propaganda have appeared in the *Journal of Mass Media Ethics*, *Journalism Studies*, *The Communication Review*, *Public Relations Review*, *Journalism History* and *American Journalism*. He is currently working on a book about U.S. press professionalization and propaganda.

Aaron Barlow teaches English at New York City College of Technology, City University of New York. He is the author of *The Rise of the Blogosphere* (Praeger, 2007) and *Blogging America: The New Public Sphere* (Praeger, 2008).

James K. Batten died in 1995. In 1990, when he wrote and presented the talk that appears in this volume, he was the 54-year-old chairman and chief executive of Knight-Ridder Inc., publisher of 29 daily newspapers including the *Miami Herald*,

Philadelphia Inquirer and *Daily News*, *San Jose Mercury News*, *Wichita Eagle* and *Charlotte Observer*. His career included work as a reporter for the *Observer* and also in Knight-Ridder's Washington bureau. He was an assistant city editor of the *Detroit Free Press* and returned to the *Observer* when he was named executive editor there in 1972. In 1975, he moved to Knight-Ridder corporate headquarters in Miami as a vice president. He became president of the company in 1982, CEO in 1988 and chairman in 1989. He was still chairman when he died on June 24, 1995, of a brain tumor. In tribute and memorial to him, the James K. Batten Awards for Civic Journalism were presented annually from 1996 to 2002 by the Pew Center for Civic Journalism. Since then, the Knight–Batten Awards for Innovations in Journalism – which honor novel efforts that involve citizens in public issues – have been presented annually by the Knight Foundation and J-Lab: The Institute for Interactive Journalism.

Serena Carpenter is an assistant professor at the Walter Cronkite School of Journalism and Mass Communication at Arizona State University. Carpenter researches in the areas of online communication and media sociology. Her research concentrates on predicting and explaining what leads to variations in news content. She is the author of several articles on the topic of citizen journalism, which have been published in *New Media & Society*, *Journalism & Mass Communication Quarterly* and in the book *Web Journalism: A New Form of Citizenship?*

Cathy DeShano is a doctoral student in the University of Wisconsin-Madison's School of Journalism and Mass Communication, where she studies citizen journalism, communities, and public deliberation. Before beginning graduate studies, she worked as an editor and reporter for newspapers and online publications for a decade.

Lewis A. Friedland is a professor in the School of Journalism & Mass Communication and an affiliated professor in the Department of Sociology at the University of Wisconsin-Madison, which he joined in 1991. He earned a B.A. in sociology from Washington University in St. Louis and a Ph.D. in sociology from Brandeis University in 1985. Friedland teaches courses in journalism, communication and society, communication research methods, and civil society and public life, and helped to found Madison Commons.org. His publications include three books: *Public Journalism: Past and Future* (Kettering Foundation Press, 2003); *Civic Innovation in America: Community Empowerment, Public Policy and the Movement for Civic Renewal*, with Carmen Sirianni (University of California Press, 2001); and *Covering the World: International Television News Services* (Twentieth Century Fund Press, 1993). He has published articles and monographs on topics including the structure of international television news, coverage of Tiananmen Square, the changing structure of public television, new media technologies and electronic democracy, community and communication, and civic and public journalism. His research has been supported by major foundations, including the Ford Foundation, the Pew Charitable Trusts, the Knight Foundation, the Kettering Foundation, the Center for Information on Civic Learning and Engagement (CIRCLE) and others.

Tanni Haas (Ph.D., Rutgers University, 1999) is a professor of Communication Studies in the Department of Speech Communication Arts & Sciences at Brooklyn College – The City University of New York. He is the author of *The Pursuit of Public Journalism: Theory, Practice, and Criticism* (Routledge, 2007) as well as more than 30 scholarly journal articles and book chapters on public journalism, citizen journalism and related topics. His research on public journalism has followed two interrelated trajectories. The first has been to articulate a theoretically based public philosophy for public journalism that specifies how journalists should conceive of the public, what forms of public deliberation and problem-solving journalists should help promote, and how journalists, as a matter of practice, should facilitate public discourse. His second and related objective has been to apply this public philosophy for a number of different purposes, including to outline future avenues for empirical research on public journalism, respond to criticism directed at public journalism by its detractors, specify what given public journalism initiatives could have done differently and better, evaluate the appropriateness of widely used deliberative methods, and assess whether the newer, citizen-based forms of journalism are furthering public journalism's principles and practices.

Kirsten A. Johnson is an assistant professor in the Department of Communications at Elizabethtown College in Elizabethtown, PA. She has a Ph.D. in Information Science and Technology from Drexel University, an M.S. in Telecommunications from Kutztown University, and a B.A. in Broadcast News from Drake University. She teaches courses in new media, broadcast news writing and television production, and also advises the student newspaper the *Etownian*. Prior to joining Elizabethtown College she worked for WGAL-TV in Lancaster, PA and WOI-TV in Des Moines, IA as a news producer. Her research interests include citizen journalism, credibility of websites and media convergence.

Nakho Kim is a Ph.D. candidate at the School of Journalism & Mass Communication, University of Wisconsin-Madison. His academic focus is on citizen and civic journalism, how they function in the media ecology, and how to enhance them via community social networks and media technology. He has been working as a developer and administrator for Madison Commons, a citizen journalism project based in Madison, WI.

Suzanne McBride is associate chair of the Journalism Department at Columbia College Chicago, where she teaches community news and investigative reporting. She is co-founder and co-publisher of ChicagoTalks.org, a local news website that covers the neighborhoods of the nation's third-largest city. ChicagoTalks has won national awards from Investigative Reporters and Editors and the Society of Professional Journalists for investigations of the Chicago City Council. The site was launched in 2007 with a New Voices grant from J-Lab: The Institute for Interactive Journalism. McBride has lectured in the United States and Asia on civic journalism and the rise of hyper-local news sites. Before joining Columbia College's faculty in 2005, McBride was a reporter and editor for *The Indianapolis Star* and now-defunct *Indianapolis News*. Her positions included leading the local news and business operations, and working with the newspaper's convergence partner, the Indianapolis NBC-affiliate (WTHR-Channel 13). McBride has also worked as an editor at the Terre Haute (IN) *Tribune-Star*, a business reporter for *The Journal Gazette* in Fort Wayne, IN and as a legislative aide in Washington, DC, for an Ohio congressman. She is a Phi Beta Kappa graduate of the University of Iowa and earned a master's degree with distinction from Northwestern University.

Donica Mensing is an associate professor at the Reynolds School of Journalism, University of Nevada, Reno. Mensing studied public journalism during her graduate academic work and then for three years at the University of Nevada worked with Cole Campbell, one of the leading practitioners of public journalism who went on to an academic career focused on the practice. This experience was an immersion course in thinking about the evolution of public journalism and how it fits within the larger context of journalism and democracy today. She has worked with her Nevada colleague, David Ryfe, to apply some of the principles and practices of public journalism in a graduate program in environmental journalism. Mensing teaches online journalism, social media and media ethics, and conducts research on the evolving practices of journalism. She holds a Ph.D. in political science from the University of Nevada, master's degrees in technology and public policy, as well as journalism and an undergraduate degree in political economy of natural resources from the University of California, Berkeley.

Davis "Buzz" Merritt, a reporter and editor for 43 years, wrote the first book about public journalism (*Public Journalism and Public Life*, 1995) during a leave of absence from his position as editor of *The Wichita Eagle*. He was a consultant for Knight-Ridder newspapers (1998–9) on the subject, conducting seminars in 25 states and eight foreign countries and contributing dozens of papers to journals and books. After retiring from the *Eagle* in 1999, he taught media ethics and seminars on journalism and democracy at the University of Kansas and Wichita State University, and was visiting professor at the University of North Carolina (2006). He co-authored (with Maxwell McCombs) a public affairs reporting text, *The Two W's of Journalism* (2004), and wrote *Knightfall: Knight-Ridder and How the Erosion of Newspaper Journalism is Putting Democracy at Risk* (2006). He was a Morehead Scholar at the University of North Carolina, graduating in journalism in 1958. His newspaper career included reporting and editing at *The Charlotte Observer*, and he held positions as editor of the *Boca Raton News*, news editor of Knight-Ridder's Washington Bureau and editor of the *Eagle*.

Joyce Y.M. Nip is an assistant professor of journalism at the Hong Kong Baptist University. In 2004–5 she was a Fulbright Visiting Scholar at the Philip Merrill College of Journalism, University of Maryland, College Park, researching on the practices of public journalism in the United States. Her work on public journalism has been published in *Journalism Studies* and *Journalism Practice*.

Sue Robinson worked for a dozen years as a reporter before attaining her Ph.D. from Temple University in 2007. She became an assistant professor at the University of Wisconsin-Madison, where she teaches skills and theory classes to both undergraduates and graduate students. Her main research interests center on citizen journalism, online journalism, new media technologies and collective memory as these affect or illustrate the transforming nature of journalistic authority in society. She has also helped Lewis A. Friedland restructure the Madison Commons citizen journalism project.

David M. Ryfe is an associate professor of journalism in the Reynolds School of Journalism, University of Nevada Reno. He has published widely on the history of American journalism, the practice of deliberative democracy and the sociology of news, and has published a book, *Presidents in Culture* (Peter Lang, 2005), on presidential communication. He is currently working on an ethnographic study of the transformation under way in the American newspaper industry, which is tentatively titled *Transforming the News*.

Jan Schaffer is executive director of J-Lab: The Institute for Interactive Journalism (j-lab.org) and a leading thinker in the journalism reform movement. She left daily journalism in 1994 to lead pioneering journalism initiatives in civic journalism, interactive and participatory journalism, and citizen media ventures. She launched J-Lab in 2002 to spotlight new forms of digital storytelling. J-Lab rewards novel ideas through the Knight-Batten Awards for Innovations in Journalism, funds cutting-edge citizen media start-ups through its New Voices project and McCormick New Media Women Entrepreneur initiative, and produces Web tutorials on digital and citizen media at the Knight Citizen News Network (kcnn.org) and J-Learning. org. Schaffer previously directed the Pew Center for Civic Journalism, a $14 million initiative that funded more than 120 pilot news projects to engage people in public issues. She is a former business editor and a Pulitzer Prize winner for *The Philadelphia Inquirer*, where she worked for 22 years as a reporter and editor. As a federal court reporter, she helped write a series that won freedom for a man wrongly convicted of five murders. The stories led to the civil rights convictions of six Philadelphia homicide detectives and won several national journalism awards, including the 1978 Pulitzer Prize Gold Medal for Public Service.

Index